THE SOCIAL AND
EDUCATIONAL THOUGHT
OF HAROLD RUGG

THE SOCIAL AND EDUCATIONAL THOUGHT OF HAROLD RUGG

PETER F. CARBONE, JR.

DUKE UNIVERSITY PRESS   DURHAM, N.C.   1977

© 1977, Duke University Press
L.C.C. card no. 75-36176
I.S.B.N. 0-8223-0355-8
Printed in the United
States of America

For my wife, Claire

CONTENTS

PREFACE

My interest in Harold Rugg dates back to the early 1960s when I was a graduate student at Harvard. I had been intrigued for some time with the concept of the school as an agent of social change and had discovered that Rugg, when compared with other leading educator-reformers (or "social reconstructionists" as they were often labeled), had been neglected by educational historians and philosophers. Apart from a master's thesis (by Mark Phillips, Columbia University, 1961) that focused mainly on Rugg's early writings, and a number of publications that dealt with his controversial textbook series *(Man and His Changing Society)*, the bibliography on him at that time consisted merely of a few scattered articles and an occasional reference to his work in various books on educational theory or curriculum development. (Recent dissertations on Rugg by Virginia Wilson and Elmer Winters are referred to in the text and listed in the bibliography of this volume.)

This struck me as a curious oversight in view of the fact that Rugg's career had reflected so many developments in American education during the progressive era. Early in his career, between 1915 and 1920, for example, he was involved in the pioneering attempts to apply the quantitative methods of science to educational problems. Then in the 1920s he was identified with the popular "child-centered" approach to teaching, and during the thirties and after he was a leading spokesman for the reconstructionist point of view. In 1947 he published what is still the most comprehensive treatment of educational "foundations" *(Foundations for American Education)* and the fifties found him in the front rank of those searching for the secrets of the creative process.

Clearly, then, Rugg had been associated with most of the

significant educational developments of his day. In addition, he had managed to generate a fair amount of controversy both within progressive circles and among the general public. To the progressives and reconstructionists, most of whom were strongly influenced by the pragmatists, Rugg was something of a maverick. Although he was himself of the pragmatic persuasion to some extent, he was also sharply critical of Peirce, James, and Dewey for what he took to be their overemphasis on scientific procedures for acquiring knowledge. Rugg was convinced that in addition to the scientific method there is an intuitive way of knowing, and that the two approaches should be merged into a comprehensive theory of learning. These ideas presented an interesting contrast to the views of his colleagues, who were for the most part less disposed than Rugg to question the efficacy of scientific methods of inquiry.

Rugg's general notoriety stemmed from the public furor over his social science textbook series. The books were warmly received when they were first published in the 1930s, but by 1940 they had been labeled "subversive" in some quarters and were quickly removed from school bookshelves all over the country. The dispute generated a great deal of heated debate at the time and is still an instructive case study of censorship in education.

All of this seemed to me to confirm Rugg's credentials as a major figure on the educational scene and to warrant a critical analysis of his views. The outcome was a doctoral dissertation in 1967, two follow-up articles in the next four years, and finally a transformation of the dissertation into this book.

As the study has evolved through these several stages, I have incurred my full share of scholarly debts. I am particularly grateful to Professor Israel Scheffler, my adviser at Harvard, who helped me immensely with his constructive criticisms of my first draft. I am further indebted to Professor Scheffler for his friendship, encouragement, and advice at all points of the study.

Special thanks are due as well to Professors Kenneth D. Benne, Lawrence A. Cremin, and Wilbur A. Murra, each of whom read the manuscript in its entirety and contributed a number of valuable suggestions for improving it. I wish to express my thanks also to Professors Henry Aiken, A. Stanley Bolster, Roderick F. McPhee, Donald Oliver, and Theodore Sizer for their helpful comments on earlier versions of the study.

Information provided by Rugg's family, friends, and colleagues proved to be invaluable, especially in view of the fact that his personal papers have not yet been made available. Mrs. Elizabeth Rugg was particularly helpful in this respect, and I am deeply indebted to her for several conversations and letters concerning her husband's career. I am indebted also to Rugg's brother, the late Professor Earl Rugg, and to Professor William Withers for the useful information furnished in their correspondence with me.

Professors Kenneth Benne, Theodore Brameld, and James E. McClellan, Jr. all kindly consented to be interviewed during the course of the study, and shared with me their personal knowledge of specific aspects of Rugg's career. I wish also to acknowledge the assistance of the late Dr. Lawrence K. Frank, who provided me with tapes of several of Rugg's speeches, and I am grateful to Mr. Henry Halvorson of Ginn and Company for the time he spent discussing the Rugg textbook controversy with me.

I also wish to express my gratitude to Dr. Virginia S. Wilson for assistance with the bibliography, to Janet Robinson and Anne Smith for their excellent typing of the manuscript at various stages, to Anne Poole and Carol Thompson of Duke University Press for editorial suggestions, and to Jackie Ward for help in preparing the manuscript for publication.

Finally, I want to thank my wife, Claire, not only for typing the first draft of the manuscript and for help at every step in its preparation, but also for her indispensable encouragement and unfailing support throughout the entire course of this work.

ACKNOWLEDGMENTS

I should like to express my gratitude to the Duke University Research Council for a subsidy that helped defray publication costs.

I wish to thank Ginn and Company and Prentice-Hall Incorporated for granting me permission to reproduce the materials that appear in the Appendixes to this book.

Parts of this volume were first published in *The Journal of Creative Behavior* (Spring 1969) and *History of Education Quarterly* (Fall 1971). I am indebted to the editors of those journals for permission to use that material in revised form here.

THE SOCIAL AND
EDUCATIONAL THOUGHT
OF HAROLD RUGG

INTRODUCTION

Few, if any, educational leaders were associated with more significant aspects of the progressive education movement than Harold Rugg. Teacher, engineer, historian, educational philosopher, student of sociology and psychology—his career was marked by a versatility seldom encountered in the history of American education.

Before America's entry into World War I, for example, Rugg distinuished himself in the field of educational statistics under Charles Judd at the University of Chicago and earned an opportunity to serve during the war with Edward L. Thorndike on the army's Committee on Classification of Personnel, the first group to use aptitude and intelligence tests on a mass scale.

During the 1920s at Teachers College, Columbia University, Rugg began to attract attention as educational psychologist at the experimental Lincoln School and as the author of a series of social science pamphlets designed to comprehensively interpret modern industrial civilization for school children. His professorship at Teachers College and his active participation in the Progressive Education Association brought him into contact with several of the leading educational innovators of the day—men such as John Dewey, William H. Kilpatrick, George S. Counts, and Boyd H. Bode. For Rugg the twenties were also years of close proximity with many of the artistic and literary figures in the New York area. These contacts helped him develop an enduring and active interest in the creative, self-expressive activities so characteristic of progressive schools at the time.

Apart from his work at Teachers College, Rugg became involved during his long career in a number of other significant educational activities. He was, for instance, one of the charter members of the John Dewey Society and one of the founders of the National Council for the Social Studies. In 1934 he helped organize *The Social Frontier,* a journal of remarkable vitality during its ten years of existence, and later served as editor after the name of the journal had been changed to *Frontiers of Democracy.* He also served for over a decade as social studies editor of *Senior Scholastic* and for eleven years as editor of the *Journal of Educational Psychology.* At various times in his career he was an educational consultant or visiting lecturer in the Middle East, the Far East, Western Europe, South Africa, Australia, and New Zealand. In addition, he came to be widely regarded as a sort of unofficial spokesman for the PEA in the international New Education Fellowship.

Rugg was also a prolific author. In addition to numerous articles and books prepared for an adult audience, his writings include a fourteen-volume series of social science textbooks (the earlier pamphlets in revised form) for elementary and junior high school students. He was, therefore, one of the few professor-reformers whose point of view on educational and social reconstruction actually found its way into the schools, at least temporarily.

What exactly was his point of view? Harold Rugg was a man with a vision. He saw on the horizon a better society—referred to in various writings as "the great society," "the great technology," and "the great new epoch"—emerging out of the harnessing of America's industrial resources, provided that the American people would consent to large-scale social and economic planning.

More than mere social engineering was needed to bring forth this new epoch, however. According to Rugg, a sound (i.e., more humane, tolerant, socially cooperative) society of lasting duration was also contingent upon the development of multitudes of cultured, "integrated" personalities, and, because of its "integrity-producing power," he regarded creative expression in the various art forms as an indispensable element in the production of such personalities.

Thus there were two basic factors involved in Rugg's conception of social reconstruction: social engineering and self-cultivation. Education cut across both these factors in the sense that social and economic planning were to take place within the framework of democratic institutions, and this implied proceeding only with widespread popular consent. But if people were to grant consent based on intelligent reflection, they would first need to be made more aware of existing social problems and then alerted to various suggestions for reform. They should also be given an opportunity, said Rugg, to engage in creative activities—again because of his assumption that creativity and integrity were inextricably related— and various other cultural pursuits. To serve these educational needs of adults, Rugg recommended the formation of culture groups that would function as open forums for the discussion of social issues and at the same time as centers for participation in the arts and crafts; for children the obvious place to carry out the necessary educational functions was the formal school system. Education was thus an integral part of Rugg's plan for social betterment. As a matter of fact, he conceived of a "school-centered community," in which all the principal social agencies would study local and national problems and formulate proposals for social reconstruction. For Harold Rugg, then, education was indeed an instrument of social change.

This study will focus on the two essential components of Rugg's social and educational reformism: his prescriptions for social reconstruction and his views regarding self-cultivation through creative activity. My main objective is to deal critically with Rugg's thought, but my approach will be historical as well as analytical. Although Rugg's thinking remained essentially consistent over the years, certain shifts in emphasis are discernible, and it will be necessary to point these out against the background of changing social and cultural conditions.

Although I shall naturally be concerned with Rugg's reconstructionist philosophy of education, it should be emphasized at the outset that he never held himself out to be a systematic philosopher as such. Hence, he never formulated a complete philosophy of education if that phrase means, as Price holds, that "a philosophy of education consists in an analysis of educational terms and in metaphysical, ethical, and epistemological reflection on education. . . ."[1] Rugg had neither the training nor the inclination to construct a philosophy of education in this sense. He did have a theory of knowledge of sorts, but he rarely concerned himself with metaphysical support for his statements of fact or with detailed ethical arguments to justify his recommendations. That is to say he did not offer explicit statements of this nature in support of his program of reconstruction; nor was he overly concerned with an analysis and clarification of the terms he used.

Price's definition is by no means the final word on the matter, but anyone who formulates a theory of social and educational reconstruction must in the end grapple with these issues, whether or not he sets forth his premises in a systematic fashion. Whatever changes are proposed are a function of one's set of values, conception of knowledge and learning, and ultimate world view. And since Rugg did not always clarify the connections between his personal philosophy and the proposals he made, part of our task is to uncover his assumptions and implicit premises and to evaluate them along with the recommendations they yield.

These, then, are some of the issues with which I shall deal in the remainder of this study. The discussion is divided

---

1. Kingsley Price, *Education and Philosophical Thought* (Boston: Allyn and Bacon, 1962), p. 15.

into six chapters as follows: In chapter 1 an outline of Rugg's career will be sketched against the social and intellectual environment in which he functioned. The historical account, though undeniably oversimplified, may nonetheless be expected to illuminate certain aspects of Rugg's career in relation to recent social and educational history. The next two chapters are devoted to Rugg's social thought. The main concern in chapter 2 will be with his prescriptions for social reconstruction and in chapter 3 I shall analyze his politcal, ethical, and psychological views. I shall examine Rugg's account of the creative process in connection with this theory of self-cultivation in chapter 4. The analysis of creativity will lead, in turn, to a consideration of this theory of knowledge as well as his conception of mind. The fifth chapter will provide an opportunity to consider the role assigned to the school within Rugg's overall plans for social reform. Since I am primarily concerned with his views on education as an instrument of social change, I will not attempt to provide a comprehensive treatment of his educational writings, however. Chapter 6 will include a summary of the earlier portions of the study and an appraisal of Rugg's efforts from a contemporary perspective. In this final chapter I shall also inquire into the relevance of Rugg's thought for the educational concerns of the 1970s.

1. THE MAN AND HIS TIMES: A BIOGRAPHICAL SKETCH

THE EARLY YEARS

Harold Ordway Rugg was born in Fitchburg, Massachusetts, on January 17, 1886. He attended the Fitchburg public schools, finishing high school in 1902. Apparently he found little to admire in the Fitchburg school system, for he related several years later that he could not recall a single experience in school that had stimulated in him any creative thought or activity.[1]

This early disillusionment with formal education may have contributed to Rugg's decision to forego college in favor of a position in a textile mill, where he met for the first time the realities of modern industrialism. This experience undoubtedly contributed to the aversion for unrestrained business operation that later became the core of his social philosophy, for in describing the mill some forty years later he wrote, "I saw the ruthlessness with which an uncontrolled industry could exact precision of skill in a world in which dividends apportioned bread."[2]

Evidently conditions at the mill were distasteful enough to induce him to reevaluate the merits of formal education, and in 1904 he enrolled in Dartmouth College, where he was disappointed once again. He described Dartmouth as a place where the football was superb and the curriculum as good as most, which was to say, rather uninspiring.[3] He received his

1. Harold Rugg, *That Men May Understand: An American in the Long Armistice* (New York: Doubleday, Doran and Company, 1941), p. 176.
2. Ibid.
3. Ibid., p. 177.

B.S. in 1908, nevertheless, and stayed on for another year to earn a degree in civil engineering from the Thayer School.

Rugg spent the next few years gaining practical experience, first as a railroad surveyor and then as instructor of civil engineering at the James Milliken University in Decatur, Illinois. Finally he went on to graduate study in education and sociology under the direction of William C. Bagley at the University of Illinois, taking his Ph.D. in 1915.

Having completed his graduate work, Rugg began his association with Charles Judd at Chicago. There he embarked upon his long, productive career as a writer, concentrating his initial efforts in the areas of measurement, statistics, and mathematics. In 1916, for instance, he published *The Experimental Determination of Mental Discipline in School Studies,* a comprehensive summary of all the experimental work on formal discipline up to that time. This was followed by *Statistical Methods Applied to Education* (1917) and (with John R. Clark) *Scientific Method in the Reconstruction of Ninth Grade Mathematics* (1918). In relation to this study these early efforts are interesting only as they provide some insight into the personal reorientation involved in the transformation of Rugg the engineer into Rugg the social scientist, a transformation that did not coincide exactly with his shift from engineering to education. In fact, the transition to education involved no radical alteration in Rugg's interests. He later described it as "merely changing the job, the data with which I worked—not my fundamental interest. Society had made me a technician, and the change from engineering to education left me still a technician—and to a very considerable extent ignorant of the new world order that was being fashioned all around me."[4]

The turning point came in 1918 when Rugg, then working for the army, became friendly with Arthur Upham Pope, who introduced him to Van Wyck Brooks's *America's Coming of Age* and *Letters and Leadership.* These works opened up new areas of thought for Rugg, and gradually he became

4. Ibid., p. 181.

familiar with the work of Waldo Frank, Randolph Bourne, and other contemporary social critics, particularly those who had written for *The Seven Arts*, a highly regarded literary journal founded in 1916 by Brooks, Frank, James Oppenheim, and Paul Rosenfeld.

John Coss, another colleague on the army's Personnel Committee, also had a hand in influencing Rugg at this time. Coss's plans for building an undergraduate orientation course at Columbia University that would integrate the social sciences into a general introduction to contemporary civilization seem to have started Rugg thinking about his own social science pamphlets.[5]

Late in 1918 Rugg returned to Chicago for another year of work under Judd, but his talks with Pope and Coss had widened his intellectual horizons, and he was eager to try out some ideas for reorganizing the social studies curriculum. Thus when the opportunity presented itself in January, 1920, he accepted a post as associate professor of education at Teachers College, Columbia, and educational psychologist at the experimental Lincoln School, an adjunct to Teachers College. (He was promoted to full professor in 1924.) The decision to take these positions was another crucial factor in Rugg's intellectual development, since it brought him into contact with the avant-garde in the New York area. His subsequent participation in Frederick Howe's School of Opinion at Nantucket, his association with creative artists such as Alfred Stieglitz, John Marin, Marsden Hartley, and Georgia O'Keefe in Greenwich Village, and his residence in the art community of Woodstock, New York (after 1930), contributed profoundly to Rugg's intellectual development, particularly to his interest in the nature of the creative process.

This interest was in accord with the thinking of a large segment of the progressive education community at that time, for one of the chief postulates of postwar experimental

5. Ibid., p. 193.

schools was that the means to the "good society" lay in the development of individual creative potentialities. Remove the artificial restraints that hamper this development, so the argument ran, allow the child real freedom to express his unique, growing personality, and we need not fear for the society of tomorrow.[6]

The roots of these notions can be traced back through Froebel and Pestalozzi, among others, to Rousseau, and perhaps even back to Comenius. In late nineteenth- and early twentieth-century America, they were modified and adapted to the exigencies of modern formal schooling. "Child-centered" schools that had begun to appear sporadically during the first two decades of the 1900s multiplied rapidly in the years immediately following the war.[7] The significant point to be noted here, in order to make clear the intellectual currents that influenced Rugg's thinking, is that when he arrived in New York, the emphasis in many of the progressive schools, especially the private ones, was on creative self-expression.[8]

The decision to go to Teachers College also afforded Rugg an opportunity to sharpen his thinking about social issues. John Dewey and William H. Kilpatrick were already at Columbia, and George S. Counts, John L. Childs, Jesse Newlon, R. Bruce Raup, Goodwin Watson, Harold F. Clark, and F. Ernest Johnson arrived during the 1920s. These men formed a discussion group in 1927 which met regularly to discuss American culture in general. Rugg described this informal association as "a fairly cohesive group taking our stand together for the general conception of a welfare state, but critically

6. Lawrence A. Cremin, *The Transformation of the School: Progressivism in American Education, 1876–1957* (New York: Alfred A. Knopf, 1961), pp. 201–202.

7. See Harold Rugg and Ann Shumaker, *The Child-Centered School: An Appraisal of the New Education* (Yonkers-on-Hudson, N.Y.: World Book Co., 1928), pp. 48–52 for a partial, though representative, listing.

8. It should be noted that Freudianism was also an important element in the pedagogical theories of several progressive educators. (See Cremin, *Transformation of the School*, pp. 207–214.) This aspect of progressive education has little bearing on this particular study, however.

appraising all platforms, creeds, strategies, and tactics. This was practicing what we preached—vigorous adult education."[9]

During the twenties the strong interest in social justice evident in the Teachers College discussion group was to some extent atypical of progressive education in general. This is not to say that the reform strain was nonexistent during the twenties, but simply that it was somewhat overshadowed by the prevailing emphasis on self-expression. Nonetheless, reformism did have sturdy roots in the progressive education movement. Before the 1920s, in fact, a strong reformist orientation had been at least as much of a distinguishing characteristic of the movement as had the expressionistic element. This is not really surprising once the connection between progressive education and the broader progressive movement for political and social reform is perceived.

Cremin, for example, argues that progressive education originated in the nineteenth century as "part and parcel" of "progressivism writ large."[10] Similarly Rush Welter, in his analysis of the political and social implications of the traditional American faith in education, says, in effect, that the progressive movement in politics and the progressive movement in education were two sides of the same coin.[11] Both movements sprang from the same middle-class motive to protect democracy from threats inherent in the development of modern industrialism, a point which receives further support from Timothy L. Smith:

> An initial survey of the evidence at hand indicates that the movement to reform American education may have been a catalyst of this larger crusade for social justice. . . . By 1899, when he [John Dewey] published *School and Society*, social settlement workers, pastors of institutional churches,

9. Rugg, *That Men May Understand*, pp. 155–156.
10. Cremin, *Transformation of the School*, pp. 85–89.
11. Rush Welter, *Popular Education and Democratic Thought in America* (New York: Columbia University Press, 1962), p. 258.

directors of charitable kindergartens and industrial schools, crusaders for tenement-house legislation, temperance leaders, and the faculties of both progressive teachers colleges and of the new graduate universities had cooperated for nearly a decade in a pattern of action whose goal was to achieve a better environment for children in home, school, and community, and hence a "purer" national life.[12]

These writers may have overstated the case, however, for surely, as Paul Nash has pointed out, not all of the educators who considered themselves "progressive" in regard to educational practices were at the same time deeply concerned with social reform. Nash suggests, plausibly, that progressive education must be construed in much broader terms, that it encompasses a theory of knowledge and certain pedagogical attitudes about how children learn as well as a social outlook.[13] The point seems well taken in view of the obvious affinities between progressive education and the pragmatism of James and Dewey or the romantic naturalism of Rousseau and Froebel.[14]

Yet, even with this qualification noted, the fact remains that progressive education did receive much of its impetus from the larger progressive movement. In this connection, Dewey's work is the obvious paradigm. At the turn of the century he had spoken out against excessive competition among school children and pleaded for teaching that would instill a spirit of service in the child, which could be carried over into adult life.[15] Later he held that it was a function of the school to purify existing social customs and, through proper

12. Timothy L. Smith, "Progressivism in American Education," *Harvard Educational Review* 31 (Spring 1961): 170.

13. Paul A. Nash, "The Strange Death of Progressive Educaton," *Educational Theory* 14 (April 1964): 69–70.

14. See John S. Brubacher, *Modern Philosophies of Education*, 2d ed. (New York: McGraw-Hill Book Co., 1950), chap. 14, for a discussion of some of these affinities.

15. John Dewey, *The School and Society* (New York: McClure, Phillips and Co., 1900), pp. 29, 44.

habit formation, to initiate changes in the environment.[16] Dewey and his followers, many of whom came to hold influential positions in the field of education, never tired of the theme that the role of the school, in part at least, was to function as an agent of social betterment.

Further, there were definite connections between progressivism and education in the settlement-house programs, notably exemplified in the work of Jane Addams at Hull House; in the development of nature-study and agriculture clubs, both inspired by the vision of Liberty Hyde Bailey; in the municipal reform efforts of the Public Education Association; in Felix Adler's Ethical Culture Schools; and in the involvement of the University of Wisconsin with problems of government during the La Follette administration.[17] The common element in these diverse programs was "uplift," "regeneration," or "reform" of one kind or another, and education was the key to achieving the desired goal. The list is by no means exhaustive, but it is perhaps extensive enough to support the claim that education and social progress were, in fact, closely related during the progressive era. Reformist zeal subsided a bit during the twenties, perhaps, but it survived the decade and became revitalized during the thirties.

Once again, the significance of all of this in our context lies in its influence upon Rugg's thought. For these two vital elements of progressive education—creative self-expression and social reform through education—provided the foundation for his philosophy of education. The rest of his social and educational thought rests as an arch upon these two pillars.

Previous to his conversations with Pope, Rugg had shown little interest in social problems or, for that matter, with the "life of the mind" in general. Nothing in his early background had prepared him for such concerns. He described

16. John Dewey, *Democracy and Education* (New York: The Macmillan Co., 1916), pp. 27, 55.

17. See Cremin, *Transformation of the School*, chap. 3, for a full treatment of these developments.

the New England life of his boyhood as

> thin and arid like the soil; norm domineered over the spirit.
> All social forces—home, community and education—
> made for acquiescence, molding my contemporaries and
> myself to the standards of adult life. Independence of
> thought was minimized; loyalty was canonized. . . . Cer-
> tainly for most of us in the Neo-Victorian era conformity,
> not adventure, was the governing concern of conduct.[18]

Rugg made it quite clear that he had found few enlighten-
ing influences in his early academic environment. His appraisal of the postwar academic community was, in fact, out-
spokenly disparaging:

> As I inventory the academic mind of 1918 . . . one
> distinct lack of mental equipment stands out above all
> others—a profound naivete about the social scene and lack
> of independence in thought and action. As word came
> through in the spring of 1919 of the kind of treaty President
> Wilson was letting Clemenceau dictate at Versailles, few of
> us in the academic world had any really critical insight
> about it; and it must be confessed that several years more
> passed before I myself had much competence. Among my
> university colleagues there was little evidence that they
> understood the . . . trends that had already brought the in-
> ternational world to an economic and political stalemate.[19]

The accuracy of Rugg's indictment may be challenged,
but in view of his later total involvement in social issues, it is a
cogent reminder of the drastic intellectual transformation that
he experienced in the postwar years. The transformation is all
the more remarkable when it is recalled that he was already
thirty-two years old in 1918. Moreover, he was building a
personal commitment to social reform at a time when, as any
number of historians have pointed out, many intellectuals

18. Rugg, *That Men May Understand,* p. 173.
19. Ibid., pp. 171–172.

were discarding the notion. William Leuchtenburg describes the prevailing climate of opinion as follows:

> In 1913 progressive intellectuals were giving the United States its first intelligent analysis of modern society and blueprinting an ebullient hopeful program of reform. By 1919 they were a disenchanted lot; discouraged by the war and the peace that followed. . . . Faced by the victory of political reaction and the disappointment of their hopes for a new international order, they felt an overwhelming sense of their own impotence. Society seemed infinitely less malleable than it once had; they were no longer certain of their ability to shape institutions to their own desires.[20]

Henry May has observed that the old faith in moral idealism and social progress that had nurtured the progressive movement was wavering even before the war. In discussing the years between 1912 and 1917 he writes, "We can see the walls of nineteenth-century America still apparently intact, and then turn our spotlight on many different kinds of people cheerfully laying dynamite in the hidden cracks."[21] Thus the ideals which Americans carried into the war were already tottering on shaky foundations; the war simply delivered the crowning blow. "After the war," May writes, "it was hard to find a convincing or intellectually respectable spokesman for the prewar faith. The old moral idealism had become a caricature of Woodrow Wilson; the old culture was an inaccurate memory of [William Dean] Howells."[22]

Subsequent events—the machinations at Versailles, the Red Scare of 1919, Harding's easy victory signifying a "return to normalcy" and a triumph for the business ethic, the Sacco-Vanzetti case, the Scopes trial, the revival of the Ku Klux Klan—further disheartened intellectuals and led many to

---

20. William E. Leuchtenburg, *The Perils of Prosperity 1914–32* (Chicago: The University of Chicago Press, 1958), pp. 124–125.

21. Henry F. May, *The End of American Innocence: A Study of the First Years of Our Own Time* (New York: Alfred A. Knopf, 1959), p.ix.

22. Ibid., p. 394.

reject the notion of social reform altogether in the 1920s. "It seemed simpler," in the words of Richard Hofstadter, "to catch the first liner to Europe or retire to the library with the *American Mercury.*"[23] Leuchtenburg describes the decade as a period "when interest in politics was at its lowest ebb in half a century. . . . At the same time, the Red Scare left a bitter heritage of suspicion of aliens, distrust of organized labor, hostility to reformers, and insistence on political conformity, which created a smothering atmosphere for reform efforts in the 1920's."[24]

Thus it would seem that Rugg had chosen a rather inopportune time to "go liberal." Nor was his choice of residence appropriate, at least on the face of it, for in moving to New York and making friends in Greenwich Village, he was entering the very stronghold of cynical disregard for the reform impulse. Before the war the Village had, according to Malcolm Cowley, contained two types of revolt, which might be labeled "bohemianism" and "radicalism" or "the revolt against puritanism" and "the revolt against capitalism." With the war over, the former flourished while the latter all but vanished. "The bohemian tendency triumphed in the Village," Cowley writes, "and talk about revolution gave way to talk about psychoanalysis."[25] In contrasting the attitudes of the prewar residents of the Village with those of later arrivals (including himself) Cowley writes: " 'They' had been rebels: they wanted to change the world, be leaders in the fight for justice and art, help to create a society in which individuals could express themselves. 'We' were convinced at the time that society could never be changed by an effort of the will."[26]

Thus radicalism, and with it liberalism, was simply out of vogue with the postwar Village cognoscenti.[27] Cowley, inci-

23. Richard Hofstadter, *The Age of Reform: From Bryan to F.D.R.* (New York: Alfred A. Knopf, 1955), p. 286.

24. Leuchtenburg, *Perils of Prosperity,* p. 81.

25. Malcolm Cowley, *Exile's Return: A Literary Odyssey of the 1920's* (New York: W. W. Norton & Company, 1934), p. 77.

26. Ibid., p. 82.

27. Ibid., pp. 76–78.

dentally, had an interesting observation to make regarding the attitude of his generation toward progressive education: "The idea of salvation by the child was embodied in progressive education; a topic that put us to sleep."[28]

Why then did Rugg, with little previous interest in social problems, suddenly become engrossed in such cares in a seemingly unreceptive environment? Clearly his introduction (through his conversations with Pope) to the social criticism of Van Wyck Brooks, Waldo Frank, and other contributors to *The Seven Arts* had a great deal to do with it.[29] Although Brooks, in *America's Coming of Age*, had led the way in articulating the alienation of writers and artists from an excessively materialistic, acquisitive society, he had never abandoned the ideal of reform. On the contrary, he had coupled his indictment with a plea to writers to point the way to a cultural renaissance within a general socialistic framework. Later, in *Letters and Leadership*, a collection of his *Seven Arts* essays, Brooks wrote: "For poets and novelists and critics are the pathfinders of society; to them belongs the vision without which the people perish."[30] Brooks went on to argue that significant social change was highly unlikely "till a race of artists, profound and sincere, have brought us face to face with our own experience and set working in that experience the leaven of the highest culture."[31] This view put forth in *America's Coming of Age*, further developed in Brooks's articles for *The Seven Arts*, and repeated in *Letters and Leadership*, was endorsed by Waldo Frank (whose influence on Rugg, along with that of Brooks, cannot be overestimated) and others who contributed to *The Seven Arts* and became an

28. Ibid., p. 83.

29. Rugg, *That Men May Understand*, p. 323. Here Rugg acknowledges his profound indebtedness to Frank, Brooks, and others who wrote for *The Seven Arts*. See also Mark Phillips's illuminating study: "*The Seven Arts* and Harold Rugg: A Study in Intellectual History" (Master's Thesis, Columbia University, 1961).

30. Van Wyck Brooks, *Letters and Leadership* (New York: B. W. Huebsch, 1918), p. 119.

31. Ibid., p. 127.

integral part of Rugg's personal philosophy throughout his career.

Rugg's late arrival at an interest in social problems and a liberal orientation for solving them may have been still another factor in his ability to fend off the skepticism so prevalent in the twenties. It is entirely possible that he resisted disillusionment partly because neither his generally austere New England background nor his formal education had provided him with the kind of intellectual commitment that would prove vulnerable to the events of the war and its aftermath.

Moreover, the so-called revolt of the intellectuals during the twenties and the description of the decade as a period when reformist sentiments were all but eliminated require some qualification.[32] It is true that these generalizations are fairly accurate with regard to creative artists—there is no denying the exodus to Paris—and to other intellectuals as well. But several spokesmen for another segment of the intellectual community, the scholars, were in the process of restating liberal philosophy. This group, spearheaded by Dewey, Charles Beard, Thorstein Veblen, and Herbert Croly, was concerned less with the specific reforms and moral regeneration that had interested so many early progressives than with a general orientation to social planning based on an empirical approach to society and its institutions.[33] It was marked by what Morton White has called "the revolt against formalism."[34] Observation and experience rather than logical abstractions were to

32. In this connection, see Henry F. May, "Shifting Perspectives on the 1920s," *Mississippi Valley Historical Review* 43 (December 1956): 405–427; Arthur S. Link, "What Happened to the Progressive Movement?" *American Historical Review* 64 (July 1959): 833–851; and Clarke A. Chambers, *Seedtime of Reform* (Minneapolis: University of Minnesota Press, 1963). Chambers provides an illuminating account of the activities of various voluntary reform associations and social service agencies during the 1920s.

33. Arthur M. Schlesinger, Jr., *The Crisis of the Old Order, 1919–1933* (Boston: Houghton Mifflin Company, 1957), pp. 130–139.

34. Morton White, *Social Thought in America: The Revolt Against Formalism* (New York: The Viking Press, 1949).

be the foci of the new outlook, and the commitment was not to a blueprint for a better world (because that might lead to a new rigidity, a new dogmatism), but rather to intelligence as an instrument of social change.

Before starting work on the social science pamphlets, Rugg immersed himself in the works of these men while at the same time turning to the books of James Harvey Robinson, Frederick Turner, John Maynard Keynes, Sidney and Beatrice Webb, John A. Hobson, Harold Laski, R. H. Tawney, Graham Wallas, and many others. At first the new ideas encountered in his reading, clashing as they did with attitudes formed during his youth, had an unsettling effect on Rugg. "I had always believed," he recalled, "that the machinery of industrial civilization was essentially admirable and that capitalism was to be accepted on its proved merits and not really to be challenged."[35] For some time he vacillated between these older attitudes and the views of the social critics he was reading, but eventually his investigations led him to discard his earlier assumptions. The effect on him was to instill in his mind an ideal of social engineering along collectivist lines, which took its place in his thinking alongside the already germinating idea of redemption through the arts.

Thus, in the 1920s Rugg was being influenced from two directions. On the one hand he was plunging into the available library of social criticism and feeling the thrust of various arguments for social engineering; on the other, he was seriously investigating the views of those who felt that artists and writers should lead the way to social uplift. The two strains were to mature in him during the 1930s and provide him with a dual approach to social reconstruction that was rather distinctive among educational reformers. His proposals for collective social action have received due consideration in the educational literature, but the other side of Rugg, the insistence that we must look to the creative artist for guidance

35. Rugg, *That Men May Understand*, p. 202.

in the quest for the good life, has for the most part been neglected in published works.[36]

THE MIDDLE PERIOD

By the late twenties the forces in Rugg's new environment had done their work, and he was completely caught up in the main currents of progressive education. In 1928 he published, with Ann Shumaker, what was easily his most important book of the decade, *The Child-Centered School*. Cremin calls this book the characteristic progressive work of the twenties.[37] It was an appraisal of the various progressive schools of the day—favorable in tone, but not lacking in constructive criticism. The greatest significance of the book, however, was its emphasis on creative self-expression. The authors saw the task of the school as one of drawing out the creative power which lay latent within every child.[38] This drawing-out process required a flexible, sympathetic teacher who understood child psychology and was personally acquainted with the creative act.[39] It required, in short, an artist-teacher. Thus Rugg, in stressing the creative process, was clearly reflecting the prevailing ideology of progressive educators in the twenties.

The Depression led to a shift in emphasis or, rather, a return to the concern with social reform that had been so important to progressive-minded educators a generation earlier. I have already suggested that it is inaccurate to describe the 1920s as bereft of the reform impulse. Similarly, the progressive schools were not totally unconcerned with the larger society. As already noted, their emphasis on self-

36. However, this aspect of Rugg's work has been dealt with in Phillips, "The *Seven Arts* and Harold Rugg." My own appreciation of this segment of Rugg's thought owes much to Phillips's study.
37. Cremin, *Transformation of the School,* p. 183.
38. Rugg and Shumaker, *Child-Centered School,* p. 229.
39. Ibid., pp. 321–323.

expression was frequently accompanied by a rationale that included benefits for society at large. It would be erroneous, therefore, to assume that the social consciousness displayed by educators in the 1930s was a new development evoked by the Depression. True, the Depression served as a catalyst, but, as previously mentioned, social reform had been very much on the minds of a number of educators before World War I. In fact a strong case has been made for the view that American education has *never* been without a strong commitment to social progress.[40] Nevertheless, just as the twenties reveal less concern than the progressive era for reform in the society at large, so in the field of education the reform impulse was relegated to the background by the primacy of child-centered expressionism after the war. Thus with the onset of the Depression, a renewed interest is clearly discernible on both levels.

Everyone, it seemed, had a plan. Apart from the by-now-familiar Marxist prescriptions and the rather extreme suggestions offered by such groups as Technocrats, Townsendites, Share-the-Wealthers, and the Union for Social Justice—some of them on or near the lunatic fringe—there were a number of more moderate suggestions for coping with the situation that clearly demonstrated the shift in attitude from individual to social concerns. Charles A. Beard, for example, presented a five-year plan in 1931, and the League for Independent Political Action produced a four-year plan in 1932. In addition, there appeared a number of solutions from the pens of individual writers, such as Stuart Chase, Philip F. La Follette, George Soule, and Gerard Swope, to name but a few.[41]

The impact upon education in general, and upon progressive education in particular, of the emphasis on social problems was manifested in a renewed concern with the role

40. Welter, *Popular Education,* passim.
41. See Harold Rugg, *The Great Technology: Social Chaos and the Public Mind* (New York: The John Day Company, 1933), pp. 300–302, for a listing of proposals to deal with the Depression.

of the school in an era of social change. Among educators, Rugg was one of the first to make the intellectual readjustment, though in his case it was less a readjustment than a fusion of this thought into an integrated philosophy of social and educational reconstruction. Actually he had been directing his attention to an analysis of modern civilization and its sputtering economic system since the early twenties when he had begun writing his social science pamphlets. His work during the 1930s was simply a continuation of these earlier efforts, although it was given a fresh impetus by the terrible effects of the Depression.

Rugg produced three major works during the thirties: *Culture and Education in America* (1931), *The Great Technology* (1933), and *American Life and the School Curriculum* (1936). All three were concerned with the problems of contemporary American society and the role of the school in solving them. Taken together, these three volumes are a comprehensive statement of Rugg's mature thought. Nearly all of his work in later years was essentially an elaboration of the themes developed at this time. I shall examine these themes in some detail in chapter 2.

Throughout the Depression years, Rugg was a prominent member of a group of professor-reformers (often referred to as "reconstructionists" or "frontier thinkers") whose educational philosophy included the tenet that the school ought to be in the vanguard of social change. The nucleus of this group—which in addition to Rugg looked to Dewey, Kilpatrick, Counts, Boyd H. Bode, and Childs, among others, for its intellectual leadership—was located at Teachers College and was instrumental in organizing the John Dewey Society, an organization which published a number of significant yearbooks around progressive themes during the thirties. These men also helped establish *The Social Frontier,* the reformist journal that attracted to its pages many of the influential liberal writers of the day. For nearly a decade this journal was the leading voice of educational reform, and not a few of the proposals originating within its covers were taken up for general debate in other professional journals of the period.

Yet, with all the talk about the school as an agent of social change, Rugg, as noted in the introduction, was the only member of the group who actually managed to get a significant part of his program directly into the schoolrooms of the nation. His vehicle was the textbook series that later drew the wrath of a wide assortment of self-appointed censors. The series evolved out of the pamphlets he had written in the 1920s and eventually grew into six volumes for the junior high school, which were published by Ginn and Company between 1929 and the middle thirties. Later five of the books were revised, and by 1939 eight additional volumes had been produced for the elementary grades. The entire series was published under the general title of *Man and His Changing Society.*

In general, the material in the books written for the elementary grades was noncontroversial. In one glaring exception, however, Stalin seemed farily bursting with compassion and benevolence as he declared, "Our people live in dirty, dark huts. We shall teach them how to live in clean, light homes. They break their backs pulling those old wooden plows through the soil. We shall teach them to use tractors pulled by engines. . . . Radios will bring them the news of the whole world every day."[42] But once again it should be emphasized that this "Uncle Joe" portrait was an exception and that the elementary books on the whole were not likely to offend anyone.

The junior high texts were something else again. Because Rugg's objective was to encourage critical judgment based on understanding and reflective thinking, much of the material in these books was critical of existing conditions, and Rugg occasionally courted criticism in his eagerness to bring social inequalities to the attention of his readers. In one book, for

42. Harold Rugg and Louise Krueger, *Peoples and Countries* (Boston: Ginn & Company, 1936), pp. 155–157.

instance, after pointing out that 10 percent of the population received one-third of the total national income, he went on to allege that these recipients produced nothing in return for their affluence; according to Rugg they simply sat back and accumulated wealth in the form of stock dividends.[43]

In another volume, he stated, that Russia, with her planned economy, would probably equal in 25 years the industrial achievements that took 100 to 150 years to realize in England and the United States.[44] A third book contained photographs of Marx and Engels in a chapter about "frontier thinkers" who were showing the way to more democratic forms of government.[45]

It would be a mistake to infer from these examples that Rugg was "soft on communism." He was never a member of the Communist party or even a fellow traveler. Nor was he an ideological Marxist. In an article written for *The Social Frontier,* as a matter of fact, he emphatically repudiated Marxism as a viable solution for American social, political, and economic problems.[46] His sympathetic treatment of Stalin referred to above does seem to indicate, however, that during the twenties at least (when the pamphlets were written) Rugg, like many another liberal, saw only the possibilities of social improvement and failed to perceive the totalitarian implications of the Russian experiment.

Rugg also denied any socialist leanings, but as we shall see in chapter 3, some of his suggestions for dealing with the Great Depression placed him (perhaps more so than he realized) in a position not far removed from democratic so-

43. Harold Rugg, *A History of American Civilization, Economic and Social* (Boston: Ginn & Company, 1930), pp. 602–603.

44. Harold Rugg, *Changing Countries and Changing Peoples: An Introduction to World Geography and Historical Backgrounds,* 1st ed. rev. (Boston: Ginn & Company, 1938), pp. 410–415.

45. Harold Rugg, *Changing Governments and Changing Cultures: Democracy Versus Dictatorship: The World Struggle,* 2d ed. (Boston: Ginn & Company, 1937), p. 216.

46. Harold Rugg, "The American Mind and the 'Class' Problem," *Social Frontier* 2 (February 1936): 138–142.

cialism. At the same time, it should be made clear here that his post-Depression social thought tended to gravitate toward the moderate left and merge with the sort of piecemeal reformism characteristic of New Dealers. Thus it is probably fair to conclude that during his career as a whole Rugg's disclaimers regarding the affinities of his social thought with that of either Marxist or other varieties of socialist theory are acceptable with slight qualifications.

In any case, despite the fact that they were published in the 1930s when there was much talk of "subversion" in the schools, the textbooks were, remarkably enough, warmly received at first. In the long run, however, the series was removed from the nation's school shelves as a result of the efforts of a variety of conservative organizations. Since I will deal with the texts in chapter 5, there is no point in discussing them at length here. It might be helpful, though, to furnish some of the details of the "purge" in order to provide background information and to point out some of the pitfalls awaiting those who would introduce controversial issues into the schools.

The attacks began in earnest in 1939. In one of the books Rugg had pointed out that advertising costs were passed on to consumers.[47] He also cited instances of the misrepresentation of products,[48] and he suggested that one of the purposes of advertising was "to persuade the purchaser to buy whether he wants to or not."[49] The American Federation of Advertising took exception to these remarks and began attacking the book in pamphlets and letters sent out to thousands of Federation members.[50]

Bertie C. Forbes, publisher of _Forbes Magazine_ and long-time Hearst columnist, joined the attack in his writings and, using his position on the board of education in that city,

47. Harold Rugg, _An Introduction to Problems of American Culture_ (Boston: Ginn & Company, 1931), p. 454.
48. Ibid., p. 465.
49. Ibid., p. 459.
50. "The Crusade Against Rugg," _New Republic_ 104 (10 March 1941): 327.

tried (unsuccessfully) to have the books removed from the schools in Englewood, New Jersey.[51] E. H. West, a business executive and American Legion official, entered the Englewood controversy and used his Legion post as a platform for further attacks on Rugg.[52]

In the spring of 1940 *Liberty* published three articles by George Sokolsky, a publicist for the National Association of Manufacturers. The articles attacked liberal educators (notably Rugg, George Counts, and Carl Becker) for endangering democratic principles and promoting Marxist teachings in their writings for children and educators.[53]

Merwin K. Hart, president of the New York State Economic Council, distributed anti-Rugg newsletters to his membership,[54] and O. G. Rudd, a retired army major, contributed to the rising chorus of protest with an attack on the Rugg books in an article entitled "Our Reconstructed Educational System: Textbooks Teach That Our Economic and Political Institutions Are Decadent."[55]

A full-scale attack on the Rugg series by the American Legion in 1940 and 1941 produced one particularly unsavory article by O. K. Armstrong that "blacklisted" the Rugg books and presented a cartoon in which a teacher was shown leering at frightened children while pouring slime upon four books labeled "Constitution," "Religion," "U.S. Heroes," and "U.S. History."[56] Finally, the National Association of Manufacturers commissioned Ralph W. Robey to make a study of American textbooks. Robey concluded that a number of social studies

51. Rugg, *That Men May Understand*, chap. 2. This chapter and chap. 4 provide a detailed account of the attacks on the textbooks, as does Elmer Arthur Winters, "Harold Rugg and Education for Social Reconstruction" (Ph.D. dissertation, University of Wisconsin, 1968), chap. 5.

52. Ibid., p. 28. See also "The Crusade Against Rugg."

53. "Hard-Boiled Babes," 16 March 1940, pp. 49–50; "Our Children's Guardians," 6 April, 1940, pp. 33, 36; "Is Your Child Being Taught to Loaf?" 4 May 1940, pp. 41–42.

54. Rugg, *That Men May Understand*, pp. 77–78.

55. *Nation's Business* 28 (April 1940): 27–28f.

56. "Treason in the Textbooks," *American Legion Magazine* 29 (September 1940): 8–9, 51, 70–72.

texts (including two of Rugg's) tended to be "derogatory of the American form of government and critical of free business enterprise."[57]

The attitude of many of the attackers was perhaps best summed up by Mrs. Elwood Turner, corresponding secretary of the Daughters of the Colonial Wars, though it was seldom, if ever, so boldly stated. Rugg, Mrs. Turner declared, "tries to give the child an unbiased viewpoint instead of teaching him real Americanism. All the old histories taught my country right or wrong. That's the point of view we want our children to adopt. We can't affort to teach them to be unbaised and let them make up their own minds."[58]

The most spectacular incident was the actual burning of the books in Bradner, Ohio.[59] Far more serious in the long run, however, was the virtual disappearance of the series from the nation's schools. By 1940, 5,500,000 copies, including workbooks, had been sold and were being used in over five thousand school systems.[60] In 1938 alone, sales of the reading books had totaled 289,000 copies. By 1944, sales had dropped to 21,000, a decrease of some 90 percent.[61] Thus ended Rugg's dream of bringing controversial issues into the classroom.

THE POSTWAR PERIOD

Rugg attributed the attacks on his texts partly to social unrest caused by the Depression and also to a wave of irrational fear and suspicion sweeping the country because of the fear of

57. "Excerpts from Various Textbooks Criticized in the Survey," *New York Times,* 22 February 1941, p. 6.

58. *Boston Transcript,* 21 February 1940, quoted in Alonzo F. Meyers, "The Attacks on the Rugg Books," *Frontiers of Democracy* 7 (15 October 1940): 17.

59. *Cleveland Press,* 9 April 1940, quoted in Rugg, *That Men May Understand,* p. 3.

60. "Rugg Critics Lose Ground," *Publishers' Weekly,* 12 October 1940, p. 1492.

61. Jack Nelson and Gene Roberts, Jr., *The Censors and the Schools* (Boston: Little, Brown & Company, 1963), p. 39.

impending war;[62] and there can be little doubt that the fear of war, and later the war itself, had unfortunate consequences for those of the progressive-liberal persuasion. *The Social Frontier,* for instance, despite its consistent high quality, was unable to make a satisfactory adjustment to the changing times, and it faded from the scene in the early 1940s. Overshadowed by the war, the old progressive exhortations that it continued to expound did not seem quite so relevant any more.

The passing of *The Social Frontier* marked the end of an era. During and after World War II, with the Depression over, many social critics of the thirties found they had little left to offer in the way of social prescription. Rugg, however, continued to publish through the forties and fifties, attempting to synthesize the diverse strands of his thought into solid educational foundations.

In this period he focused his attention on the problems of working out a proposed structural design for the postwar American school, devising an adequate program of teacher training, and developing a coherent theory of creative imagination that would be relevant to formal education. His more important books in these later years included *Now Is the Moment* (1943); *Foundations for American Education* (1947); *The Teacher of Teachers* (1952); *Social Foundations of Education,* coauthored by William Withers (1955); and *Imagination,* published posthumously and edited by Kenneth Benne (1963).

In comparison with his earlier work, Rugg's proposals for social reform were somewhat subdued after the war, but the concept of reconstruction continued to be a vital part of his social and educational philosophy. By this time, however, he was finding it increasingly difficult to find a receptive audience. The notion of large-scale economic and social planning had never really been part of the mainstream of traditional American ideology. True, it had been partially accepted—in

62. Rugg, *That Men May Understand,* p. 83.

many cases with serious misgivings—during the Depression, but, with relative prosperity restored, it seemed to bear too close a resemblance to socialist doctrine for the tastes of most Americans.

In fact, the country at this time seemed more receptive to the call of a rising "new conservatism." A generation that had endured two world wars, a terrible depression, and the partial disintegration of its value structure was now faced with the grim prospect of an indefinitely long cold war. Weary of change, its unrest was compounded by the paradoxical fact that continual change seemed to be the only permanent quality of twentieth-century America.[63]

Faced with such unsettling circumstances, significant numbers of people longed for some sort of security, something stable to fall back upon. But the viewpoint that Rugg represented could offer nothing of the kind. Instead, it called for continual readjustment to ever-changing conditions, for new modes of thinking in the light of new problems. It was, in other words, precisely the sort of outlook most likely to elicit a hostile reaction at that point in American history.

Further, the brutality of the war had called into question the optimistic liberal conception of human malleability, given optimum environmental conditions. Confronted, say, with the facts disclosed at the War Crimes Trials, it seemed absurd to some to take seriously the view that the major inequities and injustices besetting the race would succumb to the efforts of social planners. Rather, it seemed to many that the traditional view of evil as an inherent part of human nature was more sensible and ought to be revived. Reckless, overoptimistic, liberal thinking, so the argument ran in some quarters, had led us into mistaken notions regarding human nature and society, which later proved disastrous. Liberalism, it would appear, was somehow responsible both for the serious crises we faced on the international scene and for the collapse of traditional mores at home.

63. Eric Goldman, *The Crucial Decade: America, 1945–1955* (New York: Alfred A. Knopf, 1959), p. 119.

As early as 1943 Sidney Hook noted sadly that the liberal orientation, marked by confidence in the application of scientific methods to social problems, was being superseded by a renewed interest in theology and metaphysics.[64] And again, while the war was still in progress, Friedrich A. von Hayek's *The Road to Serfdom* (1944), which argued that all forms of governmental economic planning deteriorated finally into totalitarianism, quickly became a best seller.[65]

As the postwar period moved on, the conservative protest, given added volume by Communist advances in Europe and Asia, grew louder. As Eric Goldman has observed, 1949 was a particularly crucial year. The fall of China and the explosion of an atomic bomb in Russia set the stage for the Alger Hiss trial, which in turn added new impetus to the growing suspicion that perhaps there was indeed a Communist-liberal conspiracy afoot in the land.[66]

Following the McCarthy era, the tension lessened somewhat, but if there were fewer outcries from the extreme right, the left-of-center was also conspicuously quiet. In point of fact, moderation was fast becoming the national temper. "Somehow, amid all the bitter disagreements of the post-World War period," Goldman writes, "the United States had found its way to a genuinely national mood. . . . It was nothing more or less than the decision on the part of a people who were so in-between in so many of their attitudes to go on cautiously, hopefully, maintaining equilibrium."[67]

Midcentury America, then, was not a particularly promising place to put forth models of a substantially reconstructed society to be achieved by virtue of a public school system committed to social reform. The Reconstructionists were able to attract only a limited following even during the Depression when the nation's economic system had faltered badly. The circulation of *The Social Frontier*, for example, never ex-

64. Sidney Hook, "The New Failure of Nerve," *Partisan Review* 10 (January-February 1943): 2–23.
65. Goldman, *Crucial Decade*, p. 8.
66. Ibid., pp. 121–125.
67. Ibid., p. 289.

ceeded five thousand or so in its very best years. It is hardly surprising, therefore, that their program was coolly received in the relatively prosperous fifties.

Moreover, the entire progressive education movement, social reformism included, was clearly foundering by 1955. In that year the Progressive Education Association disbanded, and two years later its journal, *Progressive Education,* was discontinued. A tide of criticism of the new education that had begun to rise in the 1940s had reached flood proportions subsequent to the launching of Sputnik 1 in 1957. The inclination of the critics was to equate progressive education with a philosophy of life adjustment, and then to point out that such an educational philosophy was obviously inadequate to meet the challenge of Soviet scientific achievement. That this argument had reached a large and sympathetic audience by the early 1960s was evident in the emphasis of that period on intellectual training and academic achievement, and in the enlistment of scholars and scientists in such projects as the Physical Science Study Committee, the Biological Sciences Curriculum Study, and the School Mathematics Study Group. Israel Scheffler described the changed mood concisely:

> We now hear constantly of "excellence," "mastery," "structure," and "discipline" where we once heard of "adjustment," "interest," "growth," and "self-expression." In place of the autonomous humanistic ideal of self-development, and the progressive concern with the child as the center of the educational process, we now find an increasing appeal to the model of the academic disciplines, and an increasing effort to shape schooling in their image.[68]

Given the then-prevailing academic orientation, one would have expected to observe a marked deterioration of reconstructionism as a philosophy by the late fifties and early

68. Israel Scheffler, "Concepts of Education: Some Philosophical Reflections on the Current Scene," in *Guidance in American Education: Backgrounds and Prospects,* ed. Edward Landy and Paul A. Perry (Cambridge, Mass.: Harvard Graduate School of Education, 1965), p. 20.

sixties and by and large such was the case. Not so, however, for all of its adherents. A few have continued to espouse its credo,[69] and while he lived Harold Rugg was certainly notable among them. Rugg never lost his enthusiasm despite the fact that the progressive education movement was disintegrating all around him in his last years. On the contrary, he retained his faith in the school as an agent of social change right up until his death in 1960.

69. Theodore Brameld is perhaps the leading contemporary spokesman of the reconstructionist view.

2. SOCIAL RECONSTRUCTION

RUGG'S SOCIAL CRITICISM

As noted in the introduction to this study, Rugg sees the possibility of a great new American culture, a "new epoch" emerging in the future. He thinks of the new culture as

> that epoch in which the fear of economic insecurity can be obliterated from the face of the earth and labor can become a pleasant experience for all mankind. It is that epoch in which universal literacy can be extended to encompass widespread, tolerant understanding, in which the scientific method can be applied to government and social relations as well as to the production of physical things, and in which the artist in every man can be liberated.[1]

In order to bring forth this new epoch, however, people must shake off the effects of what he refers to as the exploitive tradition in our society. The exploitive tradition, according to Rugg, is the unfortunate progeny of the union between industrial technology and laissez faire economics. Although this combination has given us our present high productive capacity, it has also instilled in us an acquisitive attitude that manifests itself in unrestrained competition with our neighbors and in the periodic crises that shake our economy.[2] In addition, the exploitive tradition has been established within the framework of Puritan attitudes of thrift, industriousness, austerity, and conformity—traits that have augmented our industrial growth

1. Rugg, *Great Technology*, p. iv.
2. This is Rugg's general view and is expressed in nearly all of his books. From this point on, I will cite the reference which in my judgment provides the clearest statement of his position.

but have tended equally to stifle the development of the arts in America.[3]

Here the pervasive influence on Rugg of Van Wyck Brooks and other contributors to *The Seven Arts* is clearly evident. In *America's Coming of Age* Brooks had commented on "the idealization of business" in America and observed that the best minds were drawn into commercial activities.[4] It was in this book that he differentiated so memorably between "highbrows" and "lowbrows," the former being mainly concerned with "high ideals," the latter with "catchpenny realities," and neither coming into contact with the other.[5] Brooks criticized those authors who he felt had abandoned their high ideals and succumbed to commercialism in order to please the lowbrows, but his more severe indictment was reserved for writers who had retained their high ideals at the cost of estrangement from the mainstream of American life.[6] He maintained that we needed writers who could live in both worlds and map out a middle ground of theory and action between them. In this connection, he thought we could learn much from Emerson and Whitman. "Emerson's idealism," he wrote, "was double-edged: it was concerned not merely with the spiritual life of the individual, but also with the individual in society, with the 'conduct of life.'"[7] But the real harbinger of the middle ground was Whitman, who had successfully fused the idealistic and practical strands in American life.[8] It was Whitman, said Brooks, who initially "gave us the sense of something organic in American life."[9]

All of these themes are to be found in Rugg's writings,

3. Rugg and Shumaker, *Child-Centered School*, p. iv.
4. Van Wyck Brooks, *America's Coming of Age* (New York: B. W. Huebsch, 1915), p. 137.
5. Ibid., pp. 3–8.
6. Ibid., pp. 37–70.
7. Ibid., p. 79.
8. Ibid., pp. 118–119.
9. Ibid., p. 112.

particularly in his *Culture and Education in America*. Echoing Brooks, Rugg finds the American "mass mind" regrettably preoccupied with materialistic and acquisitive goals and unreceptive to the development of indigenous creative expression. With exploitation, acquisitiveness, and social conformity in the ascendancy, the creative mind, he thinks, has in large part either been rendered inarticulate or diverted into technological or business pursuits.[10] Only a few literary giants (Emerson and Whitman notable among them) have been able to transcend the prevailing climate of opinion and emerge as forerunners of a potentially great native literature.[11]

Rugg also thinks that the arts have been neglected in the general exaltation of science resulting from the technological breakthroughs that have built our industrial civilization.[12] He lays part of the blame for this state of affairs at the doorstep of the pragmatists, who, he believes, have overemphasized experimental inquiry and problem solving at the expense of feeling, appreciation, and contemplation. In this connection, Rugg goes so far as to describe the pragmatists as "rationalizers" of American industrial culture. There is something odd about Rugg's reasoning here. It is not that he has misconstrued certain pragmatic catch phrases like "the cash value of an idea" as some critics have, and thereupon concluded that pragmatism must be the philosophy of American business life. Rather, the oddness resides in his equation of absorption in logic, science, philosophical speculation, and the like with approval of marketplace values. For instance, immediately after commenting on Charles Peirce's competence in the fields of science, mathematics, and logic Rugg writes: "Out of these sprang the inevitable rationalization of the American climate of opinion. In Charles Peirce the economic man found his pragmatic philosopher."[13] Later he adds

10. Rugg, *Culture and Education in America* (New York: Harcourt Brace & Co., 1931), pp. 4, 92.

11. Ibid., pp. 145–146.

12. Ibid., p. 111.

13. Ibid., p. 106.

the following statement to a brief discussion of James's radical empiricism: "So William James became the great rationalizer, reflecter (*sic*), and interpreter of the new industrial culture."[14]

Rugg seems to be charging the pragmatists with guilt by association in these and similar passages. His reasoning apparently runs somewhat as follows: Our industrial culture, which is based on applied science and therefore on experimentation and problem-solving, fails to do justice to the arts, to appreciation and contemplation; the pragmatists, with their emphasis on experimental inquiry and problem-solving, are deficient in much the same way; therefore our industrial culture and pragmatism must be closely related. Now the conclusion certainly does not follow from Rugg's premises, if indeed these are his premises. It is possible, of course, to make a case for the same conclusion on other grounds. Several commentators have observed that the stress on action, consequences, and "practical" matters so evident in some of the writings of Peirce, James, and Dewey marks pragmatism off as a distinctively American philsophy. But, as we have seen, Rugg does not argue in this vein. Instead, he concentrates his attention on the empiricist tendencies in pragmatism and fails to reveal the connection, if there is one, between these tendencies and the values of an industrial culture.

The Exploitive Tradition

Returning now to his account of the exploitive tradition, we find that Rugg thinks acquisitiveness and overly competitive attitudes are common wherever industrialization has occurred without benefit of careful design, but he feels that these traits were reinforced in the United States because of the unique physical obstacles that had to be overcome in conquering the wilderness. The advancing frontier, he believes, helped build attitudes of aggressiveness which underscored the already dominant individualism in America. Then,

14. Ibid., p. 115.

as manufacturing became more refined, individualism (originally an admirable quality) became more and more rugged until the "gospel of success" sanctioned all manner of expediency up to and including the ruthless exploitation of others in the frantic quest for profits.[15] In *That Men May Understand* Rugg describes this development as follows:

> In the restless haste to get immediate profits the earth was mined: the topsoil, the forests, the grasses, the coal and the oil, the iron, the copper and other metals. The people, too, were mined—their security in the land, in neighborliness, in sanity, in confidence, in human integrity. Everything in and on the earth was taken in a swift, unrestricted, race for gain. As a result many phases of the culture were *eroded*—men as well as land.[16] [Rugg's italics]

Thus, according to Rugg, was born the exploitive tradition in America; and from it followed the American "mass mind," the cluster of ideals, beliefs, fears, desires, and attitudes that constitute the prevailing "climate of opinion."

Rugg finds this climate of opinion filled with incongruities. As he looks out on the American scene, he sees a culture lacking in integrity and, in fact, permeated with hypocrisy because in conflict with the competitive norm there exists a norm of conformity, one that exhorts us to serve the best interests of the group, to cooperate with others, and to practice self-sacrifice for the common good. On the one hand we are encouraged to compete with and if possible best our neighbor, and on the other to seek his welfare; hence we frequently find ourselves advocating cooperation and fraternity at the very time that we are taking advantage of him for personal aggrandizement. Rugg questions the ability of a society to endure under such inconsistent standards.[17] He also

---

15. Harold Rugg, *American Life and the School Curriculum: Next Steps Toward Schools of Living* (Boston: Ginn & Company, 1936), pp. 77–93.

16. Rugg, *That Men May Understand*, p. 258.

17. Rugg, *Great Technology*, pp. 190–192.

detects a general feeling of anxiety caused by economic uncertainty and the fear of being cast adrift from the security of
old meanings, values, attitudes, and allegiances. The anxiety
increases as our lives are continually disrupted under the impact of expanding scientific knowledge and the industrial developments and social changes which follow.[18]

Rugg sees our industrial-democratic culture as the second phase of a two-stage transition from an agrarian to an
industrial civilization. The first stage, which he calls the
machine age, began with the start of the Industrial Revolution
and was characterized by economic expansion, urban
growth, wasteful exploitation of natural resources, and ram-
pant individualism. The second stage, the "power age" of
technological sophistication, started late in the nineteenth
century and has advanced almost to the point of total automation.[19]

Cultural Lag

The current transitional period, Rugg insists, demands new
modes of thought, new values, and new institutions in order
to accommodate the changing technology. But here, he cautions, we encounter the phenomenon of cultural lag. Drawing
upon William Ogburn's social theories,[20] he argues that scientific breakthroughs lead eventually to technological advances, which quickly lead in turn to rapid increases in productive capacity. These increases in production require adjustments in our social institutions, but the latter tend to
change very slowly. While people cling to outmoded ideas,
productive capacity runs far ahead of needed social change,

18. Rugg, *American Life,* p. 269. See also Harold Rugg, "Strains and Problems
of a Depressed Society," chap. 4 in *Democracy and the Curriculum,* Third Yearbook
of the John Dewey Society, ed. Harold Rugg (New York: D. Appleton-Century Co.,
1939), pp. 103–131.
19. Rugg, *American Life,* pp. 215–220.
20. William Ogburn, *Social Change with Respect to Culture and Original Nature* (New York: B. W. Huebsch, 1922).

and institutional control is rendered inept. Thus we have a society bewildered and out of step and an economy that is inadquate to supply the economic security for all that modern technology is capable of providing.[21]

Stated another way, we are dealing, in Rugg's view, with three social elements: economic productivity, social invention, and popular consent; and it is imperative, he thinks, that these three elements keep pace with one another in order to insure social stability. In point of fact, however, social invention and popular consent (based on understanding of changing conditions) always lag behind technological improvements.[22] Clearly, then, given Rugg's premises, an educational program—one that will reach adults as well as children—is needed if we are to gain popular consent to the social adjustments required in an age of advanced technology. The problem here, according to Rugg, is that the school has always lagged far behind contemporary social conditions and problems. "Not once in the century and a half of national history," he writes, "has the curriculum of the school caught up with the content of American life."[23] Instead, it has occupied itself with "passing on descriptions of earlier cultures and . . . perpetuating dead languages which were useful to no more than a negligible fraction of our population."[24] Hence, the first step toward social change is a thoroughgoing reconstruction of the school curriculum, one that will close the gap between the school and society and eventually help to reduce cultural lag. I will return to this notion in the next section of this chapter and again in chapter 5.

Observations

Much of the material for this first section has been gleaned from books that Rugg published during the 1930s, but it

21. Harold Rugg, *The Teacher of Teachers: Frontiers of Theory and Practice in Teacher Education* (New York: Harper & Brothers, 1952), pp. 152–155, 249–250.

22. Rugg, *American Life*, pp. 443–448.

23. Rugg, *Culture and Education*, p. 58.

24. Ibid., p. 5

would be a mistake to construe his views strictly as a response to the Depression. Much of his social criticism was formulated in the 1920s, and some of the work he completed before 1930, such as the social science pamphlets that preceded his textbook series, clearly anticipated his later writings. Moreover, *Culture and Education in America* (1931), from which I have drawn liberally, was originally drafted in 1926–27. Further, a virtual outline of *Culture and Education* appeared in the foreword to *The Child-Centered School* (1928). The Depression influenced him, of course. As we shall see later in this chapter, it led him to concern himself more with specific economic issues than he had previously, but even so, his writings during and after the thirties are perfectly compatible with his earlier social criticism.

As already observed, his social thought owes much to others. His criticism of American culture stems directly from the work of Brooks and other contributors to *The Seven Arts*; his critique of capitalism mirrors the ideas of R. H. Tawney, Graham Wallas, the Webbs, and other collectivist writers on both sides of the Atlantic; he borrows the notion of cultural lag from William Ogburn; and his complaint that the school lags behind the society of which it is a part is an old hobby horse of Dewey's.

But if Rugg's social diagnosis lacks originality, it nevertheless pulls together a number of themes and presents them to an audience of educators in a manner seldom equaled in the educational literature. Rugg was at his best at this sort of thing. Energetic, dedicated, possessed of an almost encyclopedic mind, and gifted with a flair for turning a phrase, he was at home with the ideas of natural scientists, social scientists, technologists, philosophers, and creative artists. He was able to integrate these diverse ideas and reproduce them in a way that could not fail to expand the horizons of his audience. He was, in short, a great teacher. And although he may not have been quite so successful in devising sound prescriptions for social reconstruction, his efforts along those lines were certainly no less interesting. I shall examine those efforts in the remainder of this chapter and again in chapter 3.

PRESCRIPTIONS FOR SOCIAL REFORM

As we saw in the previous section, Rugg obviously finds much in American society with which to quarrel. His is a lover's quarrel, however, and even when he is most critical—as when he scores the "exploitive tradition"—it is clear that his criticism is intended to be constructive, that he is interested in building a better America and certainly not in subverting the "American way of life," as some of his critics would have it.

Rugg gives full credit to the "exploiters," the practical men of action, for their technical achievement in converting agrarian America into an industrial giant. He writes, "It is difficult indeed to restrain one's language and not to turn appreciative appraisal into fulsome eulogy."[25] He even acknowledges their creativity: "One can have nothing but admiration for a creative mind that can turn a creaking inefficient age of wood-and-leather into one of steel, aluminum-magnesium alloys and plastics and near-manless production of quantity goods."[26] Yet, Rugg feels, as we have already observed, that the creative impulse has not fared so well in the arts. Still, he does see in this area of American life signs of change that indicate promise for the future. In order to understand Rugg's social thought, particularly with respect to the role of the artist in society, it is necessary, once again, to grasp the extent to which he was influenced by Van Wyck Brooks. Brooks's *America's Coming of Age* was more than just a critique of American literature. It was also an invitation to writers to follow Whitman's lead, to see American society whole, and in fact to show the way to a general elevation of American culture. The middle ground between "vaporous

25. Harold Rugg, *Now Is the Moment* (New York: Duell, Sloan and Pearce, 1943), p. 71.
26. Ibid., p. 72.

idealism and self-interested practicality" that Brooks wanted writers to occupy was not explicitly marked out, nor was it entirely clear just how the better life was to be lived. Brooks did outline some of its features, however. For one thing, it involved personality development apart from the quest for wealth. "You cannot have personality," he wrote, "you cannot have the expressions of personality so long as the end of society is money."[27] In addition to the pursuit of life interests or goals other than the purely economic, the good life involved a kind of creative self-fulfillment, a release of personality that would, he hoped, be channeled into various forms of useful social activity.[28]

These Brooksian notions could serve almost as a prologue to Rugg's social thought, for the same themes— personality development, disdain for the pursuit of wealth, creative self-expression, and social cooperation—may be found in all of his major works. We shall meet these themes again and again in the course of this study, particularly in the remainder of this section.

As noted earlier, Rugg, again following Brooks, had great admiration for Emerson and Whitman, who between them had provided an "organic," integrated view of individual and group life and had anticipated the work of later literary and social critics such as Brooks himself (presumably), Waldo Frank, and Randolph Bourne.[29] Rugg felt that with one exception the tradition established by Emerson and Whitman had lain dormant through the remainder of the nineteenth century, victim once again of "the hampering bonds of industrialism." The lone exception was architect Henry Louis Sullivan, whom Rugg regarded as another of the great "integrators," one who combined the skills of the technologist with those of the artist and who valued man's individuality as highly as his social responsibility.[30]

27. Brooks, *America's Coming of Age*, p. 33.
28. Ibid., p. 32.
29. Rugg, *Culture and Education*, pp. 163, 205–210.
30. Ibid., p. 165.

"Then after 1900," Rugg writes, "an increasing host of young creative artists appeared—poets, painters, dramatists, social and literary critics—rediscovering the concepts first affirmed by Emerson and Whitman."[31]

At this point it becomes difficult to discern the connection that Rugg is attempting to establish. His group of creative artists includes a wide variety of European and American writers, painters, sculptors, dramatists, musicians, and critics who seem to have had little in common other than that they were all innovators of sorts, people eager to depart from the conventional in their various art forms.[32] Rugg refers to some of them as "integrators of imagination and intellect,"[33] and apparently it is their "integrating" function that he sees as a link to the work of Emerson, Whitman, and Sullivan.

The concept of "integration" is clearly of the utmost importance to Rugg, but he has a tendency to apply it rather indiscriminately to artistic personalities with a flair for originality. Moreover, he never really provides a satisfactory description of the integrative process. Hence there is frequently an enigmatic quality attached to passages in which the term appears. What is apparent is Rugg's commendation of Emerson, Whitman, Sullivan, and a number of early twentieth-century artists and writers (notably the *Nouvelle revue Francaise* group in Paris and the *Seven Arts* group in New York) for their various cultural syntheses, including the "integration" of self and society, science and art, intellect and imagination; and, for reasons that will become clear presently, he thinks these achievements are important preparatory steps toward the overall improvement of American society. As we saw at the outset of this chapter, Rugg is very optimistic regarding prospects for social and cultural betterment. In fact, as the following passage indicates, he thinks the necessary ingredients—natural resources, technology, artistic vision, and scientific knowledge—are already available.

31. Ibid., p. 164.
32. Ibid., pp. 179–211.
33. Ibid., p. 192.

As a consequence of these achievements of the scientist and the artist, the constituents with which to bring forth a great culture are at hand. There are vast energy resources, an efficient machine technology and trained technicians enough to completely wipe out the economic problem. There are creative leaders on the frontiers of thought and feeling who are equipped to design a centrally coordinated economic-political system, a humane social organization and a regime of beauty. There are many millions of persons who, taken together, constitute a potential informed thinking minority whose opinions can form the supporting intellectual climate for the new designs. These are, indeed, the constituents for a magnificent culture.[34]

The Description of Society

How then does Rugg propose that social reconstruction proceed, and to what end? He recommends first a "creative portrait," a comprehensive description of American society. This description would deal with the external elements of our civilization, that is, our various economic modes of production and distribution; political, legal, and religious institutions; the family, language, science, mass media of communication, as well as the veiled forces that operate at a deeper level. The latter would include the psychological and philosophical beliefs, attitudes, and desires of the people, that is to say, the general climate of opinion that shapes the surface features of a civilization.[35]

Rugg feels that the materials for this description have already been uncovered by scholars and artists working on the frontiers of knowledge. He divides these "frontier" thinkers into three groups: "students of the interrelationships between economics and political life," comprising economists, political scientists, and the "new" historians; "students of culture," including philosophers, psychologists, anthropolo-

34. Rugg, *Great Technology,* p. 284.
35. Rugg, *Culture and Education,* pp. 259–260.

gists, and sociologists; and a twofold group of creative artists and cultural critics.[36] The scattered individual inquiries of these workers need to be woven together (or "integrated") into the proposed total description, which would reveal the basic characteristics and problems of contemporary society.

Once the description is completed, the next step is to impart it to children and adults alike. With respect to the former, this task can be performed in the formal school setting by making the description of society the basis of the social studies curriculum.[37] To digress for a moment, this was precisely the purpose of Rugg's textbook series, which in fact he offered as a tentative description of society. To illustrate, one volume is concerned with a historical exposition of what Rugg considers to be the basic trends in American government and culture. The extension of our role in international affairs and the increasing influence of government in relation to the lives of our people are examples of the topics dealt with.[38] Another volume analyzes problems of contemporary life in the United States within the context of a wide variety of community settings. The impact of industrialism and urbanization on family and community life is one of the main themes considered.[39] A third book attempts to describe the changes that have taken place in nine selected foreign countries as a result of the Industrial Revolution and subsequent events.[40] The texts and their underlying rationale will be considered in greater detail in connection with Rugg's philosophy of curriculum construction in chapter 5.

With respect to adult education, Rugg anticipates the

36. Ibid., pp. 269–274. A few of the more prominent thinkers he had in mind were Tawney, Wallas, Marx, Beard, J. H. Robinson, and Turner in the first group; Dewey, Lippmann, Cooley, Freud, Jung, and Adler in the second; and Brooks, Bourne, Stieglitz, Sandburg, Lindsay, and Frost in the third.

37. Ibid., p. 323.

38. Harold Rugg, *A History of American Government and Culture: America's March Toward Democracy* (Boston: Ginn & Company, 1931).

39. Harold Rugg, *An Introduction to Problems of American Culture* (Boston: Ginn & Company, 1931).

40. Harold Rugg, *Changing Civilizations in the Modern World: A Textbook in World Geography with Historical Backgrounds* (Boston: Ginn & Company, 1930).

formulation of cultural discussion groups—modeled after Frederic Howe's Nantucket group and similar associations in Provincetown, Massachusetts, and Woodstock, New York, all of which Rugg was familiar with during the twenties and thirties—in every community of at least moderate size across the country. He believes that each of these communities has a few potential leaders who should be encouraged (by educators, apparently) to take the initiative in forming discussion groups in their respective localities for the serious consideration of local and national problems.[41]

In addition, Rugg wants all the various community organizations to take on an education function. This is part of his conception of the "school-centered community," a society in which government, industry, business, agriculture—all the various social agencies—would attempt to define an improved individual and social existence for all by exploring alternative suggestions for social reconstruction. Coordination of these diverse agencies would be the responsibility of the superintendent of education and his advisory board. The school system would thus accept adult education as part of its responsibility.[42]

The feasibility of Rugg's school-centered community has been questioned, and he has often been criticized for a tendency to set unrealistic goals. As we shall see later in this chapter, there is some basis to these charges. Nonetheless, there is much to be said for the notion that the school should be considered as only one (though the most important) of the community's educative agencies. (This idea deserves further discussion, and it will be considered at greater length in chapter 5.) Meanwhile, we need to consider the all-important question of what Rugg sees as the outcome of his educational program.

Assuming that the description of society could be completed and incorporated into both the school curriculum and

41. Rugg, *Culture and Education*, pp. 283–288.
42. Ibid., pp. 288–291.

the agenda for Rugg's proposed discussion groups, what, then, are his further objectives? Rugg writes:

> Toward what are the description and analysis of our society to be directed? There shall be two foci: first, an expressive theory of individual and group life constructed out of the conditions of American civilization and culture; second, a program of collective action—a planned regime for economic, political, and social life. Both of these—a theory of living for the American and a plan of action for the Americans—are indispensable and the latter rests indubitably upon the former.[43]

It is worth noting here that since Rugg distinguishes between a theory of group life and a program of collective action, it appears that he really has three tasks in mind. "First and foremost," he continues, "we need a theory of individual life. . . . But we must also construct a theory of group life in America. . . . Upon it must be built a program of production and distribution of physical goods, and a mechanism of effective political institutions."[44] The theory of individual life and the theory of group life should be constructed together in Rugg's view. "Our goal is a cultured society," he writes, "but we can produce a cultured society only by producing cultured individuals. We know full well that neither is antecedent to the other, both develop together."[45]

In terms of sequence, then, the theories of individual and group life should be formed together, and should precede the program of collective action. Two years later, however, in *The Great Technology*, Rugg wrote, "The first problem is to design a social structure which can turn the potential economy of abundance into an actuality; the second is to design a way of complete personal living within it."[46] He thereby re-

---

43. Ibid., p. 10.
44. Ibid.
45. Ibid., p. 254.
46. Rugg, *Great Techonology*, p. 19.

versed the sequence given in *Culture and Education*. Since the order provided in *The Great Technology* was reiterated in 1936[47] and again in 1939,[48] it was, apparently, the one Rugg finally decided upon.

The total revised sequence, then, would have the description of society coming first. This would be followed by a program for social reconstruction based upon conditions and problems revealed in the description. And finally, a theory of individual and group life would be worked out within the reconstructed society. This version seems by far the more reasonable of the two since the steps follow naturally one after the other. In our discussion, however, we shall deal with the theory of individual and group life first in order to show more clearly the development of Rugg's thought. In *Culture and Education*, where these ideas were first presented, he chose not to develop a plan for social reconstruction on the grounds that this task would require the joint efforts of a number of "far-seeing and critical minds."[49] Later he changed his mind and did offer at least the outline of such a plan. But this later effort was prodded by the Depression,[50] and it will be more appropriately discussed in the section devoted to Rugg's response to the Depresssion.

The Theory of Individual Life

Rugg introduces his theory of individual life by pointing out what he considers to be the limitations of pragmatism as a guide to living. Although he concedes that the pragmatic emphasis on the experimental method of inquiry has contributed much to building our present industrial civilization, he nonetheless finds pragmatism less than adequate as a dynamic philosophy of life. Agreeing with Randolph

47. Rugg, *American Life*, p. 418.
48. Rugg, "Strains and Problems," p. 128.
49. Rugg, *Culture and Education*, p. 11.
50. *Culture and Education*, it will be recalled, was first drafted in 1926–27; hence much of it represented a pre-Depression view.

Bourne,[51] he remarks, "Here is an instrument but no power. An engine has been created, perfect in design and construction, but—without motive force."[52] In addition to the scientific, experimental habit of mind, with its emphasis on intellect and problem-solving, we must also pay heed, according to Rugg, to the concepts of imagination, contemplation, appreciation, and "feeling-import." And it is the artist's guidance that we must seek in understanding these concepts:

> Through centuries of utterance Culture—men—Artists —have given us additional concepts for the good life. Listen to them: self-cultivation . . .conscious—appreciative— awareness . . . detached . . . contemplation . . . the integrity of the natural thing . . . feeling import . . . imaginative reason . . . confident belief in self . . . the whole self and the whole society . . . society conceived as a multitude of proud affirming selves.[53] [Ellipses and capitalization appear in the original.]

As Rugg himself acknowledges, some of these concepts are elusive, and he attempts to clarify his meaning as follows: "I think the essence of the attitude which I am trying to delineate is a gathering-together-of-the-self. Like one's personal philosophy, it is a mental and emotional synthesis. It is a unitary thing, a fusion of total physiology, emotion, meaning."[54]

Now this does not seem to take us very far, either. Here again we meet the notions of "fusion" and "synthesis" that appear frequently in Rugg's work, and, as in other instances, we are left wondering exactly what the process entails. Just how does one "gather one's self together" and achieve the desired "mental and emotional synthesis"?[55] We can grasp what Rugg is driving at, generally speaking. In the tradition of

51. Randolph Bourne, "Twilight of Idols," *The Seven Arts,* October 1917, pp. 688–702.
52. Rugg, *Culture and Education,* p. 141.
53. Ibid., p. 229.
54. Ibid., p. 230.
55. Here I am indebted to Boyd H. Bode for his criticism of Rugg's *Culture and Education* in Bode's article, "The Problem of Culture in Education," *Educational Research Bulletin* 10 (30 September 1931): 339–346.

Brooks, Bourne, and Frank, he is stressing the need for fostering the development of artistic personality and creative spirit
(associating "creative" with the arts, primarily) in American
life, and he finds that this need has been left unsatisfied in
modern industrial society. He finds, moreover, no signs of its
being met by contemporary science or by the dominant
American philosophy of his day, pragmatism. Thus he stands
convinced that we must look to creative artists and to writers
like Emerson and Whitman for help in defining the "good
life." Essentially, then, Rugg is seeking a merger of science
and art, intellect and imagination. He phrases it as follows:

> In the synthesis of pragmatic and artistic concepts we
> have a sound basis for a description of our society. Thus we
> shall utilize a broad array . . . the experimental method of
> inquiry, but also appreciation, awareness . . . Man Thinking
> and Man Feeling . . . creative desire and creative intelli-
> gence . . . vision cooperating with Technique . . . the cir-
> cumscription of science and sanctity . . . the marriage of
> intellect and imagination.[56] [Ellipses and capitalization ap-
> pear in the original.]

To anyone familiar with the writings of Brooks, Bourne,
and Frank, there is a familiar ring to this passage, for Rugg's
social criticism is basically an extension of theirs. Interestingly
enough, furthermore, Rugg's effectiveness diminishes at the
same point at which his mentors encountered difficulties,
namely when they attempted to move beyond social criticism
to positive suggestions for improving the conditions that dis-
turbed them. It was all very well for Brooks to point out that
creativity in America was being smothered in an overly acquisitive society and to call for writers and artists to establish a
new creative spirit in America—Brooks's social criticism was
always perceptive and well taken—but as Alfred Kazin has
observed, it was never quite clear what the new spirit was to
be.[57]

56. Rugg, *Culture and Education*, p. 211.
57. Alfred Kazin, *On Native Grounds: An Interpretation of Modern American
Prose Literature* (New York: Harcourt, Brace & Co., 1942), p. 181.

Similarly, many of Rugg's critical observations are telling, but his account of "self-cultivated" individual life is, as noted above, rather slippery. It is not an easy task to get a firm grip on terms like "gathering-together-of-the-self," "feeling-import," and "mental and emotional synthesis."

Further, it seems fair to ask how these and similar characteristics, even if they can be defined more precisely, add up to a mode of living that can be labeled "good," for we have seen that Rugg counsels us to look to the artist for clues to the "good life." The question is, does he mean morally good or nonmorally good, or both? If he were using the term "good" in a nonmoral sense exclusively, we could accept more readily his assumption that the "self-cultivated," "cultured" life of artistic achievement and appreciation is, other factors held constant, a "good" life. Surely these pursuits provide satisfaction and pleasure for any number of people. But Rugg seems to think that a life-style of this sort is also good in the moral sense. He writes:

> This attitude of self-cultivated awareness seeks as its consummation the production of honest, integral things, the life of honest, integral acts. To it the current widespread mode of hypocrisy is an incredible way of life. The very basis of individual and social living is the integrity of the human act. . . . Each of these must be an honest objectification of the self. That, I think, is the chief criterion for an integrated personality in the Man-as-Artist. He constantly strives to speak, to write, to make, to live, what he feels and thinks, in short, what he *is*, at a given moment. This is the measure of a sound personal philosophy of living. . . . The objects of allegiance which govern these human acts of integrity are found in the assimilated internal experience of the man. . . . If his personal philosophy constitutes an honest program of life, he can utter only what he is. . . . Hence the thundering affirmation of the Answerers throughout history that it is the integrity of the self which is the gathering-together principle. This has been the theme of every great

religion and the true measure of works of art and of philosophies of life.[58]

Thus the "cultivated" life is marked by honesty, integrity, a sound personal philosophy of life, and honorable social relationships—a far cry from Rugg's conception of the predominant mode of American life, which he describes throughout his writings as exploitive, hypocritical, and sadly lacking in integrity. It would appear, then, that he considers the cultivated or cultured life to be "good" in the moral as well as in the nonmoral sense of the term.

But why should this be the case? Why does Rugg think that people who engage either actively or vicariously in creative activities, especially in the arts, are more likely than others to demonstrate integrity? The answer rests in his assumption that if one wishes to complete successfully a creative project, one must be prepared to engage in a good deal of hard work, sacrifice, and self-criticism; and these are the kinds of activities, Rugg holds, that develop self-discipline and moral fiber.[59] Elsewhere he says:

> It is the art experience, the creative act, that contains within itself the psychological power to develop the sound individual and hence the sound society. That power is the concept and attitude of Man-as-artist's integrity as set forth in the constant attempt to objectify himself—to speak, to write, to make, to do only what he thinks and feels, only what he is. . . . I can only conclude, then, that the creative art experience, because of its integrity-producing power, is an indispensable vehicle for social integration.[60]

Touching on the same point in another context, Rugg states: "Between the Man-As-Artist's opinions and his life there will be no gaps. . . . There will be no lacuna between his theory and his behavior. Defense mechanisms will be re-

---

58. Rugg, *Culture and Education,* pp. 230–232.
59. Rugg and Shumaker, *Child-Centered School,* pp. 282–286.
60. Rugg, *American Life,* p. 440.

duced to a minimum. Hypocrisy will not exist in human be-havior."[61]

Rugg reaches for altogether too much in these passages. He is probably right in his contention that the self-discipline which is so important a part of the creative process is also a prime factor in the development of character; furthermore, self-expression would seem to be one way of coming to a better understanding of one's abilities, capacities, and uniqueness of personality. The resulting increase in self-awareness, in turn, might well be a significant step toward achieving an autonomous individuality that relies mainly on internal norms of conduct rather than on external patterns of conformity. And all of this no doubt contributes to one's mental and emotional well-being. Hence, Rugg's references to a mental and emotional synthesis, an integrated pesonality, a "gathering-together-of-the-self" are presumably meaningful to the creative artist (and perhaps to the psychologist as well). But even supposing, for the sake of argument, that this is the case, there is still a gap here between the psychological con-notations of "integration" and the moral connotations of "in-tegrity" which he bridges a little too easily in his discussion of the self-expressive, creative person. Even if we grant that self-expression is a factor in developing an integrated person-ality and that the term "integrated personality" implies men-tal and emotional stability, we can still question the claim that an individual so endowed is also a person of integrity. The term "integrity" connotes moral soundness or uprightness, and these terms suggest the concept of "virtue." One won-ders, then, whether Rugg is implying that the creative or ap-preciative individual is by definition also a virtuous individu-al. If this is in fact his intent, he is clearly mistaken for there is nothing illogical in the assertion that a creative person may be morally deficient. A swindler, for example, or better still a forger, could conceivably be an artist in his own right.

Thus it simply does not follow that the creative person is

61. Rugg, *Culture and Education*, p. 232.

necessarily a person of integrity in any of the usual senses of the term. It may be the case that creative self-expression is one element in building character or developing integrity, but it seems clear that Rugg has exaggerated its importance and offered an approach to individual and social betterment that is both overly optimistic and rather limited in scope. Unless he can establish a firm connection between creativity and integrity his theory is somewhat unconvincing, and it has been the burden of the preceding analysis to show that the suggested connection is precarious at best.

The Theory of Group Life

At the start of this discussion it was pointed out that Rugg mentions the need for a theory of group life in addition to the theory of individual life. Actually, he never gets very far in the formulation of the former because his emphasis is so often on the individual. Indeed this emphasis reveals another of his points of contention with the pragmatists. He feels that pragmatism overstresses social adaptation, thereby minimizing the importance of the individual and his esthetic experiences, many of which are asocial.[62] Whatever the merits of this charge, Rugg errs in the opposite direction. He stresses the need "for a theory which will embrace the coordinate concepts—'the individual' and 'the social' "[63]—but he pays scant attention to the latter. For him society is simply the interaction of two or more individuals.[64] "Social life," he says,

> consists of nothing but men and women, boys and girls, living together, influencing one another in various and subtle ways. . . . There is no 'social mind,' 'American mind,' 'crowd mind,' 'group mind,' apart from the interpenetrating give and take of the individuals who compose these groups.

62. Ibid., pp. 251–254.
63. Ibid., p. 252.
64. Rugg, *American Life*, p. 259.

These terms, therefore, are merely phrases designed for the convenience of abstract thinking and discussion. Hence my constant emphasis upon basing our social program upon an expressive program of individual living.[65]

This terminology is confusing because earlier Rugg had said that a social program should also be related to a theory of group life, but his theories of group life and individual life are hardly distinguishable. One is simply a slight extension of the other. I have already noted his assertion that the goal of a cultured society can be achieved only through the production of cultured individuals. And that is all there is, really, to his theory of group life. That, and the added proviso that the cultured, "integrated" individuals who make up the society, must recongize the true worth of one another.[66] As the following passage indicates, Rugg is remarkably confident with regard to the kind of society that would emerge out of the interaction of his cultured individuals:

The society that springs from the interpenetration of such personalities will be of the highest order of social good. It will approximate social purity; it will be relatively free from an hypocrisy which is dictated by the compulsions of self-defense. The very need for social self-defense, for preparing attitudes to get what we want, will tend to disappear. Instead of each individual's trying to defeat other individualities (as in the regime of competition for success, *laissez faire*), each will strive only to be his best self. Correspondingly, because of mutual respect, differences among individuals will be settled by honest, frank compromise. The current widespread order of hypocritical anti-social competition can then give way to true social cooperation.[67]

Rugg apparently believes that if we can only produce enough cultured men of good will, we can all but eliminate

65. Rugg, *Culture and Education*, p. 248.
66. Ibid., p. 255.
67. Ibid.

social conflict. In a complex pluralistic society such as ours, with its myriad social groups, the values of which are bound to clash sooner or later as a result of competing claims on available goods and services (not to mention divergent ideas), this is a somewhat simplistic point of view.

Rugg's theory of group life is therefore open to criticism similar to that leveled against his theory of individual life. It is oversimplified and optimistic to an extent that renders it almost utopian. These excesses are all the more remarkable because, as we shall see in the section on human nature, Rugg is not unaware of the social forces that impinge on the individual and shape his attitudes. He elects, however, to hold this awareness in abeyance in his efforts to formulate a theory of individual and group life. Perhaps he is overreacting to his long-time adversaries, the pragmatists. At any rate, his one-track analysis of what is needed to set American social relationships aright simply fails to accomplish its purpose.

Social Engineering: Rugg's Response to the Depression

Earlier in this discussion, it was noted that in *Culture and Education* Rugg demurred from submitting a plan for "collective social action" because he felt that an undertaking of such magnitude required the joint efforts of several creative minds. As the grim conditions of the Depression gradually emerged into sharper relief, however, he was stimulated to offer some suggestions of his own, most of which were set down in *The Great Technology* (1933). But even in this book his proposals were intended to provide no more than an outline of a program for social reconstruction. Here, as in most of his work, he saw his role as one of pointing out the conditions that in his view made reconstruction imperative, summarizing the events that had led to these conditions, and providing the educational leadership required to convince the general public of the need for social change.

On the whole these tasks were carried out effectively. Although his social criticism contained few new insights, it did recapitulate the best of liberal (in the contemporary sense) and socialist thought quite forcefully and persuasively. And some of his proposals for educational reconstruction were among the most inventive offered during the progressive education era. Conversely, his proposals for dealing with the social impasse described in his writings were not so impressive. This was partly because his approach to social engineering, like his approach to a theory of individual and group living, was too restricted. At first glance it appears comprehensive enough, since he called for social and political as well as economic reconstruction to cope with the changing times. But a closer look reveals that for the most part he limited his analysis to the economic phase of the problem, thus sidestepping the related social and political questions. I shall return to this limitation and its consequences in the next chapter. Meanwhile we need to consider the positive recommendations for social reconstruction that Rugg did offer.

A program for collective action.   As noted above, Rugg's most specific suggestions for social engineering appeared in *The Great Technology*. The ideas presented in this book were inspired in part by Thorstein Veblen and Howard Scott (leader of the technocracy movement that gained a wide following during the early thirties), both of whom had proposed that in the interest of efficiency, control of the economy should rest with engineers and technicians rather than with financiers who were interested only in profits.[68] Rugg, a former engineer himself, had long admired Veblen and had made a careful study of Scott's views in the early thirties. Although his own proposals differed from theirs in specifics, the call was essentially the same: for technological experts to design and operate the economy in the public interest. Hence Rugg took the word "engineering" in the term "social engineering" quite seriously. He wrote:

68. See Thorstein Veblen, *The Engineers and the Price System* (New York: The Viking Press, 1921), and Howard Scott, *Introduction to Technocracy* (New York: Technocracy, 1936). Scott had been expounding his theories for years in Greenwich Village before the publication of this book.

The scientific student recognizes at the outset only two factors: a people needing physical goods and a physical world containing the resources from which these can be produced. The economic problem, then, is to design and operate a system of production and distribution which will produce the maximum amount of goods needed by the people and will distribute it to them in such a way that each person will be given at least the highest minimum standard of living possible. Thus the scientific student does not recognize the right of any person to take an undue share of the goods produced *until all have received that minimum* [Rugg's italics] which the scientific study of physiology and psychology determines is necessary for the maintenance of a healthful life and which the study of the national resources shows is possible. Whether some persons, on account of greater creative ability and initiative, should be permitted to take more than the minimum and how much more is a question that can be answered only by future social experimentation. Personally I should say they should, with definite restriction of the "ceiling" to a low multiple of the minimum.[69]

In passing, we might note Rugg's interesting assertion in this passage that a value question involving the distribution of goods (i.e., who should receive what?) is to be answered by experimentation. I shall deal with the implications of this and similar assertions in the section on Rugg's ethics in chapter 3 and again in chapter 5, but it is worth noting at this point that the failure to distinguish between factual statements and value judgments is a recurrent problem in his writings.

In any case, Rugg believed that the nation possessed an abundance of natural and human resources. The problem, therefore, was to plan and design the economy to take advantage of this abundance. "It is now axiomatic," he said, "that the production and distribution of goods can no longer be left to the vagaries of chance—specifically to the unbridled com-

69. Rugg, *Great Technology*, p. 106.

petitions of self-aggrandizing human nature."[70] In Rugg's view the choice (if it could be called that) was between the economic security that could be achieved through social reconstruction and the social chaos that seemed imminent under a system of laissez faire capitalism. In order to avoid the latter, Rugg recommended three steps toward reconstruction: design, consent, and technical operation under democratic control.[71] I shall first explain each of these steps separately, and then return to Rugg's overall plan for further discussion and criticism.

By "design" Rugg meant planning for an economic and political system through the cooperative efforts of technologists, political scientists, philosophers, psychologists, economists, and artists.[72] There is an ambiguity here in that this group is almost identical with the one charged with the task of furnishing the description of society. Apparently several of the scholars mentioned are assigned to both phases of the reconstructive process—description and design. The precise role of the teacher is also unclear. Obviously one of his tasks would be to impart the description of society to the nation's youth, but in some of Rugg's writings the teacher, too, is referred to as a social engineer, notably in the final chapter of *American Life and the School Curriculum.*

To Rugg "consent" meant a supporting body of public opinion made up of the intelligent minority. He was a "realist" on this point. His experience with mass testing during the war had apparently convinced him that universal understanding of political and economic issues was unlikely in a complex industrial society. Hence he was prepared to settle for a well-informed, articulate minority.[73]

Finally, "technical operation" meant turning the system over to technicians who would run basic industries such as farms, factories, and mines so that production would be regu-

70. Ibid., p. 172.
71. Ibid., pp. 186–187.
72. Ibid., p. 172.
73. Ibid., pp. 199–201.

lated according to consumer needs.[74] The design and management of the system were to be carried out under the authority of elected political representatives who, acting on the wishes of the people, would leave the working details to the experts.[75] Rugg thought that this scheme was an ideal merger of democracy and science. "Such a procedure," he claimed, "bears both the democratic and the scientific sanctions. It is based upon scientific design by experts, the adoption of the design by the true consent of the people, and practical administration by chosen legislators, executives, and judges."[76]

Difficulties in Rugg's proposal.   Rugg's proposal suffers from a scarcity of detail that makes evaluation difficult. Presumably he did not provide an operational description of how his designed system would function because he felt that this task should be undertaken by the designers and technicians themselves. This is fair enough, perhaps, except for his skirting of a fundamental issue that he should have considered even on the general level at which he chose to carry on the discussion.

This issue involves the relationship between political representatives and those who were to design the economy, a relationship that Rugg never clarified. The key question is where does control reside? Now assuming, as Rugg did, that the design and operation of the economic system are to be carried on within a framework of democratic political institutions, control must rest ultimately with the elected representatives of the people, and Rugg said as much himself.

In view of some of the other things he said (and did not say), however, it seems permissible to wonder whether he wished to minimize this control, at least in 1933. It is possible that his reticence concerning the limits of the planners' authority and the mechanism for exerting governmental control over them may have stemmed from a reluctance to explicitly place the experts under the direct authority of political office-

74. Ibid., pp. 186–187.
75. Ibid., pp. 174–175.
76. Ibid., p. 172.

holders. His problem was to provide the means by which an aristocracy of talent could set economic policy within a democratic framework of government, but he had little confidence, it seems, in the integrity of politicians. He was afraid that under the sway of private business interests and out of self-seeking political motives they would fail to give the system designed by scholars and operated by technological experts a fair trial. Thus on the few occasions when he discussed their role in the designed system he did so with an unmistakable note of disparagement. In one passage, for instance, he expressed serious misgivings about the likelihood of freeing politicians from the influence of businessmen.[77] In another, he argued that "the basic industries must be taken from the sphere of political manipulation and carried on purely as a scientific and technological enterprise."[78] In still another, he called for "the exertion of public compulsion upon elected officials to put the new design to experimental trial."[79]

All of this conveys the distinct impression that Rugg regarded political representatives and appointees as a necessary evil whose participation in the reconstruction of society should be kept to a minimum. Their role seems to have been reduced to that of performing necessary administrative, legislative, and judicial duties in compliance with the recommendations of expert social engineers who would emerge as the real policy makers. In particular, his explicit statements (quoted above) regarding the administrative function of politicians and the need for public compulsion to ensure their cooperation with the social engineers indicate that he may have desired rather sweeping de facto power for his proposed planning group.

This possible interpretation of Rugg's position is reinforced by a consideration of his views on popular consent. He

77. Ibid., p. 180.
78. Ibid., p. 175.
79. Ibid., p. 172.

insists that "the consent of an organized body of the people is the desideratum of prolonged stability in social action. . . . The consent of the people is indeed basic to the democratic method."[80] And yet the elitist implications in his outlook are unmistakable for as we noted earlier the consent Rugg had in mind was that of an "intelligent minority." In this connection he wrote, "No permanent reconstruction can be brought about that does not rest upon the consent of at least an effective minority of considerable size."[81] He went on to describe the "effective minority" as individuals with sufficient intelligence to understand the complexities of modern society, to choose capable leaders, and to evaluate suggested policies intelligently. The "rank and file," on the other hand, were described as "followers," many of whom could not be expected to comprehend the difficult problems and issues of contemporary society or the relative merits of proposals for social reconstruction.[82] It was primarily the "thinking minority" whom Rugg hoped to enlighten with his program of adult education,[83] and although he did not spell it out in so many words, the tacit assumption was clearly that members of the intellectual elite would help to mold public opinion in favor of social change.[84]

Thus the reconstructed society would be one in which artists and writers provided clues to the "good life," while scholars and technologists designed social institutions, and an intelligent minority built consensus among the people. There is an autocratic ring to this scheme that is faintly audible in much of Rugg's work and which signals difficulties for his concept of democracy as government according to popular

80. Ibid., p. 187.
81. Ibid.
82. Ibid., p. 200.
83. Ibid., p. 201.
84. He came close to spelling it out in the following passage: "Just as a Tammany precinct leader knows that he carries his precinct if he delivers his allotted 'five votes,' so we can create intelligent social reconstruction if we can produce five thoughtful Americans in each of our million neighborhoods." Ibid., p. 202.

consent. In a review of *The Great Technology* Lawrence Dennis made these comments:

> For Professor Rugg the problems of the hour are those of design for the new order and consent of the people. Technological experts will draw up the best hypothetical designs for an economic and political system that their cooperative thought can produce.... The intelligent minority will then take care of the problem of consent by creating a large supporting body of public opinion.... The result will be democratic control and technical operation. To call such an achievement "democratic control" seems to me either a piece of crass stupidity or intellectual dishonesty.[85]

On the whole, Dennis's criticism, particularly his objecting to Rugg's use of the term "democratic control," was justified, but it was also a bit harsh. Clearly Rugg was neither stupid nor intellectually dishonest. He was intellectually untidy, however, in that he took an eclectic approach to issues that frequently led him to entertain conflicting ideas. Good democrat (in the broad sense) that he was, Rugg felt that popular consent based on an understanding of the issues was a necessary prerequisite to social reconstruction. At the same time, he felt that only a minority of the population was capable of fully understanding present social conditions, their antecedents, and the need for change. This minority had to be used, therefore, to create a nationwide climate of opinion favorable to social reconstruction. The fact that for most people this plan would result in their granting consent based on something akin to conditioning rather than on understanding seemed not to bother Rugg in the least. Indeed, it may never even have occurred to him, given his capacity for simultaneously entertaining the most incongruous ideas. We shall en-

85. Lawrence Dennis, "Is Capitalism Doomed?" *Saturday Review of Literature* 9 (27 May 1933): 615.

counter this characteristic again in connection with his theory of knowledge, which will be considered in chapter 4.

Social Engineering: Rugg's Later Writings

Rugg's social thought was generally consistent over the years. He may have been somewhat harsher in his criticism of existing conditions before and during the Depression than he was later on, but his social prescriptions remained essentially the same. Moreover, he never repudiated the views set forth in his earlier writings. On the contrary, he frequently took pains in later books to refer the reader to such early works as *Culture and Education* and *The Great Technology* for a better understanding of his then current position.[86] By the early 1940s, however, Rugg was more willing than he had been during the Depression to acknowledge some promise in New Deal policies. In discussing the Roosevelt administration, for example, he wrote,

> Here, on the very threshold of consummation, is the thing we have dreamed about and pled for and worked for— science in government, research in government, brains in government. Here are the makings of a government of welfare and creative ability . . . a government motivated by good will and guided by brains . . . emerging at the very moment we need it most. [Ellipses appear in the original.][87]

The forties and fifties likewise found Rugg more receptive to the concept of a "mixed economy," partly planned and partly unplanned. In a sense, a mixed economy was always his goal, but during the thirties he was convinced that a large measure of centralized planning was necessary in order to operate the system successfully. His views on this point are more tentative, more hesitant, in his later work.[88] Yet, even in

86. Rugg, *Teacher of Teachers*, pp. 278–279, 281, 292, 295, 296, 298.
87. Rugg, *Now Is the Moment*, pp. 140–141.
88. See, for example, *Teacher of Teachers*, pp. 75–76, 164–166.

this later period, Rugg very definitely wanted an economy designed to an extent that exceeded any planning programs the nation had previously experienced.[89]

At this point in his career Rugg was also attempting to clarify his position regarding the mechanism by which social planning could be accomplished. In 1933 he had called for the establishment of councils of cultural reconstruction "in every community in America" to study the economic, social, political, aesthetic, and educational needs of their respective communities and to design plans for meeting these needs. In addition, he suggested that Congress create a National Council of Reconstruction, to be appointed by the President.[90]

Later, in 1943, he sought a network of planning agencies or "councils of design" that would start on the community level, extend up through state and regional levels, and culminate in a national council to be located in Washington. The latter would function as a kind of clearing house for the other councils and would also enjoy certain discretionary powers regarding the implementation of plans formulated by the state and regional groups, though these powers were not made explicit.[91]

Still later, in 1952, Rugg elaborated on this idea. Here we find him sketching an ideal history of the next generation, in which he sees a bipartisan National Planning Board being created in Washington sometime in the 1970s. This board would coordinate the activities of a dozen regional valley authorities, 50 state planning councils, 90 metropolitan councils, and a variety of city, town, and village councils. All of these organizations would work together to solve pressing social problems on the national, regional, and local levels. In addition, study and planning groups would be formed in the heavy industries in which representatives of business, labor, and the general public would gather to establish levels of

89. Ibid., p. 167. Here Rugg calls for planning "on a scale that this nation has never succeeded in attaining in the past."

90. Rugg, *Great Technology*, pp. 251–253.

91. Rugg, *Now Is the Moment*, pp. 175–176.

prices and purchasing power. Meanwhile, a system of educational councils for community development would be built on both the regional and national levels. This is Harold Rugg's vision of 1984. He called it a flight in imagination, yet he believed that part, if not all, of it could eventually become a reality.[92]

Throughout his career, many of Rugg's proposals for immediate action were equally ambitious. In the midst of the Depression he had called for an annual budget of three billion dollars for his proposed National Council of Cultural Reconstruction.[93] During the war he wanted President Roosevelt to promote an Office of Education for Peace which would have unlimited resources and be capable of reaching thirty million Americans daily with a barrage of progressive ideas. There were, he estimated, about five hundred thousand Americans well enough informed to elect a Congress of welfare-minded representatives. We needed, he felt, at least ten million to solve the problem of consent.

The new office would be under the direction of the U.S. commissioner of education, and it would use all the mass media of communication to reach and inform the people. In addition, Rugg appealed to the nation's superintendents of schools to lead in the organization of his proposed community discussion groups.[94]

None of this ever came to pass, of course, and perhaps Rugg never really expected that it would. It is possible that he looked upon these recommendations as ideals rather than as tangible plans to be converted into action in the near future. At any rate, we should notice certain differences between his earlier and later statements regarding the planning process. During the 1930s, as we have seen, the social engineers play a clearly dominant role in Rugg's program, whereas political officeholders seem little more than hirelings. In the fifties,

92. Rugg, *Teacher of Teachers*, pp. 256–266.
93. Rugg, *Great Technology*, pp. 251–252.
94. Rugg, *Now Is the Moment*, pp. 222–245.

conversely, there is more stress on teamwork, with representatives of government, industry, labor, academia, the arts, and the general public planning together. The nature of the authority of these planning groups, their precise relationship to the various branches of government, and, for that matter, the affiliation of national with regional and local groups are, however, issues that remain cloudy.

The threat of automation.   A strong sense of urgency is a familiar theme in Rugg's writings. During the Depression, for example, his discussions of social conditions frequently included warnings that unless democratic reforms were quickly undertaken, some form of dictatorial control—either by the extreme left or the extreme right—was likely to be imposed in the not-too-distant future.[95] These fears were somewhat abated, though by no means eliminated, with the return to relative prosperity after the Depression. But at that point Rugg saw the possibility of "technological unemployment" as a growing threat to individual and social well-being. Looking ahead a generation or so, he observed that advancing automation would inevitably lead to increased displacement of men by machines in industrial occupations. He assumed, apparently, that the physical needs of workers so displaced would be met through an extension of already existing welfare programs; what worried him was the intellectual and spiritual needs of these workers. "The persons displaced from all work," he said, "will be men with food, shelter, and clothing in abundance, but they will be idle men; men with all-day 'leisure' and with nothing to do; men degenerating, their souls and their minds inert."[96]

Of course Rugg saw a way to avoid these intolerable consequences, and that way, not surprisingly, involved the substitution of creative activity—arts and crafts, for example—for

95. For a sampling, see "Strains and Problems," pp. 122–125; *American Life,* pp. 11–14; and *Great Technology,* pp. 185–186.

96. Rugg, *Teacher of Teachers,* p. 8.

the rapidly disappearing industrial occupations. In other words, people should be taught to employ the increased leisure time available to them in activities that would contribute to their intellectual and spiritual self-fulfillment. Since Rugg regarded the intrinsic value of the creative experience of prime importance, he felt that neither creative labor nor its products should be construed as competition for the automatic processes and standardized products of industry.[97] Seeing, moreover, that full automation would mean that eventually industry would require the services of far fewer workers than is now the case, Rugg argued that an equitable way must be found to distribute both purchasing power and the goods and services provided by modern industry to people, regardless of whether these people had any direct part in the production of such assets.[98]

In effect, then, Rugg was calling for the subsidization of displaced workers in order to enable them to pursue creative activities for self-fulfillment. Here again the precise nature of the social changes required to implement this plan were not spelled out, though Rugg was well aware, of course, that the implied changes were considerable. He was once again interested not so much in the details of changing the system as he was in establishing the fact that changes were necessary and in alerting others to the need. With respect to the latter consideration, Rugg called, as he had so many times in the past, for the use of schools as forums for the discussion of social conditions and issues.[99] Since, in Rugg's view, the teachers who would lead these discussions would need preparation superior to that now offered in professional courses, he urged those responsible for teacher education to rid training institutions of their "trade school temper" and convert them into "centers of ideas."[100] In this connection, he

97. Ibid., pp. 8, 48.
98. Ibid., p. 48.
99. Ibid., p. 10.
100. Ibid., pp. 17–18.

charged that educators had too long been "faint echoes of the practical men" who had built the exploitive tradition.[101] It was time, he said, for them to join the creative men of the "great tradition" by redesigning the theory and content of teacher education in order to properly train teachers for their roles in the reconstructed lower schools. The teacher of teachers would thereby take his place among society's truly creative leaders.[102]

In chapter 5 I will examine the foundations program that Rugg recommended for teacher trainees, but here it is worth noting once again the continual emphasis on creativity and cultural uplift in his writings. His message in *The Teacher of Teachers* was very similar to that delivered in *Culture and Education* some twenty years earlier, namely that in the last analysis we could have a "great society" only if we could produce enough cultured, reflective, sensitive individuals; and the key to the process was a high-quality educational system. Rugg thought that a reconstructed social system could provide everyone with an adequate standard of living, but this alone would not produce a better society. It would merely free individuals from want and anxiety so that they could engage in self-fulfilling activities, thus directly elevating the plane of their personal lives and, indirectly, that of society as well. For Rugg, then, the affluent society was just a step toward the cultured society, his ultimate end.

A brief note on Social Foundations of Education.   There is a marked change in tone in Rugg's next-to-last book, *Social Foundations of Education,* written in collaboration with William Withers.[103] The authors critically discuss various economic theories, including classical free enterprise, Marxism, and Keynesian planned capitalism, and conclude that although some variation of the Keynesian model (appro-

101. Ibid., p. 12.
102. Ibid., pp. 12–16.
103. Harold Rugg and William Withers, *Social Foundations of Education* (New York: Prentice-Hall, 1955).

priately modified in the light of evolving economic theory) is probably the view most adaptable to present conditions in the United States, none of the proposed economic theories is free of difficulties. Moreover, they point out that the American people may not even accept the relatively small amount of planning required in the Keynesian model.

There is a dispassionate and objective tone to all of this and a "let's-wait-and-see" attitude that one does not usually find in a Rugg book, but this is partly because of its intended use as a college textbook in education classes, whereas many of his other works are frankly polemical. Moreover, the coauthor, a professional economist, contributed most of the material on economic theory.[104] In any case, it is very unlikely, considering the consistency of the rest of Rugg's later work with his earlier books, that the subdued style in this one instance reflects any significant change in his views over the years.[105]

104. Letter from William Withers, April 19, 1966.
105. *Social Foundations of Education* also contains an interesting application of scientific terms and concepts to social and cultural phenomena. The first draft of this study included a discussion of the use of scientific terminology for this purpose and a criticism of certain analogies between the physical and social sciences that were drawn in the book. Subsequently, however, I learned through correspondence with Professor Withers that he had written nearly all of the material in question. It therefore seemed inappropriate to include an analysis of this material in a study of Rugg even though Rugg coauthored the book. It did seem necessary, though, to explain the omission.

3. POLITICS, MORALITY, AND SELF-INTEREST

RUGG AND POLITICAL IDEOLOGY

The Great Technology—clearly written in response to the Depression, though by no means incompatible with Rugg's earlier critiques of laissez faire capitalism—was frequently cited in later years by detractors of Rugg's textbook series. Having neglected to avail themselves of his other writings, these critics erroneously concluded from Rugg's stinging attack on the economics of capitalism in *The Great Technology* that Rugg was at least a "fellow traveler," if not an outright Communist, that, in fact, he was so enamored of the Soviet system that he would actually applaud its transplantation to American soil. In reply to these charges, Rugg attempted to set the record straight in 1941:

> I am not a Communist. I have never been a Communist. I have never been a member of or affiliated with the Communist party, directly or indirectly, in any way whatsoever. I am not a Socialist. I have never been a Socialist. I have never been a member of or affiliated with the Socialist party. Nor have I taken part in the work of that party.[1]

Rugg was convinced, as the following passage shows, that Marxist theory was largely irrelevant to the social and economic realities of American life.

> Thus, neither from the study of the process of government, nor the history of the American mind, nor from the current

1. Rugg, *That Men May Understand*, p. 89.

eye-witness appraisals, can I find support for the Marxian dictum that the American people are divided today into two antagonistic conflict groups in which a class of property-less workers will shortly fight it out with a small but powerful propertied class. Moreover, a careful study of the American Marxians' data, which purport to apply Marx's theses to twentieth-century America leaves grave doubts as to their validity.[2]

His rejection of Marxism as a viable alternative for this country was based, then, on his conviction that the concept of two warring classes is inappropriate to describe the facts of the American situation. Rugg viewed political reality in the United States as the interplay of many small special interest groups. Hence America, in his view, encompassed a number of "shifting groups, some of which, from time to time, are mutually exclusive and antagonistic, but most of which overlap in membership and interest and are both partly conflicting and partly co-operative."[3] For Rugg, the notion of two independent social classes locked in bitter conflict was simply unrealistic in the American context.

Rugg's attitude toward socialism was less clear. Despite his repudiation of the label, he often talked like a Socialist. For instance, after reviewing the plans for economic recovery submitted by Charles A. Beard, Stuart Chase, George Soule, and others during the Depression, he wrote:

A study of the comprehensive plans shows very clearly that our students of reconstruction do not want to abolish private capitalism but that they tend decidedly toward the imposition of collective control at the top—either by industry, by national government, or by both. They recognize that free competition, laissez-faire, and "rugged" indi-

2. Harold Rugg, "The American Mind and the Class Problem," *Social Frontier* 2 (February 1936): 140.
3. Ibid., p. 139.

vidualism are incompatible with the complicated, interdependent mechanism upon which a hundred million people depend for a livelihood.[4]

Rugg then went on to say, "Hence, although these plans are in no sense a solution to the problem of a new design for the economic system, they are a striking indication of the changing temper of thinking people concerning the imperative need for social reconstruction."[5]

Now the question is, if these plans would not solve the economic problem, if collective control of production and distribution would not go far enough in designing the economy, wouldn't the next step be collective ownership, that is to say, socialism? It is difficult to see what possible middle ground between collective control and collective ownership Rugg could have had in mind here. A few pages further on he commented as follows on the issue of collective control versus collective ownership: "I personally anticipate very great difficulty in alienating the direct influence of owners upon legislators, executives, and judges."[6] He went on to say that in his opinion some form of collective control without collective ownership would in fact be attempted, but the quoted statement implies that he was rather dubious regarding its prospects. He seemed to think that stronger medicine was called for.

During the Depression, furthermore, Rugg not infrequently sounded a socialistic note in criticizing New Deal policies. He objected, for example, to what he felt were tinkering, half-way measures intended to revive private capitalism rather than to accomplish the "fundamental" reconstruction he deemed necessary.[7] In addition, he often made proposals to "integrate" key industries into a national sys-

4. Rugg, *Great Technology*, p. 170.
5. Ibid.
6. Ibid., p. 180.
7. For a sampling, see *Great Technology*, p. 105, "Strains and Problems," p. 106, and (especially) *American Life*, pp. 451–452.

tem, to redistribute the wealth, to establish fair-profit figures, to set ceilings on salaries, and to provide for minimum standards of living that were certainly more extreme than the prescriptions of most New Dealers. These examples do not prove that Rugg was a Socialist, of course. They merely indicate that his stance during the thirties was well to the left of New Deal liberalism. My purpose is not to establish his presence in the Socialist camp (since his political affiliation has nothing to do with the quality of his thought) but rather to show that his views were not so far removed from those of the Socialist persuasion as his statements to the contrary would seem to indicate at first glance.

His exact position is not easy to determine, even with the assistance of his own attempts to clarify it. In one such attempt, for example, he said, "I believe in private enterprise. But I believe in social enterprise too. I believe we should leave the play of individual initiative as free as possible and in as many areas of life as human ingenuity can contrive."[8] But surely this expression of Rugg's beliefs would be acceptable to representatives of almost any political-economic ideology. The statement can have little meaning until we know how much free enterprise, how much social enterprise, how much individual initiative, and in what spheres of social life. Unfortunately, Rugg did not provide answers to these questions on this particular occasion. In a later book (*Now Is the Moment,* 1943), however, he does give us some indication of what he considered to be a desirable balance between free enterprise and social enterprise. Looking back over the Depression years from the vantage point of 1943, it seemed to Rugg that such a balance had already been achieved by the Tennessee Valley Authority. He had nothing but praise for the TVA:

> And it did come about in that Valley—a fine fusion of centralization of sovereignty and financing, design and total

8. Rugg, *That Men May Understand,* p. xiv.

administration, hand in hand with a decentralized ownership and a "grass-roots" operation. Both federal and local
authorities, they said, should take part—the federal government doing the things for which it was best equipped,
the state and local government doing others, and the private companies, the co-operative associations and individuals doing still others.[9]

Elsewhere he described TVA as a model of cooperation between public and private interest: "Here we see a Mixed
Economy, part centralized, part decentralized—working dem-
ocratically. Here is the object lesson for a century to come."[10]
  It seems fair to conclude, then, that in the 1940s Rugg
accepted TVA as a model for social reconstruction and would
have been pleased to see it duplicated, wherever conditions
warranted, throughout the country. Whether he would also
have found it acceptable in 1932 when he was writing *The
Great Technology* is, of course, another matter. He was less
disposed at that time to concur with New Deal policies than
he was during the forties and fifties. All we can say for sure is
that by the 1940s the TVA represented for Rugg the desirable
mixture of public and private enterprise that he had been
groping for earlier in his career. There are those who would
argue that his wish to extend the type of planning that went
into the TVA to other sectors of the economy demonstrates his
socialistic leanings, but it is also clear that Rugg would reject
this appraisal of his position. The point is a disputable one,
and the dispute leaves unanswered the question of exactly
where Rugg stood ideologically. The best we can do is plot
his position somewhere between New Deal liberalism and
democratic socialism and resist the temptation to force him
into either camp.

  9. Rugg, *Now Is the Moment*, p. 32.
  10. Harold Rugg, *Foundations for American Education* (New York: World Book
Co., 1947), p. 416.

Piecemeal or Utopian Social Engineering?

Rugg's position might also be described as vacillating between what Karl Popper has called "utopian" or "holistic" social engineering and "piecemeal" social engineering. Popper describes the piecemeal engineer as one who strives to combat specific social ills by making small adjustments in social institutions. He does not attempt to reconstruct society as a whole. Further, he proceeds cautiously and with an open mind, ready for unexpected consequences at every step. The utopian social engineer, on the other hand, rejects the experimental "tinkering" of the piecemeal approach. He wants to redesign the entire society according to a preconceived plan or blueprint.

Popper argues that in practice the utopian or holistic method is unworkable because the greater the task of reconstruction undertaken, the greater are the unexpected consequences, a result that eventually forces the utopian engineer to improvise, to adopt, in other words, the piecemeal method. Thus the utopian method turns out to be impossible, and the doctrine that a blueprint for remodeling society as a whole can be prepared and applied without modification is false. This doctrine is also dangerous, according to Popper, because having decided a priori that sweeping reconstruction is feasible, the utopian or holistic engineer is susceptible to the use of dictatorial methods in his attempt to realize his ideal society. Having decided beforehand that social institutions invulnerable to human error or weakness can be constructed, for example, the utopian engineer is likely to attempt to control the human factor by shaping human impulses in such a way that they will be adaptable to his new social order.[11]

Although the merits of Popper's thesis need not be dis-

11. Karl R. Popper, *The Poverty of Historicism* (Boston: Beacon Press, 1957), pp. 64–70. See also chap. 9 of Popper's *The Open Society and Its Enemies*, vol. 1: *The Spell of Plato*, 4th ed. rev. (London: Routledge & Kegan Paul, 1962).

cussed here, he certainly seems right in his analysis of the dangers inherent in the utopian approach. A review of the history of Russian communism, to cite only the most obvious example, would appear to demonstrate that his fears regarding the threat to individual autonomy posed by holistic social engineering are not unfounded.

To what extent does Popper's critique apply to Rugg? This is another nice question. Rugg never submitted anything approaching a blueprint for a new social order himself, but he did seem to charge his social planners with the construction of such a blueprint. Moreover, he stressed, as we have seen, the need for an overhaul of social and political, as well as economic institutions, and during the thirties he derided the efforts of New Dealers to "prime the economic pump." Further, there are elements of authoritarianism to be found in his treatment of popular consent. On the other hand, he did wish to try out on an experimental basis whatever plan the experts delivered, and, as already observed, he was much more receptive to New Deal proposals after the Depression. Finally, one cannot read Rugg without feeling the sincerity of his concern for individual freedom. In short, it is very difficult once again to classify Rugg. The fairest answer to our question seems to be that although he leaned toward utopian or holistic social engineering in the 1930s and was therefore open to the objections to that point of view raised by Popper, his position in later years was more tentative and open-minded, and therefore more tenable.

Freedom and Control

Rugg's oversimplified approach to the problems of individual and social life in a planned society did not, as we have seen, emanate from a systematic social philosophy. His prescriptions stemmed rather from an engineer's point of view and were concerned chiefly with the economic problem of working out an equitable distribution of goods. But this approach is certain to be inadequate simply because economic issues cannot be separated from social and political isues. It is impossible to initiate major changes in the economy without also affecting the social and political structure within which economic activities are carried on. This observation is, of course, little more than a truism, and Rugg would no doubt agree to it. In fact, he might well point to his own statements regarding the need not only for changes in the economic system, but also for social and political reconstruction as well. But as we have seen, he furnished little indication of what reconstruction in this broader sense would entail. Rather, he left this question to the "experts," that is, the scholars and artists referred to earlier. There is sparse consideration in his own writings of the limits of state authority, the grounds for political obligation, relationships between the state and the individual or the state and lesser associations, or the nature of democratic government; nor does he offer more than a cursory treatment of such basic political concepts as "liberty," "authority," "equality," "justice," or "rights." Yet these elements of our social and political lives are sure to be affected by any significant changes made in our economic institutions. Rugg needs some sort of public mandate for a planned economy, but he cannot reasonably expect public support in the absence of information regarding the probable impact of economic changes in other aspects of our individual lives and social relationships.

Of particular importance in this respect is the preservation of democratic control in step three of Rugg's sequence. On the face of it at least, the adoption of centralized planning and control of the economy would pose some threat to individual freedom. How, we may ask, is individual liberty to be reconciled with social stability in "a designed social order"? Rugg acknowledged the significance of this question but was unable to provide a staisfactory answer. He referred to the issue as the problem of freedom and control or the relation between "I" and "We." (These terms stand for a whole cluster of concepts representing private or individual interests on the one hand and social interests on the other.) Society, he insisted, must allow the individual sufficient freedom to realize his potential, it must "maintain a climate of opinion marked by spiritual freedom."[12] How this is to be done in the face of increasing collectivization was not explained, however, and he left open the question of what areas of private or individual life the government or "We" should enter.

What Rugg was striving for here was the best of two worlds: the high degree of individual freedom associated with classical liberal theory together with the kind of governmental intervention postulated by contemporary liberals as a necessary condition to providing everybody with an even start, so to speak, in the pursuit of life goals. This is an admirable aim, certainly, but there are two very large questions here that Rugg never really came to grips with: Is it possible to have it both ways? And if so, how? Democratic Socialists and New Dealers answered the first question affirmatively and provided answers to the second question that were at least plausible, but Rugg did not seem to want to align himself on the side of either; nor did he work out a detailed position of his own. Thus he could furnish no solution to the difficult problem of balancing freedom and control. This omission together with some of the others noted above undoubtedly contributed to the widespread misunderstanding of his views. As I have already pointed out, a careful reading of Rugg reveals unmistakably his genuine concern for the individual, but it is not very difficult to understand how some of the "skimmers" missed this quality and concluded that he harbored a one-sided interest in the extension of centralized authority.

The relationship between the self and society in Rugg's writings will be taken up again in the last part of this chapter, but first we shall examine his views on ethics.

12. Rugg, *That Men May Understand*, p. 255.

ETHICAL THEORY

Rugg thinks the realities of modern industrial society call for a transformation of ethical theory. The moral-ethical problem of the present, he maintains, is to create new principles and rules of conduct, based on an understanding of human nature, within the framework of an ever-changing society.[13]

Rugg's approach to ethics is somewhat oversimplified because he is not interested in philosophical questions as such, but only in passing, as it were, when he needs philosophical concepts to deal with social and educational problems. "By morals," he writes, "I shall mean rules of conduct developed through the social practices of the people; by ethics, the principles which determine the rules."[14]

This definition is too confining, for at the very least ethics includes the consideration of judgments of value on the one hand and judgments of obligation on the other, and Rugg fails to accommodate the former. Moreover, "the social practices of the people" is an ambiguous yardstick. The term "social practices" does not necessarily imply moral rules if morality, as opposed to convention, is, in part, concerned with the critical evaluation of existing societal rules. Morality involves the establishment of normative principles as the outcome of reasoned deliberation, and sometimes this process leads the individual to discard accepted social practices. William K. Frankena describes morality as follows:

> Morality fosters or even calls for the use of reason and for a kind of autonomy on the part of the individual, asking him, when mature and normal, to make his own decisions, though possibly with someone's advice, and even stimulating him to think out the principles or goals in the light of which he is to make his decisions. Morality is a social

---

13. Rugg, *Foundations for American Education,* p. 511.
14. Ibid., p. 475.

institution of life, but it is one which promotes rational self-guidance or self-determination in its members.[15]

The crux of the matter is that Rugg fails to distinguish adequately between morality and custom or tradition. He writes, "Ideas of value or worth become moral only when they are defined against a code of behavior—either written or unwritten—that has been made by the larger social group; in fact our term moral derives through the Latin-term "moral" from *mores* or customs. Customs, *mores,* moral acts, are acts approved by the social groups."[16] [Rugg's italics.]

Thus he is really describing the development of a moral code, a collection of norms which should be distinguished from ethical judgments in order to preserve the distinction between custom or conventional morality and ethics or critical morality. His distinction between moral rules and ethical principles indicates that he is aware, at least to some extent, of the differences involved here, but he never clarifies these differences satisfactorily. In his discussion of ethical principles, for example, he seems to minimize the critical factor. "At intervals of considerable length," he maintains, "professed philosophers and students of society and the culture stand above the current of events, *study the culture patterns,* the ontology of the people, and *the emerging rules* of moral conduct and formulate new statements of ethical principles."[17] [My italics]. Thus, on this account, an ethical principle seems to be little more than a brief description of incipient social norms, a summary of unfolding cultural patterns. In fact, there is, considering Rugg's emphasis on the formulation of ethical principles in light of emerging cultural patterns, a hint of "moral futurism" in his view, that is, the idea, as Popper phrases it, that "the morally good is what is ahead of its time in conforming to such standards of conduct as will be

---

15. William K. Frankena, *Ethics* (Englewood Cliffs, N.J.: Prentice-Hall, 1963), p. 7.

16. Rugg, *Foundations for American Education,* p. 478.

17. Ibid., p. 480.

adopted in the period to come.''[18] This view, as Popper points out, is frequently adopted by historicists, social theorists who believe that they can detect certain rhythms, trends, and laws of historical evolution that will enable them to predict the future course of events and to facilitiate the emergence of the social conditions that are destined to occur. The writings of Karl Marx are, of course, a classic illustration of this view.

That Rugg's view of morality should contain traces of historicism is not surprising in view of the fact that historicists often supplement their prophesies with prescriptions for social engineering that can be characterized (again following Popper) as "utopian" or "holistic."[19] And as we noted in chapter 2, Rugg's brand of social engineering, at least as set forth during the Depression, was essentially holistic. In addition, there are historicist tendencies not only in his ethical views, but in other areas of his thought as well. These tendencies are brought out in passages such as the following: "The march of democracy is . . . the main line of social advance. Against it each rise and fall of a dictator is a mere side-track from the central course of human evolution. Even though one of them may persist in power for a generation or so, each is a mere flurry of disturbance from the main line of progress."[20] But it should be pointed out that passages such as this are countered by the "crisis" passages mentioned earlier, in which Rugg takes the position that unless we take action to preserve democracy, we shall be overwhelmed by some form of dictatorship. In other words, the world's "march toward democracy" (a favorite phrase in Rugg's textbook series) requires our active support in order to reach its destination. There is, of course, a conflict here,[21] which Rugg somewhat

18. Popper, *Poverty of Historicism*, p. 54. See also Karl Popper, *The Open Society and Its Enemies*, Vol. 2: *The High Tide of Prophecy: Hegel, Marx and the Aftermath* (London: George Routledge & Sons, 1945), chap. 22.

19. Popper, *Poverty of Historicism*, pp. 73–76.

20. Harold Rugg, "Democracy vs. Dictatorship," *Scholastic* 29 (5 December 1936): 12.

21. It might also be argued that a conflict exists between the points of view of the historicist and *any* activist who wants to change society. But as Popper points out,

characteristically leaves unresolved. At any rate we cannot regard him as a thoroughgoing historicist, since historicism holds that what is coming is inevitable and the most we can do is to "ease the birth pangs." Rugg does not consistently hold this view, though he does express it in passages like the one quoted above.

Seeing that Rugg's historicism is largely implicit, fragmentary, and not consistent, we need not delve into Popper's criticism of the doctrine, except to point out that he offers a number of telling arguments against its tenability. Notable among these is his point that, since history is significantly affected by the growth of human knowledge, and since it is impossible to predict precisely our future growth in knowledge, we are unable then to predict the future course of history.[22]

Returning again to Rugg's views on morality, I need only apply my earlier remarks to the moral futurism that seems to be implied in his account of how ethical principles become established and point out that one cannot claim to be doing moral philosophy if one simply studies the culture for emerging rules of conduct and then formulates ethical principles based on the rules or norms that he sees developing. This is a useful enterprise but it is sociological rather than ethical in nature, and the two tasks should not be confused. An individual could be well aware of what the emerging norms are, be convinced, moreover, that these norms will constitute the moral standards of the future, and nevertheless decide, after critical reflection, to reject these standards as acceptable moral principles. Again it is this insistence on rationality and critical evaluation that is the sine qua non of moral philosophy, and these are the very characteristics that are given insufficient consideration in Rugg's exposition.

the two are compatible provided that plans for changing society fit in with the main trends of historical evolution. (See *Poverty of Historicism,* pp. 7–8, 49, 52–53, 71–76.)

22. Popper, *Poverty of Historicism,* pp. ix–x.

Rugg's discussion of "moral acts" and the rules which govern them also reflects this basic confusion between moral judgments and descriptive statements about mores. He puts forth three criteria for distinguishing the moral act from the nonmoral one: The moral act is voluntary, it involves a choice between alternatives, and it includes the weighing of conflicting values, which must be measured "against social standards."[23] Here he appears to be moving toward a more convincing explanation of morality, but as he continues his account, it becomes increasingly difficult to perceive any significant difference between his conception of moral rules and the kinds of rules we normally think of as pertaining to custom or law. In accounting for the development of a moral climate of opinion, for instance, he speaks of "the people's naive responses to the current of events"; "the moral interpretation of events by special agents" such as politicians, educators, and the clergy; and the transformation of critical moral judgments into law.[24] Thus moral rules are equated with evolving customs, the most important of which become, in due course, incorporated into the prevailing legal code. Once again insufficient consideration is given to the individual and critical elements that set morality apart from custom or law. Morality, it must be emphasized, entails the critical evaluation of normative rules by rational, autonomous agents, and this process might well call existing customs or laws into question. Hence, as Benn and Peters have it, "a moral rule differs from a custom in that it has been critically examined in accordance with some criterion other than the degree to which it is generally accepted or the competence of the authority prescribing it."[25] Just what this other criterion might be differs, of course, according to the ethical theory to which one subscribes. The point to be made here is that though morality resembles cus-

23. Rugg, *Foundations for American Education*, p. 477.
24. Ibid., pp. 478–480.
25. S. I. Benn and R. S. Peters, *Social Principles and the Democratic State* (London: George Allen & Unwin, 1959), p. 28.

tom in its normative function, it differs from custom in its critical insistence on reasons as support for the rules that are established.

Likewise, morality must be distinguished from law, though there are surface similarities in this case also; we often speak, for example, of "the moral law." A little reflection, however, convinces us of the crucial difference between the two, namely, that a law is ordinarily created and made binding by legislative fiat, whereas a moral rule is accepted voluntarily. In this connection, Kurt Baier has pointed out that it would be absurd to say, "The moral law against lying was promulgated on May 1st."[26] Furthermore laws, unlike moral rules, are supported by institutionalized sanctions up to and including physical force.

Moral rules, then, are those formulated by autonomous individuals as the result of critical inquiry, or, as Benn and Peters state it, "Morality arises when custom or law is subjected to critical examination."[27] Rugg's analysis simply fails to make this distinction explicit.

Throughout his discussion of ethics Rugg is concerned with right actions and moral rules of conduct. He does not concern himself directly with values, but it will be recalled that he does describe the moral act partly in terms of a choice between conflicting values within the context of existing social standards. But how does one decide which values take precedence over others? Again, Rugg insists that modern society requires a restated morality, and presumably this would include a new set of values to replace those that he thinks have become outmoded. But how does he know that the new values would be superior to the old? Would he argue that these questions can be answered on empirical grounds? Or by virtue of intuition? Or would he be driven, finally, to some form of ethical noncognitivism or nondescriptivism? What

26. Kurt Baier, *The Moral Point of View* (Ithaca, N.Y.: Cornell University Press, 1958), p. 178.
27. Benn and Peters, *Social Principles*, p. 31.

we need from Rugg, at this point, are his criteria for justifying value and moral judgments, but these he never furnishes.

This criticism is intended to show that Rugg's ideas with regard to ethics needed further development in certain directions in order to resolve the difficulties and ambiguities that have just been discussed. It should be remembered, however, that Rugg was not concerned with the problems of technical philosophy. He was interested in philosophy insofar as it could help modern man come to grips with the changing dimensions of modern society. His objective was to establish the need for new modes of thinking in a variety of disciplines, but he did not claim that he could solve the technical problems involved.

On the other hand, a scholar must be held responsible for that which results when he ventures beyond his sphere of competence. The problem becomes one of whether to remain on one's "home ground" and be safe but somewhat isolated; or, in striving for an integration of knowledge, to move out where the terrain is less familiar. Rugg chose the latter, and while it is easy to point out his inadequacies in so doing, it should also be noted that the alternative, which sharply reduces communication between disciplines, is equally unsatisfactory.

In any case, Rugg thinks that the changing times call for new ethical principles and rules of conduct (apparently in the sense that we have just criticized), and he sees two major barriers to the development and acceptance of such principles. The first is the tendency of people to cling to the existing system of moral principles even though these have become, in Rugg's view, largely obsolete. The elimination of this barrier is an educational task, one of alerting the public to the problems, conditions, and issues of contemporary society so that they may see the need for revised guides to action and become more receptive to needed changes. The second obstacle that must be overcome is the egoistic trait of self-interest, which Rugg believes is inherent in human nature.

HUMAN NATURE

Rugg's concern with self-interest leads him naturally into a discussion of human nature, which for Rugg, as for every reformer, is a major consideration, since it is argued in some quarters that men are aggressive and exploitive by nature, that most of the "evil" in the world stems from within man himself and not from faulty social institutions. This more or less Freudian view of human nature is a challenge that reaches right to the core of reformist psychology, and Rugg recognizes an obligation to deal with it.

In Rugg's view the infant comes into the world with no built-in personality, but simply with the raw materials out of which a personality later develops. These raw materials consist of the physical organism itself, temperament, and intellectual capacity. For Rugg, "temperament" is comprised primarily of tempo—"the basic time beat and rhythm of movement which marks us as individuals"—and characteristic individual mood. He defines "intelligence" in terms of the ability to learn, the ability to adapt to novel conditions, and the power to make reasonable judgments.[28]

Though he believes that education can play some role in total personality development, he concedes that there is little or nothing it can do to alter these basic elements. In his own words, education

can change human habits, traits, and play a large role in determining the total personality; but educators should make up their minds that the physical, temperamental, and intellectual qualities of the young people in their charge are not going to change much through their entire educational careers. . . . Unless the physiology is altered, the physique, the temperament, and the intelligence will be approximately the same *general level* throughout life.[29] [Rugg's italics.]

28. Rugg, *Foundations for American Education*, pp. 169–183.
29. Ibid., pp. 188–189.

Further, he apparently believes there is something inherent in these ingredients that causes egocentricity to develop concurrently with self-awareness. Generalizing from experiments that he had conducted at the Lincoln School and drawing on the experimental findings of Caroline Zachry[30] and others, he writes, "We know then that by the time the child is ready to enter the nursery school—at two or three years—he is a little egocentric self."[31]

Rugg goes on to point out that with the onset of self-assertiveness the problem of how to reconcile "I" and "we"—a difficulty with which the individual is confronted for the rest of his life—begins to emerge.[32] Eventually self-interest becomes a dominant factor in human motivation. "Its will-to-power, will-to-security, will-to-comfort, will-to-glory is in every moral act, and is confirmed by the competitive drives in the individualistic culture surrounding it."[33] In addition, he agrees with Niebuhr[34] that the egoistic impulse may be even stronger when it is extended from individuals to groups. In this connection, he cautions that "we must not count on the accelerating spread of group loyalties to transmute the selfishness of the individual into a better moral force in the world."[35]

How are we to cope with self-interest and its effects? Rugg sees a cohesive force at work in the very nature of current social change. As crises resulting from rapid change arise, people are forced to cooperate in meeting new challenges: "The necessities imposed by advancing social trend has [sic] increasingly compelled men to work together; the accumulating record of the controls laid upon the social

30. Caroline B. Zachry, "The Growth Process," chap. 12 in *Democracy and the Curriculum*, Third Yearbook of the John Dewey Society, ed. Harold Rugg (New York: D. Appleton-Century Co., 1939), p. 319.
31. Rugg, *Foundations for American Education*, p. 191.
32. Ibid., p. 192.
33. Ibid., p. 496.
34. Reinhold Niebuhr, *Moral Man and Immoral Society* (New York: Charles Scribner's Sons, 1932).
35. Rugg, *Foundations for American Education*, p. 496.

system in the past seventy-five years is the proof."[36] But there appears to be another conflict here. Rugg first tells us that we cannot count on group loyalties to mitigate selfishness, and then he proceeds to list social cooperation as a resource in combating self-interest. This is yet another instance of his tendency to entertain conflicting ideas without explaining how the apparent conflict can be resolved.

Rugg goes on to list love, reason, or intelligence, and the "self-affirmation of integrity" as additional resources for containing self-interest. He finds the efficacy of love and reason somewhat limited, however. In his evaluation of "the spirit of love," for example, he argues that while love is sometimes effective in smoothing direct interaction between individuals, it has enjoyed little success in preventing conflict between groups. He contends:

> The laws governing political action in communities, regions, and nations are not laws of love; they are laws of power and are deeply rooted in economics and psychology. This is not to say that spiritually sensitive people should relax their efforts to spread the power of love between human beings. There is here a great moral resource, and we must work with it and expand it; but we shall never forget that it will be a minor resource in the giant struggle for power which now confronts us on every side.[37]

He points out, furthermore, that even the most altruistic gestures may be the result of self-seeking drives, and that "acts of love may themselves be revelations of the Self's skill in calculating and securing its own interests."[38]

Similarly, though Rugg considers intelligence to be of some use in the solution of moral and political problems, he insists that its limitations become obvious in the face of obstacles thrown up by self-interest. "The logic of our data," he

36. Ibid., p. 498.
37. Ibid., p. 501.
38. Ibid.

asserts, "raises serious questions as to whether knowledge and reason can produce conduct contrary to the dictates of Self-interest. . . . Thus history reminds us the will-to-owning, will-to-security, will-to-power of those who own the things that men must have will inevitably work against any widespread social success of the method of intelligence."[39]

But if all of this is true, then what is the point of calling for a new morality? What impact would it have in a world populated by "wolves and serpents"? Earlier I criticized Rugg for expounding, at least implicitly, a form of historical relativism or what Popper has termed "moral futurism." Now Rugg could adopt this view explicitly and argue that the point of calling for a new morality is simply to alert people to impending social changes so that they can facilitate the birth of the new historical period and adjust their ethical principles to conform to future social conditions. A statement to this effect would answer the question, but if what I said earlier about morality is correct, the position taken would be unsatisfactory from the moral point of view, since it would lack the critical elements outlined in our earlier discussion. On the other hand, Rugg could argue that we have misunderstood his position and insist that he had really meant to leave room for the elements of criticism and rationality that we have been stressing, even though these factors do not clearly reveal themselves in his exposition. But this would be tantamount to a repudiation of moral futurism and would reopen our question, for what possible effect could a new morality in the critical, rational sense have in a world in which we cannot rely on social cooperation, benevolence, love, or reason to allay selfishness and social conflict?

Rugg does not resign himself to the conclusion that self-interest cannot be checked nor social conflict reduced, of course. He proceeds, as one would expect, to make a case for self-integrity, "the way of the creative artist," as the most

39. Ibid., p. 503.

important source of strength for the struggle,[40] and it will be recalled that he considers self-integrity to be a product of creative activity. Since this notion was examined at some length in chapter 2, I need only repeat the conclusion drawn at that point that Rugg places altogether too much confidence in the capacity of creative activity to build integrity, character, and the like and to eliminate human frailties such as the one under consideration, aggressive self-interest. As noted earlier, creative activity may be helpful, along with other factors, in building integrity and other desirable traits of character, and thus in overcoming selfishness. If so, however, it is simply one factor among many, and there is no obvious reason for attaching to it an importance denied to the others.

At several points in this study I have stressed the centrality of notions such as "self-expression" and "creativity" in Rugg's thought, without examing in sufficient detail his views regarding the nature of the creative act. This consideration—together with an analysis of his theory of knowledge, which, as we shall see, is closely connected to his ideas concerning creativity—will be dealt with in the next chapter.

40. Ibid., pp. 505–506.

4. CREATIVITY AND INTUITION

In a review of Rugg's *Culture and Education in America,* Boyd H. Bode wrote, "Mr. Rugg is interested in social reform, but that is a personal idiosyncrasy. It is quite as logical to use his premises for the purpose of bolstering up a scheme of detached values and a negative attitude toward social improvement."[1] Bode was discussing Rugg's insistence that in addition to observation, experimentation, logical thought processes, and the like, there is another method of acquiring knowledge, namely, the "intuitive," "feeling" method, which he ascribed to creative artists. Bode's point here was that there is no logical connection between Rugg's theory of knowledge and his program for social improvement.

Strictly speaking, Bode was right, of course. There is no logical way to derive social prescriptions from the facts of how knowledge is attained. Nonetheless, though Bode's review was very perceptive and contained a number of telling arguments (some of which will be taken up later in this chapter), his criticism on this particular point, while correct, turned out to be less damaging than it seemed at first sight. To Rugg, social reform was a means to an end. He looked upon adjustment of the social machinery as a necessary condition for the emergence of cultured individuals who would comprise the cultured society he had in mind.[2] In other words, he was interested in raising the quality of American life in general, not simply in removing social injustice. The economic problem, therefore, was just one element in the total reconstruction of American life that Rugg felt was necessary. His dis-

1. Bode, "Problem of Culture," p. 344.
2. As we saw in chap. 2, this view did not emerge clearly until later in the 1930s. Thus Bode's criticism was well taken at the time it was made (1931).

agreement with his fellow reconstructionists was in part based on his contention that they tended to limit themselves to economic questions and did not take a broad enough view of society and the individual therein. (Curiously enough, Bode himself was to argue in much the same vein in taking his colleagues on *The Social Frontier* to task for their limited perspective in matters of social change.)[3]

In reply to Bode, therefore, Rugg might have argued that although there is no logical connection between his theory of knowledge and his reformism when they are stripped of context, there is nevertheless an affinity between them when his total reconstructionism is taken into account. More specifically, he might have argued that his theory of knowledge is intimately connected with his views regarding creative expression and appreciation, which in turn are the key to the "cultured multitudes" he is seeking; and that people are unlikely to pursue culture when they are beset by economic fear and uncertainty. In short, Rugg's ideas about knowledge are part of his general concern with creativity and culture, and this concern is linked to his reformism in the sense that he thinks the latter is a necessary condition for the former. Thus Bode's criticism on this particular point, though logically correct, loses some of its thrust when Rugg's total view is considered. The strengths and weaknesses of that total view are an independent question, of course, and having already discussed his reformism, I shall, in the remainder of this chapter, deal with his views on "creativity," "mind," "knowledge," "thinking," and "feeling."

In broad terms, Rugg's thesis is that there are two methods of acquiring knowledge. One is empirical, experimental, scientific in character; the other is "intuitive." The first method involves observation, hypothetical inference, deduction, induction, testing, and the like; the second is difficult to summarize other than to say that it involves "feeling" and is the "artist's way of knowing" as opposed to that of the scien-

3. Boyd H. Bode, "Dr. Bode Replies," *Social Frontier* 2 (November 1935): 42–43.

tist. The difficulty in explaining "feeling" arises from Rugg's desire to say that feeling cannot be defined in terms of sensation or emotion. In the end he associates feeling with "bodily gesture" or "total motor adjustment" and argues that as the source of the "creative flash of insight," feeling in this sense results in, or is itself (Rugg is not entirely clear on this distinction), knowledge that is certain.

Against this view, I will contend that if "feeling" is neither sensation nor emotion, then (if it is psychological) it must be belief or "primal awareness" in some sense, otherwise it is a meaningless term. But if "feeling" is either belief or "primal awareness," then it yields, or is itself, something less than knowledge "full blown," much less knowledge that is certain. If, on the other hand, feeling is "gesture" or a form of bodily motor adjustment, then it is either a physiological state or a physical action that may be a necessary condition in explaining thought processes and the acquisition of knowledge, but cannot be a sufficient condition in either case. I shall argue, further, that even if Rugg were able to provide a convincing explanation of intuition in terms of feeling, he would still be faced with the difficulties that adhere to any intuitive theory of knowledge, difficulties which may be insurmountable.

THE CREATIVE PROCESS

During the past twenty-five years there has been a rash of books and articles on the subject of creativity, whereas before 1950 there was little to be found on the subject. In that year J. P. Guilford, president of the American Psychological Association, reported that in searching through *Psychological Abstracts* for the past twenty-five years, he had found only 186 (out of some 120,000) references to creativity, imagination, or the like.[4] Thus it is to Rugg's credit that he perceived

4. James Melvin Rhodes, "An Analysis of Creativity," in *Readings in the Foundations of Education*, Vol. 2, ed. James C. Stone and Frederick W. Schneider (New York: Thomas Y. Crowell Company, 1965), p. 170.

the importance of creativity a full quarter of a century before most of his colleagues in education and in other fields as well. Rugg's interest in creativity, incidentally, is one of the characteristics that clearly sets him apart from the other so-called reconstructionists. He thinks every child possesses a measure of creative ability, and the school should take upon itself the task of seeing that this natural talent is nourished. In Rugg's view, this task can best be accomplished by "artist-teachers" who have some personal acquaintance with the creative act.[5]

This strong interest in creativity is an essential element in Rugg's thought. He is convinced that the psychological processes involved in producing a creative or appreciative thought differ from those involved in the assimilation of facts.[6] Moreover, he feels that this distinction has been ignored by the experimentalist followers of Dewey. Rugg credited Dewey with articulating the basis of a thoroughgoing reconstruction of education built on experimentation and child study, but, as noted earlier, he often criticized Dewey and his disciples for confining themselves to the scientific method of acquiring knowledge.[7] Rugg holds that there is an intuitive way of knowing in addition to the empirical method of observation, measurement, and interpretation. For him the important thing is to insure that learning will culminate in a "mental and emotional synthesis" within the individual, and this can occur only if the school becomes sensitive enough to the aesthetic needs of children to weave the two elements— experimental and creative—into a unified pedagogical theory.[8]

Rugg's early treatment of creativity was often somewhat indefinite. For example, he frequently discussed the psychol-

5. Rugg, *Child-Centered School,* pp. 321–323.

6. Harold Rugg, "The American Experimental School," *Teachers College Record* 30 (February 1929): 415.

7. Harold Rugg, "Dewey and His Contemporaries: The Frontiers of Educational Thought in the Early 1900's," *Indiana University School of Education Bulletin* 36 (January 1960): 9–10.

8. Harold Rugg, "A Preface to a Theory for the New Individualism," *Teachers College Record* 32 (May 1931): 718.

ogy of the creative act in terms of inner urges, integration fusion, flashes of insight, and glimpses of truth and beauty. Since all of this was difficult to define apart from the subjective experience of the individual, it was always difficult to see how it could serve as the basis for a coherent learning theory. Thus, even though Rugg seemed to have been on to something that some of his colleagues were unable or unwilling to deal with, one came away from his early books wondering just how much light had actually been thrown upon the mechanics of the creative act. Nevertheless, the very fact that he *was* pioneering here attests to his perceptiveness in anticipating trends in the behavioral and social sciences, as well as in the field of education. In any event, Rugg was himself unsatisfied with his early attempts to provide a theoretical framework for understanding the creative process, but until he retired from the Teachers College Faculty in 1951 he was unable to find time enough to complete the necessary research for the "big book" that he hoped would clarify his position.

Unfortunately he died before the book *(Imagination)* was finished and it had to be edited and completed without his direction. Hence it contains a number of conceptual ambiguities and inconsistencies. Despite the editor's fine work in organizing the material into a coherent manuscript, the book was clearly in need of additional work by the author himself. It is, nonetheless, an impressive demonstration of wide-ranging scholarship (which was characteristic of Rugg), and since it is the most complete statement of Rugg's inquiry into creativity and the sources of knowledge, it will be heavily relied upon in the following exposition and criticism.

The Flash of Insight

According to Rugg, the creative process begins with a sense of restlessness. The individual is dissatisfied with the "existent" and feels an impulse to produce something better. As the impulse evolves into a strong desire, he is motivated to focus all of his intellectual and volitional energies onto the object to be created and the problem of how creation is to be accomplished. Eventually an instantaneous flash of insight clarifies the problem, and the project is carried out successfully, provided the individual has command of the essential techniques. The entire process is integrative rather than analytical as in problem-solving. It is directed by an "inner fusion" of intellectual and emotional meaning which leads the self to respond in terms of its private needs and experience.[9]

For Rugg, life is experienced on a kind of conscious-nonconscious continuum, and the flash of insight occurs in the transliminal mind, a threshold state standing between the conscious and unconscious extremes. It occurs most readily in a quiet state of relaxed concentration following a prolonged period of struggle with the problem to be solved. There is a sudden grasp of new relations that allows the mind to leap over previously insurmountable barriers, and a creative idea is born.[10]

But how? Why? What are the necessary physiological and psychological conditions? In searching for answers to these questions, Rugg eventually arrives at the conviction that a full understanding of the creative act can be achieved only through a synthesis of what he regards as the two chief sources of knowledge: scientific inquiry and intuition. With respect to the latter, he turns for enlightenment to the Eastern wise men. In the doctrines of Taoism, Zen Buddhism, and Yoga (which he refers to collectively as "the Tao of the East") he finds clues to, and techniques for, the release from consciousness into the transliminal mind where the creative act occurs. According to Rugg, this "off-conscious," quiet attitude, fanciful in nature, is free from the censors and blockages that ordinarily inhibit the creative process. It allows

9. Rugg, *Culture and Education*, pp. 369–373.
10. Harold Rugg, *Imagination*, ed. Kenneth Benne (New York: Harper & Row, Publishers, 1963), pp. 19, 39.

things to happen, that is, it sets the stage for the creative response by virtue of the free association of images, memories, feelings, and concepts.[11]

Although fully appreciative of scientific accomplishment, he insists, as we have seen, that science and logic need to be complemented by "intuitive wisdom." On that account he finds the prevailing absorption of students of human behavior in the scientific method, and their neglect of the contemplative doctrines of the East, an obstacle to a complete, balanced theory of knowledge. In Eastern philosophy, moreover, Rugg finds a parallel to his own conception of the conditions necessary for creative thought:

> I find in the Great Doctrine of the East impressive validation from widely separated cultures of my notions of the transliminal mind, of the conscious-unconscious continuum, and of the autonomous forming process in the creative unconscious. I find, moreover, mutual corroboration on the technique of developing the intuitive mind of inside identification through concentration of attention and relaxation. I shall postulate that such phrases of the East as "being in the Tao," "no-mind," and "creative climax after the interval of suspense" approximately describe the state which I have called the transliminal mind.[12]

Rugg's admiration for the "Great Doctrine of the East" leads him in turn to ponder the intuitive experiences of mystics together with the work of writers and thinkers such as William Blake, Coleridge, and Bergson as the basis of a potential "Tao of the West."[13] He also regards the contemporary organic view of mind held by some behavioral scientists as a potential source of illumination. "Perhaps, ironically," he reflects, "new developments in the sciences will succeed in building acceptable foundations for a Tao of the West where

11. Ibid., p. 216.
12. Ibid., p. 184.
13. Ibid., chap. 10, passim.

mystics, poets, and intuitive philosophers have met with a very limited hearing."[14]

Romanticism and Idealism

I shall deal with Rugg's interpretation of the above-mentioned scientific developments shortly, but first it might be helpful to say something about his overall style of thought, a style that reveals traces of both romanticism and idealism. It has already been pointed out that he was an admirer of Blake and Coleridge, and in chapter 2 I noted the high regard he had for Whitman and Emerson. In addition to Bergson, moreover, his list of great philosophers included William James (who despite his radical empiricism was always interested in "feeling" and reports of mystical experiences). Rugg was originally a New Englander. Had he been born seventy or eighty years earlier, he would have felt at home in Concord, for he was in sympathy with much of the Transcendentalist spirit. The elevation of intuitive sense and imaginative creation over logical reasoning and analytical judgment, intellectual and moral individualism, utopianism, strong democratic tendencies—all find a ready welcome in Rugg's system of values. This is not to suggest that he accepted the Transcendentalist creed in toto; aside from his interest in Emerson, he may not have been very familiar with it, yet there are unquestionably a number of striking similarities between Rugg's point of view and the Transcendentalist temper.

Given this hint to Rugg's style of thought, it is hardly surprising to find that he was also something of an idealist, though not necessarily a self-conscious one. As a matter of fact, there is little in his writings to suggest that he read the system-building idealists with any great care; nonetheless, it is noteworthy how frequently his statements are similar to (though probably not influenced by) those of various spokesmen of idealism or thinkers with idealistic tendencies. When

14. Ibid., p. 210.

he discusses the acquisition of knowledge through feeling, for example, one hears echoes of Bradley's claim that experience starts with "an immediate feeling, a knowing and being in one, with which knowledge begins. . . ."[15] And again, when Rugg gives priority to intuition over logical demonstration or empirical verification, one is reminded of Husserl's complaint that empiricism does not provide an adequate account of meaning because it fails to recognize that "direct insight" is necessary to understanding.[16] Croce's "grades of thought" at which the mind operates, first intuiting and then conceptualizing what has been intuited, also come to mind,[17] as does Schopenhauer's account of knowing objects in themselves by transcending time and space, and losing oneself in the objects.[18] Finally, at the risk of belaboring the point, it might be noted that Rugg's insistence on the difference between intuitive and discursive knowledge is compatible with Kant's distinction between the faculty of imagination, which engages in intuitions, and the faculty of understanding, which deals with concepts.[19]

And yet, having said all of this, I should quickly enter a disclaimer lest it be concluded that Rugg has been neatly classified among the romantics or the idealists. For all his criticism of the pragmatists, the empiricist strain in him is equally prominent if not more so. It will be recalled that he was trained as an engineer, and he valued highly both the empirical methods of science and their philosophical underpinnings. In this connection, he often took pains to credit the empiricists with rescuing the modern world from both "the philosophy of authority" and Cartesian rationalism.

15. F. H. Bradley, "On Our Knowledge of Immediate Experience," *Mind* 18 (January 1909): 40.

16. *Logische Untersuchungen* (1901), cited by John Passmore in *A Hundred Years of Philosophy* (London: Gerald Duckworth & Co., 1957), pp. 191–192.

17. See his *Aesthetic as the Science of Expression and General Linguistic* (1901) and *Logic as the Science of the Pure Concept* (1909).

18. *The World As Will and Idea*, Vol. 1, Bk. 3, trans. R. B. Haldane and J. Kemp, 8th ed. (London: Kegan Paul, Trench, Trubner & Co., n.d.), pp. 230–234.

19. *Critique of Judgment*, trans. J. H. Bernard, 2d ed. rev. (London: Macmillan and Co., 1914), p. 32.

Thus, he could write: "Between them, Hobbes, Locke, and Berkeley built the initial solid plank in the foundation of modern thought: there are no innate ideas; there is no depository in human nature of abstract ideas. *Knowledge is derived from experience by the mental activity of the self; not by appeal to authority, but by human derivation of psychological principles.*"[20] [Rugg's italics.]

In short, Rugg once again eludes classification. As an amateur philosopher of sorts, he takes a variety of stances while attempting to effect a meaningful synthesis of ideas. As we observed in chapter 2, this makes him an unpredictable, sometimes inconsistent, but always interesting thinker.

RUGG'S THEORIES OF MIND AND KNOWLEDGE

In trying to link Rugg's notion of creativity with the specific elements of his theories of knowledge and of mind, we note that his approach is mainly psychological and that his interest in the relevant epistemological and metaphysical questions is secondary. Consequently, his views on these matters are never set down systematically, and it is necessary to integrate ideas from scattered passages in order to emerge with some semblance of a coherent theory.

The Mind

Though he occasionally speaks loosely of the mind as if it were a substantive entity, Rugg does not really want to entertain that view because it would imply a mind-body dualism, and he wants to avoid that implication in favor of the position that human responses are neither bodily nor mental acts exclusively, but responses by the total organism. "Nothing is more basic," he claims, "than the role of the body. We not only move with it, we think with it, feel with it, imagine with

20. Rugg, *Foundations for American Education*, p. 40.

it."[21] Still, Rugg is reluctant to dispense entirely with the notion of mind. "Into each act," he states, "enters something called 'mind,' something called 'purpose,' and something called 'will.'"[22] What, then, is the nature of this "something called mind" that enters into every act? Rugg describes it as "a heaving sea of rhythmical electro-chemical impulses and motor imagery, focused momentarily in consciousness as meaningful percepts and concepts."[23] The psychological components are fused with physiological activities, and together they form the integrated act.

In formulating his conception of mind, in fact in his total outlook, Rugg draws upon field-force concepts first developed in physics. His emphasis is always on functions, "fields," and relations rather than on things, on organicism rather than mechanism.[24] Thus he rejects as overly mechanistic the view that the organic act is simply a response to stimuli. Nor, apparently, does he consider it to be something initiated at whim by the individual. Instead, Rugg subscribes to the view that the individual, because of his motor set or tensed attitude of bodily anticipation, is already reorganizing his field of perception before he "picks up" the new stimulus.[25] A number of the more salient characteristics of Rugg's theory of mind are evident in the following passage:

This four-fold flux of percept, motor adjustments, images, and concepts is the stuff of creative mind. These are not separated and inert bits. They are a glowing, rippling flow of electrical and chemical movement and motor imagery. One fact we can count upon: In meeting each new situation, the body-mind organism is neither inert nor quiescent; it does not have to be "started" to produce a new flash of meaning. On the contrary, it is in continuous wave motion, ever ready to have its electrochemistry and

21. Rugg, Imagination, p. 98.
22. Ibid., p. 99.
23. Ibid., p. 57.
24. Rugg, Foundations for American Education, pp. 59–70, 157–163.
25. Rugg, Imagination, pp. 279–281.

its motor tendencies tuned in and thereby to produce the flash of meaning.[26]

Sensation and Perception

Knowledge for Rugg, given his essentially naturalistic, functional view of mind, begins with sensation and perception, with the latter defined as "awareness of external objects, qualities or relations which ensue directly upon sensory processes."[27] But the human organism does not receive impressions passively in Rugg's view. Incoming percepts are met by, and interact with, images, memories, and motor tendencies that have been stored up in the organism.[28] They are, moreover, influenced by the organism's inner drives, needs, and frustrations.[29] The perceptual field, as Rugg calls it, is a union of external stimuli and internally stored experiences. He describes the process as follows: "We not only live in two environments—the 'reality' world of the external environment and the 'autistic' world of the inner environment—but our perceptions are inevitably distorted by the molding demands of both."[30] And again, *"Perception is more than imprinting. It is a creative process in which the perceiver creates the field from which his percepts, signs, and symbols emerge."*[31] [Rugg's italics.]

Now if all of this is true, and it appears to accord with current psychological theory, it would seem that our perceptions of the external world provide us with a distortion of whatever reality exists "out there," that "things-in-themselves" remain veiled to some extent. This is a defensible view, to be sure, but difficulties can arise when, as in Rugg's

26. Ibid., p. 77.
27. Ibid., p. 36.
28. Ibid., pp. 76–77.
29. Ibid., p. 223.
30. Ibid., p. 88.
31. Ibid., p. 82.

case, the notion of intuition is introduced. It all depends, of course, on what is meant by "intuition." If one restricts intuition to immediate awareness of the "given" in experience, or, even more selectively, to direct awareness of one's bodily sensations and states of consciousness, then serious difficulties need not arise (though epistemological pitfalls abound even in these areas, and one must tread softly). Similarly, certain "basic" principles of logic such as the "laws" of contradiction and excluded middle are often regarded as self-evident or intuitive truths that are based on simple observation or inspection as opposed to mediate judgments based on a process of reasoning. Finally, the term "intuition" may be used with relative security as a synonym for sudden insight in a problem-solving situation.

These illustrations of "proper" usage are not intended to be exhaustive, but they are offered as examples about which there is fairly wide agreement. When, on the other hand, the term "intuition" is used in the Bergsonian sense of identifying with, or "getting inside" the object of knowledge, thus yielding knowledge that is held to be "absolute," yet inexpressible,[32] our credulity is strained and the very notion of intuition becomes suspect. Our task now, therefore, is to try to determine the exact sense in which Rugg intends the term to be understood, especially in view of the fact that he must reconcile it somehow with his account of perception. The problem here is that Rugg vacillates between using the term in a Gestaltist sense as a synonym for the "flash of insight" and using it in the Bergsonian sense of certain but ineffable knowledge.

His account of perception would probably be accepted, as far as it goes, by a Gestaltist, and in general Rugg is receptive to the Gestaltist point of view. It represents for him a holistic psychology, which fits into his total world view, as

32. Henri Bergson, *An Introduction to Metaphysics*, trans. T. E. Hulme (New York: The Liberal Arts Press, 1950), pp. 21–24.

opposed to associationist and connectionist psychologies, which to him represent an outmoded mechanistic outlook. Hence Rugg frequently appeals to Wertheimer or Köhler when he discusses the flash of insight, and his account of it is often Gestaltist in tone as in the following description of problem-solving: "For those who solve the problem, the solution comes suddenly, as a 'flash of insight,' a hunch, a new idea.... What was the key to the solution? A complete reorientation in the way of looking at the problem, thinking in a new dimension."[33]

This is not all that "intuition" means to Rugg, however, for he also considers the concept in connection with terms like "certainty" and "inside identification." In discussing the artist's way of knowing, for example, he writes: "So the artist, in the grip of intense concentration, strives to objectify what he sees in imagination, inside the earth, beyond the sky, inside the apple, inside the living man or woman. This is the inside way of knowing, the artist's way of identification with the object."[34]

Now it could be argued that Rugg did not intend for this passage to be taken literally, but he does appeal to Bergson on occasion, and the above quotation certainly reflects Bergson's view of intuition. Further, there can be little doubt that Rugg connects intuition and the flash of insight with knowledge that is "certain." In one typical passage he speaks of the sudden insight "coming with such certitude that a logical statement of it can be immediately prepared."[35] In another he claims, "Autobiographers of the intuitive act are equally in agreement that the flash is sudden, unexpected, and has certitude. When it comes, the discoverer knows he is right, before he verifies it logically."[36]

Thus it would appear that Rugg's intuitionism is at odds

33. Rugg, *Imagination*, pp. 23–24.
34. Ibid., p. 32.
35. Ibid., p. 6.
36. Ibid., p. 9.

with his account of sensation and perception, for it would be difficult to explain how one is to "identify" with the object when one's perception of it is necessarily distorted. Whatever "identification with the object known" means, it implies knowledge that is somehow more accurate, more reliable, than that achieved by scientific inquiry (with which intuition is usually contrasted). Yet it is hard to see how perceptual distortion can be rectified except by employing scientific laws, theories, and facts. Consider, for instance, the familiar example of the straight stick that appears bent when partially submerged in water. If we know something about the laws of physics, we can account for this illusion and thus come to a better understanding of the stick's qualities, even if we have never seen a stick partially submerged in water before and have not observed this particular stick out of water. But how could a person with no understanding of physics possibly equal or exceed this achievement through reliance on intuition alone, that is to say, without recourse to science, or logical inference?

Perhaps the intuitionist would argue that "inside identification" is something over and above scientific knowledge, that scientific inquiry is a prerequisite for the act of intuition. Bergson seems to have something like this in mind when he says, "For we do not obtain an intuition from reality—that is, an intellectual sympathy with the most intimate part of it—unless we have won its confidence by a long fellowship with its superficial manifestation."[37] Whether or not Rugg would likewise argue in this vein is questionable. If he were to take this position, he could, perhaps, reconcile his views on perception and intuition by holding that science is needed to explain away perceptual distortion and thus to set the stage for the act of intuition. Of course this would leave intuition itself still to be explained, and mention of this problem brings us to Rugg's account of the intuitive process.

37. Bergson, *Introduction to Metaphysics*, p. 60.

INTUITION VIA FEELING

Finding sensation and perception alone inadequate grounds for knowledge, other thinkers have turned to intuition as a more reliable source, but they have usually postulated an entity like "mind" or "intellect" which does the intuiting. For Rugg, as we have seen, there is no such substantive entity. Indeed, he has apparently combined an intuitive theory of knowledge with a functional theory of mind (with the latter understood as the view that mental processes amount to a set of functions or activities and capacities manifested in the behavior of the human organism), and this is a rather unusual combination. How, then, is the process of intuition carried on?

Rugg would answer, "Primarily through feeling involving the entire organism." His use of terms here is somewhat ambiguous. In one context he defines feeling as primal awareness and calls it one of the two phases of problem-solving; the other phase, he explains, is the logical, documentary one of thinking, and together the two phases constitute the complete act of thought. Then he applies the label "felt-thought" to the first phase, further defines it as "discovery" (i.e., the flash of insight), and says that felt-thought is largely based on feeling.[38] But if feeling or primal awareness is synonymous with felt-thought or discovery, how can the latter be based on feeling? The conclusion seems to be that discovery is based on itself.

Elsewhere he explains that feeling molds thought into felt-thought and that felt-thought brings about creative discovery.[39] This seems to be closer to his intent since he has to make a distinction between feeling and discovery and explain how the one leads to the other. Rugg begins by describing feeling as "the matrix in which all coming to know takes

38. Rugg, *Imagination*, pp. 269–270.
39. Ibid., p. 310.

place."[40] In this context he stresses that feeling, in his terms, is something apart from either emotion or sensation. The obvious difficulty here is that once sensation and emotion are eliminated, it is hard to see how feeling can be anything more than a kind of rudimentary nonverbal consciousness. It is not at all clear that feeling in this sense should be considered superior (in terms of approaching certainty) to thinking as a means of acquiring knowledge. Feeling might also be used as a synonym for belief, of course, but belief is not a process or an activity leading to discovery. Rather, it is the outcome to which inquiry, discovery, and possibly other factors contribute. Moreover, though belief may be colored by emotion, it is at least partly the result of thinking or reasoning, and Rugg wants to distinguish feeling from thought.

A number of points relevant to this issue have been brought out by A. C. Ewing in a discussion of reason and intuition. Ewing points out that

> "feel," as ordinarily used, has two quite different senses: (1) It is used in connexion with occurrences such as pains, pleasures, emotions, sensations. In this sense it would be absurd to speak of "feeling that something is true." (2) It is sometimes used as a synonym for "believe." It is most naturally used as such where the belief is strongly held and connected with a strong emotion but is incapable of logical proof . . . or where it is based on a vague sense of the general situation without our being in a position to give any definite ground. . . . When we use "feel" in the second sense we are talking about the cognitive and not the sensitive side of our nature. . . . It seems to me that the fact that "feel" is used in these two different senses has helped to make the anti-rationalist view seem more plausible than it really is. . . .[41]

40. Ibid., p. 269.
41. A. C. Ewing, *Reason and Intuition* (London: Humphrey, Milford Amen

Ewing's remarks show rather convincingly that neither of the two senses in which "feeling" is commonly used will serve Rugg's purposes, and Rugg would probably agree. Presumably this is why he divorces feeling from sensation and emotion while at the same time distinguishing it from thought. Of course this leaves his own conception of feeling still to be explained and justified.

Feeling As Gesture

Rugg might have taken a position similar to that of Combs and Snygg, who define feeling in terms of the individual's total perceptual field:

> What we attempt to communicate by our feelings, then, is the state of our perceptual fields including our state of tension or acceleration. Feelings differ from emotion, however, in that they symbolize *all* [their italics] of the perceptual field. The degree of tension experienced would express very little to other people without some further description of what brought on this state. To say "I felt very tense" conveys very little until we add to this a description of the meaning of the tension for us. . . . Feelings always include the emotional condition as an important factor in the total perceptual state, but usually extend far beyond body status.[42]

This broader conception of feeling has the virtue of including elements of both cognition and bodily sensation. In this respect it might seem at first glance to lend itself readily to Rugg's notion of felt-thought, but Rugg has something else in mind. The Combs-Snygg view furnishes an account of the

---

House, E.C., 1941), pp. 15–16. (First published in *Proceedings of the British Academy, vo* 27 [Oxford: Oxford University Press, 1941].)

42. Arthur W. Combs and Donald Snygg, *Individual Behavior: A Perceptual Approach to Behavior*, 2nd ed. rev. (New York: Harper & Row, Publishers, 1959), pp. 233–234.

already existing "field" of thoughts, sensations, and emo-
tions, which are encompassed by the general term "feelings,"
whereas Rugg is concerned with providing an account of how
feeling and thought first arise and then achieve discovery.
Thus he expands his notion of feeling to include "the total
tensing adjustment of the body" and introduces the concept
of "gesture." Here Rugg postulates a dynamic movement or
tensile sense throughout the body, calls it "feeling," and goes
on to link it with "gesture." In this context he writes, "Gesture
as felt-thought, therefore, is the label I give to the total motor
adjustment of the skeletal frame, muscles, tissues, organs,
nervous system, circulatory and reverberatory systems, of the
endothalamic and the autonomic systems."[43] Just before this,
he discusses the phenomenon known as "determining tendency to act."[44] By a "determining tendency" he seems to
mean an "anticipatory set" or a predisposition to respond to
stimuli in a certain way, and he apparently regards the determining tendency as a contributing factor to the tensed condition of the organism. He refers to the Würzburg group of
psychologists in connection with "determining tendencies,"
however, and this casts some doubt on the exact meaning of
the term for him. According to the Würzburg psychologist
Narziss Ach, who developed the principle, the determining
tendencies stem from an "aim-presentation" (apparently a
task to be performed) and help to elicit a specific response
upon presentation of a specific stimulus.[45] To illustrate, Humphrey explains Ach's principle as follows:

> Instructions are, for example, to lift the right index
> finger if the letter *E* appears, the left if the letter *O* appears.
> Suppose that the letter *E* appears. From part of the content

43. Rugg, *Imagination*, p. 282.
44. Ibid., pp. 279–281.
45. N. Ach, *Über die Willenstätigheit und das Denken* (Götingen, 1905), p. 187,
cited by George Humphrey, *Thinking: An Introduction to Its Experimental Psychology* (London: Methuen & Co., 1951), pp. 81–82.

of the aim-presentation arising when the instructions are given, proceed influences which work on the stimulus-presentation of the letter E to form the specific purpose of lifting the right index finger and action follows.[46]

Thus the determining tendency on Ach's account results from the idea of a specific task to be performed. It is not part of the general motor adjustment of the organism previous to presentation of the aim. Furthermore we shall discover shortly that Rugg thinks motor adjustment somehow creates meaning, whereas the meaning carried by Ach's determining tendencies is presumably derived from the idea of the task to be performed.

There are additional problems connected with Rugg's introduction of the concept of "gesture." Gesture is first called "the organ of feeling"; next it is said to be "felt-thought" (felt-thought, in turn, is defined first as "total motor adjustment" and then as "gestural symbol"); finally it (gesture) is "feeling in tensed body movement."[47] In any case, the significance of feeling as gesture or body sense for Rugg is that he thinks that somewhere in this tension there is the "firing contact" that sets off the "act of response." This hypothesis is plausible, certainly, and it would appear to avoid some of the confusion surrounding his explanation of discovery (since the order of succession would be from total motor adjustment to felt-thought to discovery). Even so, feeling in this sense remains unconvincing as a superior means of acquiring knowledge, for it seems to be little more than a brute impulse to act which does not rise even to the level of primal awareness. At best it appears to identify some of the physiological prerequisites of thought. Rugg's attempt to imbue feeling with cognitive significance leads him, moreover, to reduce psychological processes to physical conditions in his account of think-

46. Humphrey, ibid., p. 82.
47. Rugg, *Imagination*, pp. 281–282.

ing. He holds, for example, that "a man's attitude—the total gesture of the organism—*determines* [my italics] how he behaves, what he feels and thinks. The act of knowing is indeed the total gesture of hands, limbs, face, torso, autonomic and central nervous systems."[48]

Now the word "attitude" may be used in at least two ways. It can represent a mental disposition or point of view, or it may refer to a physical posture as when one "strikes" a certain attitude. Viewing it as a mental set, we can agree with Rugg that attitude may exert considerable influence on thought and behavior, but this need not be the case when, on the other hand, attitude refers to a physical stance of some kind. Yet Rugg frequently writes in this vein in his eagerness to establish a claim for feeling or gesture as the primary source of knowledge and meaning. In another place, for instance, he again equates "attitude" with "gesture" and argues that gesture both communicates and creates meaning.[49] The error in reasoning here can be brought out by putting Rugg's argument in syllogistic form:

> Attitudes create meaning.
> Gestures are attitudes.
> Therefore gestures create meaning.

The argument is invalid because "attitudes" means one thing in the major premise and quite another in the minor premise. Thus the syllogism contains in effect four terms, one more, unhappily for Rugg, than the principles of logical deducation permit.

In attempting to establish gesture as a source of knowledge, what Rugg is putting forth is essentially a motor theory of thinking and meaning (along with a touch of Watsonian behaviorism) that bears some resemblance to the work of Edward Titchener, Edmund Jacobson, Margaret Washburn,

---

48. Ibid., p. 277.
49. Rugg, *Foundations for American Education,* p. 230.

Nina Bull, and others who have stressed the importance of kinesthesis in thinking. Thus, in discussing "motor determinants of meaning," he writes:

> This brings to the fore a motor theory of consciousness and meaning as well as of attention and relaxation. It now needs to be demonstrated that we respond to ideas as well as to people, things, situations, by making appropriate incipient or overt muscular adjustments; that shifts in emotion always imply predictable changes in postural set, and that skeletal muscle patterns fit specific emotional patterns; that the new-born baby's first meanings and the aged man's last ones are motor responses to physiological tensions or needs; that electro-encephalographic and myographic measurements verify the hypothesis that motor attitude is the matrix in which perception occurs.[50]

Probably few, if any, contemporary psychologists would deny that muscular tension is somehow related to thought processes, but the nature of the relationship and the significance of muscular tension are disputed points. Humphrey lists three possibilities: (1) Muscular tensions may be an overflow from the central nervous system. (2) They might furnish a substratum for particular thought processes. (3) "Together with the perceptual changes to which they give rise," they might "form a necessary and sufficient condition for thought."[51] Rugg seems to lean toward the third possibility in the passage quoted above. Humphrey, conversely, rejects the third alternative, which he calls the "peripheral theory of thinking." "Jacobson," he writes, "has shown that muscular tension, and the electrical accompaniments thereof, always accompanied thinking in his subjects. He has further shown that when muscular tension ceased, thinking ceased. . . . Does it follow that thinking *is* muscular process, overt or

50. Rugg, *Imagination*, p. 63.
51. Humphrey, *Thinking*, pp. 197–198.

covert? Examination of the experimental results, those of Jacobson and of others to be mentioned, does not lead to this conclusion."[52]

This dispute had better be left to the psychologists, but regardless of which view is correct it is doubtful that the outcome would lend itself to Rugg's attempts to link feeling, gesture, or total motor adjustment with knowledge, for in contending that the act of knowing is total bodily gesture he carries the discussion over the boundaries of psychology onto philosophical grounds and in the process makes what Gilbert Ryle would call a "category-mistake."[53] That is, he assigns knowing, which belongs to the category of achievements (such as winning, finding, persuading), to the category of activities or performances (such as running, looking, arguing). Put another way, knowing is not an activity at all. It is, rather, the *result* of an activity, and to call it an act is to place it in the wrong category. But even if Rugg were careful to distinguish the process leading to the achievement of knowing from the achievement itself, he would still be open to the objection (as noted above) that in claiming that meanings and thoughts are motor responses, he is in essence adopting a reductionist position. That is to say, he is identifying thought with physical activities, and it is a mistake to conclude that because thought is *dependent* on physiological activities, it is also *identical* with them. Obviously, an idea is not the same thing as the bodily motion from which it stems.

With regard to the proposition that gesture determines thought, one might easily object on the grounds that thought, once set in motion, is capable of turning back on its somatic base and determining changes therein. Thus, the claim that thought determines gesture is equally persuasive, and the debate can only lead into the old mind-body morass. Here Rugg might reply that he has been misunderstood, that what he

52. Ibid., p. 201.
53. Gilbert Ryle, *The Concept of Mind* (London: Hutchinson House, 1949), pp. 16ff.

really means is simply that thought is dependent on certain physiological factors that he has subsumed under the blanket term "gesture." This defense would possess the added virtue of enabling Rugg to avoid the charge of reductive over-simplification. At the same time, however, it would pull the teeth from his hypothesis that feeling is a source of knowledge, for it would imply that knowledge ensues from thought after all, and this concession would seem to divest "gesture" and "feeling" of their intuitionist connotations.

We are now in a position to note some of the main objections to Rugg's account of feeling in summary form. If we eliminate emotion and sensation, it is difficult to see how feeling can be anything more than primal awareness, belief, or total motor adjustment in tensed readiness to act. If feeling is primal awareness, then it is a simple state of consciousness that is inferior to logical thought. If it is belief, it is psychological rather than somatic. Finally, if it is total motor adjustment, it may furnish the necessary physiological conditions for thought to arise, but it is not itself a cognitive agent.[54]

The possibilities with respect to gesture appear to be similarly limited. The choice here seems to be between regarding gesture as feeling or as the expression of feeling. (Rugg also calls gesture "felt-thought," but felt-thought is then reduced to motor adjustment, which, as we have seen, is another name for feeling.)[55] If gesture is feeling, it is vulnerable to the objections just enumerated. If it is an expression of feeling, then it is simply a sign, or possibly a symbol, but not a "creator" of meaning. Hence Rugg seems to be faced with intractable obstacles in claiming that there is another way of knowing which is based on feeling. To repeat, he thinks the

54. Alfred North Whitehead's "Philosophy of Organism" as set forth in *Process and Reality* (New York: The Macmillan Co., 1929) might have provided support for Rugg's views, and indeed Rugg ocassionally cited Whitehead in his discussions of creativity. Since he never considered Whitehead's thought in any detail, however, it is not clear how much of the latter's theory of prehension he was prepared to accept in order to bolster his own claims for the primacy of feeling in cognition.

55. Rugg, *Imagination*, p. 282.

flash of insight is "fired" somewhere within the dynamic tensing adjustment of the body, but this fact, if it is a fact, merely indicates that thought is dependent on physiological factors. It hardly demonstrates that feeling is a source of insight.

Concepts, Conceptions, and the Flash of Insight

Rugg makes yet another attempt to place feeling on an equal footing with thinking as a source of understanding by distinguishing between conceptions and concepts, assigning the former to feeling and the latter to thinking.[56] It will be recalled that he thinks the flash of insight occurs in "the quiet mind of relaxed concentration." He is never able to explain the process precisely, of course, because, as he points out himself, there are still too many gaps in our behavioral knowledge.[57] He concludes, however, that it somehow emerges out of a fusion of the ingredients of the creative mind—percepts, images, motor adjustments, and concepts—which are in a constant flow of electro-chemical interaction and motor imagery.[58] "We know," he says, "that some autonomous forming process sweeps like a magnet across the chaotic elements of mind, picks up the significant segments and, in a welding flash, precipitates the creative response. But we do not yet know the nature of the forming process."[59]

Rugg thinks the new science of cybernetics provides clues which, when related to his account of knowing and feeling, may eventually yield an adequate theory. In this respect he writes:

> How is the adjusting, searching process carried on? A series of mutually corroborative hypotheses supplies the most plausible theory: first, that the brain-mind works continually as a modeling computer, averaging through feed-

56. Ibid., p. 266.
57. Ibid., p. 314.
58. Ibid., p. 77.
59. Ibid., p. 288.

back the organism's learned (stored) assumptions; second, that the brain-mind's alpha rhythm is the mechanism that scans for best fit; third, that the mid-brain continually computes the changing space-time coordinates; fourth, that the complete freedom of the transliminal state, in which the computing is done, permits a cumulative, organic, motor-feeling factor, a suggesting, determining tendency to complete the act, a motor-adjustment of imminence; fifth, that the total act is carried on in a bipolar fusion of perception of outer-scene and drive of inner stress-system.[60]

It is not clear, however, even if Rugg is right about the functioning of the "brain-mind" being analogous to data-processing by computer, how such physiological information would contribute to a theory of learning designed to foster creativity. Since he had not fully developed this line of thought at the time of his death, it is difficult to determine what he had in mind in the way of educational application. Perhaps he would have held that we cannot solve that problem until we know more about the workings of the human brain. At any rate, what emerges out of the forming process is a conception, and conceptions are not to be confused with concepts. Rugg offers this distinction:

> It is, moreover, of the greatest importance to distinguish conception from concept, that is, the general shotgun, nonverbal response of conceptualizing from the specific rifle-shot use of the verbal label or concept.... For example, my conception of our current automated society is a *feeling* [Rugg's italics] of a social order caught between near-abundance and near-catastrophe. It can be defined and clarified only as I build an advancing hierarchy of concepts into my changing conceptions....[61]

60. Ibid., p. 309.
61. Ibid., p. 267.

He then goes on to list a number of concepts—factory, cartel, market, corporation, etc.—which together comprise the overarching conception.

It is Rugg's view, then, that a conception includes and integrates a group of concepts.[62] The main difference between the two is, apparently, their degree of generality, for he uses the word "idea" first as a synonym for "concept" and then as a synonym for "conception'" in successive sentences.[63] It is difficult, therefore, to see why conception should be defined in terms of feeling. In the passage just quoted, "belief" could have been substituted for "feeling," and this indicates that we have here a case in which feeling has cognitive rather than sensory or affective significance. The only difference between "feeling" used in this manner and "knowledge" is the difference between "belief" and "knowledge" (an epistemological problem that need not concern us in this discussion). Both terms belong in the cognitive realm, hence it is misleading to define conceptions in terms of feelings unless it is clear that the cognitive as opposed to the sensory meaning of feeling is what is intended.

There is yet another difficulty involved in Rugg's treatment of "conception," which becomes apparent when he tries to relate conception to the process of symbolization. At one point he describes the flash of insight (he substitutes the word "meaning" for "insight" in this context) "as a transformation of motor-imagery into symbol."[64] But it is not clear whether the symbol stands for the conception or the concept, or whether it is itself the conception. The former interpretation would seem to be the more credible of the two, and Rugg does discuss the capacity of the mind to create concepts and symbols. On the same page, however, he writes, "The flash of insight emerges from the unconscious as a full-blown concep-

62. Ibid., p. 266.
63. Ibid., p. 285.
64. Ibid., p. 263.

tual symbol because the organism can behave in no other way. It is an inner necessity."[65]

Later in his discussion he attempts to connect symbolizing with conceptualizing, using metaphor as the connecting link.[66] Here again it is difficult to determine the relationship between these elements or, for that matter, how they differ from one another. For having already implied that they are three distinct factors, he goes on to describe the formulation of meaning as the projection of "metaphor-image" or "concept-symbol."[67]

The apparent lack of specificity here no doubt exists because we simply do not know enough about what happens inside the human organism when a concept is formed. What Rugg is driven back to, in any case, is the notion of the "forming process" which sweeps over the raw materials of the "mind" and somehow precipitates the flash of meaning. But of course he is unable to explain the process because of limitations in our understanding of the dynamics of concept formation.

GENERAL CRITICISM OF INTUITION

A number of problems in Rugg's exposition have been pointed out. Given more time, he might have been able to solve many of them, but, as mentioned earlier, he died before *Imagination* was finished, and it had to be edited without his direction. But even if Rugg were able to overcome the objections raised in this discussion, he would still be faced with the problems inherent in any philosophy of intuition. We may agree that scientific investigators and creative artists experience sudden "intuitions" that seem to enable them to grasp previously inaccessible principles or relationships; we may

65. Ibid., pp. 263–264.
66. Ibid., p. 285.
67. Ibid., p. 286.

grant this much and still argue that what *appears* to be an intuition or insight (i.e., a knowledge achievement) may turn out to be a case of mistaken belief. In other words, there is no guarantee that a prima-facie "flash of insight" is authentic, however certain it may seem. Clearly, there is no contradiction in saying that someone feels positive that he knows something, but that he is mistaken. Henri Poincaré's comments on creativity may serve to illustrate this point. Rugg uses Poincaré's description of an insight regarding Fuchsian functions as a case in point to support his own views and quotes Poincaré as follows on page four of *Imagination:*

> "At the moment when I put my foot on the step, the idea came to me, without anything in my former thoughts seeming to have paved the way for it, that the transformations I had used to define the Fuchsian functions were identical with those of non-Euclidean geometry. I did not verify the idea; I went on with a conversation already commenced, but I felt a perfect certainty. On my return to Caen, for conscience's sake, I verified the result at my leisure."[68]

What Rugg overlooks, however, is Poincaré's clear-cut warning that the seeming flash of insight may turn out to be a false alarm. In this connection Poincaré writes:

> The need for the second period of conscious work, after the inspiration, is still easier to understand. It is necessary to put in shape the results of this inspiration, to deduce from them the immediate consequences, to arrange them, to word the demonstrations, but above all is verification necessary. I have spoken of the feeling of absolute certitude accompanying the inspiration; in the cases cited this feeling was no deceiver, nor is it usually. But do not think this is a rule without exception; often this feeling deceives us without being any the less vivid, and we only find it out

68. Henri Poincaré, *The Foundations of Science,* trans. George Bruce Halsted (New York: The Science Press, 1929), pp. 387–388.

when we seek to put on foot the demonstration. I have especially noticed this fact in regard to ideas coming to me in the morning or evening in bed while in a semi-hypnagogic state.[69]

Poincaré's disclaimer serves to remind us that we expect people to justify their knowledge claims, to offer some kind of adequate evidence in support of their assuredness. Thus, it has been suggested that X can be said to know that Q if and only if (1) X believes that Q, (2) X has adequate evidence that Q, and (3) Q (that is, Q actually is the case).[70] The three conditions specified in the example constitute what has been called the "strong sense" of knowing, and the inclusion of (2) implies that the term "intuition" (if it is to be equated with the term "knowledge") is inappropriate until some process of verficiation has been undertaken. Here Rugg could reply that verification is precisely the function of the second phase of his complete act of thought (logical thinking as opposed to feeling), but with his notions of certainty and identification with the object known he seems to regard verification as being of secondary importance in comparison with the inspirational discovery or flash of insight. For him the insight carries certainty; knowledge, therefore, can be achieved without a process of logical or scientific verification. Verification, then, is of minor importance, almost a simple verbalization of the insight. To this point of view I have already objected that verification is crucial because we sometimes think we have valid insights only to find out later that we are mistaken. In addition, it is not clear that insight overshadows verification as much as Rugg thinks, even when the insight turns out to be valid. It is quite possible for a scientist to start with a doubtful hypothesis conceived as an unlikely possibility, and

69. Ibid., p. 390.
70. Israel Scheffler, *Conditions of Knowledge: An Introduction to Epistemology and Education* (Chicago: Scott, Foresman & Company, 1965), p. 21. Cf. Roderick M. Chisholm, *Perceiving: A Philosophical Study* (Ithaca, N.Y.: Cornell University Press, 1957), p. 16, and D. J. O'Connor, *An Introduction to the Philosophy of Education* (New York: Philosophical Library, 1957), p. 73.

then find, through inquiry, that his hypothesis is borne out. In an instance such as this the insight would develop out of the thought-inquiry-verification process.[71]

I have been discussing the strong sense of knowing, which requires that adequate evidence be presented to substantiate the knowledge claim. We can, of course, settle for a weak sense of knowing simply by eliminating the second of the three conditions listed above, in which case knowledge becomes equivalent to true belief. We might then concede that X knows that Q, even though, for some reason or other, he is unable to supply evidence for his claim. But here again it is possible for X's belief, however he arrived at it, to be false. We do not concede that he has achieved knowledge, even in the weak sense, unless we are convinced that his belief squares with the facts.

The assumption underlying this argument is, of course, that Ryle is correct in insisting that knowledge (intuition, if you will) is an achievement, not an activity or a performance. Thus it is erroneous to infer that the acquisition of knowledge implies an unerring method of inquiry, and this is the mistake that Rugg makes when he thinks of knowing as an activity and describes the activity as being primarily intuitive. No method of inquiry is infalliable, though any given inquiry may result in the achievement of knowledge. If today's truth turns out to be tomorrow's falsehood, we simply acknowledge that what was regarded as knowledge was actually a case of mistaken belief, and the reasonable response is to discard the belief.

EDUCATIONAL IMPLICATIONS

Rugg's theory of knowledge has been discussed at considerable length because of its significance in terms of his attempt to

71. See the criticism of Bergson in J. H. Randall, Jr. and J. Buchler, *Philosophy: An Introduction* (New York: Barnes & Noble, 1942), pp. 105–111 for a more detailed discussion of this point.

explain the creative process. Had he been successful, he would have had a rationale for the introduction of new teaching methods intended to nourish the creative talent of children. And this, he was convinced, was the key to bringing forth the cultured individuals who would work for social reconstruction. Reform, it must be kept in mind, is the motivating force in all of his major works.

Rugg's reasoning runs something like this: The superior society is, among other things, a cultured society. But we can produce a cultured society only by producing cultured multitudes, and we can produce cultured multitudes only by encouraging creative self-expression and appreciation in the schools. To this point the argument is plausible, and it furnishes one good reason for expanding the fine arts area of the school curriculum. This initial plausibility breaks down, however, with Rugg's insistence that an intuitive theory of knowledge based on feeling is required to explain the creative process, and, further, to build a theory of instruction designed to foster creative insight, artistic and otherwise, in school children. Bode's review article, which was mentioned at the start of this chapter, makes a relevant point in this connection. In that article Bode comments, "I have no quarrel with the view that creative self-expression and appreciation give to life a beauty and a radiance that passes understanding. But why is it necessary to insist that they are themselves a kind of understanding? That way madness lies."[72] Bode went on to point out that Rugg regarded creative self-expression and appreciation as unique kinds of responses, and to this idea he (Bode) had no objection. What he did object to, and rightly so, was the notion that this fact had any epistemological relevance.

Actually Rugg's case would have been stronger if he had presented it apart from all epistemological considerations. No esoteric theory of knowledge is required to support the claim that schools should be more concerned with the arts. On the contrary, one might argue that teachers have been too ab-

72. Bode, "Problem of Culture," p. 342.

sorbed in imparting knowledge, so much so that they have failed to perceive their obligation to enrich the lives of their charges in other ways—by providing the means for spiritual as well as intellectual self-fulfillment, for example. There is more to life, after all, than the acquisition of knowledge, but previous to the past decade or so, what is now referred to as the "affective domain" was given only slight consideration in most schools. Rugg certainly made this point and made it well. Indeed his was almost a voice in the wilderness on this score for a quarter of a century. Yet the force of his argument was blunted somewhat by the epistemological complications that accompanied it. To repeat, Rugg does not need a theory of knowledge in order to buttress his demands in behalf of the arts. He can argue both for their instrumental value in producing cultured multitudes for the better society and for their inherent value in providing contemplative enjoyment. The theory of knowledge need not enter into the discussion at all.

I have been suggesting that Rugg's theory of knowledge may have hindered rather than helped his long campaign to get school officials to make room for the arts in the curriculum. I have suggested, further, that the case for the arts can be made on independent grounds and that Rugg's epistemological difficulties tend to obscure his excellent emphases with regard to expanding the range of educational experiences. I shall now try to show how these difficulties also frustrate Rugg's efforts to apply his theory to the classroom situation.

In translating his views into recommendations for educational practice, Rugg calls for a theory of learning broad enough to entail a nonverbal symbolism of the body as well as the traditional linguistic symbolism of logical and scientific thought. Such a twofold symbolism, he feels, must provide for the inside, intuitive way of knowing along with the outside way of scientific inquiry. It must provide a logic of the gesture to accompany the older verbal-symbolic logic. Rugg calls the integration of these two methods of knowing the key to a complete theory of learning.[73] He contends that "the felt-thought of discovery can be produced only by a program that provides for development of the gestural symbol through a complete movement program in the school, as well as for logical thought through a program of reasoned verbal-processes. . . . The study calls for a motor and verbal program of education."[74]

Rugg does not provide a plan for constructing such a program, hence one is left wondering how a logic of the gesture might be formulated. At first glance the very notion may seem far-fetched, but the meaning of gestures has been of increasing interest in recent years to psychologists, social psychologists, anthropologists, linguists, and others. One researcher has, in fact, produced a bibliography of some one hundred pages on the subject.[75] Moreover, there are serious attempts underway to assemble meaningful gestures into workable classes.[76] But even if a logic of the gesture could be developed, what then? Would a logic of nonverbal symbols really be a significant contribution to learning theory? In the absence of additional information from Rugg, it is difficult to see how this new logic would complement the verbal logic currently in use.

There is also the question of the manner in which the intuitive way of knowing through inside identification with the object known is to be abetted. Given more time, perhaps Rugg could have provided some credible suggestions for classroom application; but as Brubacher has observed, it is doubtful that a learning theory based on intuition can evade a large measure of sterility. Since intuition in this sense is in-communicable, there would appear to be no way for the

73. Rugg, *Imagination*, pp. 308–311.
74. Ibid., p. 312.
75. Francis Hayes, "Gestures: A Working Bibliography," *Southern Folklore Quarterly* 21 (1957): 218–317.
76. One of the leaders in this endeavor is Ray L. Birdwhistell. See his *Introduction to Kinesics* (Louisville, Ky.: University of Louisville Press, 1952).

teacher to know whether the child has achieved it. It is uncertain, therefore, that children can be taught to intuit at all.[77]

There are, however, other ways of looking at intuition. We can dispense with inside identification and feeling and conceive of intuition simply as apparent insight[78] that may or may not turn out to be knowledge. We can also think of it as the ability to make fruitful guesses regarding the best strategy to adopt in a problem situation. These approaches to intuition render the term psychologically and philosophically "respectable" and enable us to ask meaningfully how creative, intuitive thinking can be cultivated in the school setting. It might be the case, for example, that we are too conservative in our teaching methods, that we tend to overemphasize analytical, step-by-step thinking in the classroom. We may, without realizing it, have created a classroom atmosphere that inhibits imaginative, intuitive risk-taking. Perhaps we should do more to encourage students to chance "intuitive leaps" in completing their school assignments.[79] With regard to the "flash of insight," it may be possible to simulate the special conditions, described by Rugg and others, that have apparently contributed to some of the great scientific and artistic breakthroughs.

Much research needs to be done along these lines, of course. We must work out, test, and evaluate new teaching methods, and we need to inquire much further into the nature of the creative process itself. All the same, we can perceive, at least in outline form, certain researchable areas if we take intuition to mean either immediate (as opposed to mediated) insight, or intuitive thinking (as opposed to step-by-step logical analysis), or both. Viewing intuition in this light, we are,

77. Brubacher, *Modern Philosophies of Education*, p. 80.
78. As noted previously, Rugg begins by using the term in this sense (except that he thinks the "flash of insight" carries certainty), but then he links it with feeling, opposes it to thought, and becomes enmeshed in the difficulties that have been discussed in this chapter.
79. For a fuller treatment of this point, see Jerome S. Bruner, *The Process of Education* (Cambridge, Mass.: Harvard University Press, 1961), pp. 55–68.

moreover, in a much better position to appreciate Rugg's positive contribution to the current dialogue on creativity. For despite its flaws his main work on the subject, *Imagination,* is, as Kenneth Benne notes in its foreword, a remarkable achievement of exploration and synthesis in a wide variety of fields. By virtue of its scope alone, it is among the most fertile of sources available to researchers and others interested in finding out more about the mechanics of the creative act.

5. THE SCHOOL AS AN AGENT OF SOCIAL CHANGE

This chapter concerns the relationship between education and social reconstruction in Rugg's thought. Elements of Rugg's general theory of education will be discussed insofar as they relate to his reconstructionism, but his overall educational thought will not be examined in detail. Rugg wrote rather extensively on educational psychology, teaching methods, teacher training, curriculum construction, and the so called "foundations of education," and, in fact, some of his better work was done in these areas.[1] Since much of this material is peripheral to this study, however, I shall include only those parts of it that directly pertain to, or furnish perspective for, an understanding of his conception of education as a means of achieving social reform and elevating the cultural life of the individual. The focus in chapter 5, then, will be on those aspects of Rugg's educational writings that bear on the issues discussed in chapters 2, 3, and 4.

THE SCHOOL CURRICULUM

In chapter 2 it was pointed out that Rugg views education as a lifelong process, a process that ideally should involve adults as well as children in the continual study of our changing industrial society. His aim, it will be recalled, is a "school-centered community," in which various social insitutions and

1. Informative discussions of Rugg's writings on these topics are contained in Elmer Arthur Winters, "Harold Rugg and Education for Social Reconstruction" (Ph.D. dissertation, University of Wisconsin, 1968).

independent groups of adults would complement the activities of the formal school with educational programs of their own. Thus education as a lever of social reform is by no means to be limited to the elementary and secondary schools. Nevertheless, the formal school as an ongoing enterprise, attendance at which is compulsory, is naturally of great importance to Rugg, and he has some very definite ideas concerning how it should be cast.

In Rugg's view we must first of all pay more attention to student activity in the learning process. If the curriculum is to be viable and meaningful to children, it must include, according to Rugg, a wide variety of pupil activities. For him the curriculum is the total program of the school. That is to say, the curriculum consists of all the activities of students and teachers, as well as the materials—books, supplies, and equipment—that are used in these activities.[2] The activities he recommends include those of observation, such as field trips; research activities; building activities, e.g., reproductions of buildings found in the community or actual maintenance of the school building; creative, expressive, and appreciative activities; mental and manual activities for mastering the three R's and the basic business and technical skills; forum and discussion activities; and lecture or assembly activities.[3] Such a program, Rugg contends, implies full use of the school plant and facilities, as well as the resources of the surrounding communtiy.

Creativity in the School Setting

Among the examples of the experiences that characterize what Rugg calls "schools of living," the creative or expressive experiences are of prime importance. For, as we have seen, he regards the drawing out of the child's capacity for self-

2. Rugg, *American Life,* p. 18.
3. Ibid., pp. 337–339. See also *Culture and Education,* pp. 310–311, and *Foundations for American Education,* pp. 694–696.

expression as one of the chief aims of education, and, potentially, a force in effective social reform. Therefore, in addition to providing an opportunity for students to study the arts for understanding and appreciation, the school should also furnish the means for children to express themselves in various art forms: painting, music, the dance, sculpture, creative writing, the graphic arts, and dramatics. Further, the school should stress physical activities in order to help children develop the sense of rhythm necessary for successful achievement in many of the arts.[4] (Apparently this is part of what he had in mind when he called for a motor program in connection with his notion of a logic of the gesture.)

The most important consideration for Rugg is that children be allowed freedom to express their individualty through their art work. Since his goal is to draw out the child's inner capacities for self-expression, he feels that techniques, procedural rules, and the like should be kept subordinate in the lower grades and brought into prominence only after the child has gained some experience in expressing himself.[5] Actually most of what Rugg had to say about art education was drawn from his observations of progressive schools in the 1920s and is very ably presented in *The Child-Centered School,* his first major book (with Ann Shumaker, 1928). Later, in *Foundations for American Education* (1947) and *Social Foundations of Education* (with William Withers, 1955), he further articulated his views on self-expression and the creative act.[6]

In chapter 4 it was noted that in his total outlook Rugg stresses fields of force and relations rather than things. His orientation is "organistic" rather than mechanistic. He

4. Rugg and Shumaker, *The Child-Centered School,* pp. 151–153.
5. Ibid., pp. 239–243.
6. According to Rugg, the expressive or creative act (for him the terms are nearly equivalent) involves three aspects: (1) the artist's statement, what it is that he wishes to express; (2) his perception, what he sees, feels, or thinks; and (3) form, which he breaks down into organization, economy or simplicity, and functionality. See Rugg, *Foundations for American Education,* pp. 447–462; also Rugg and Withers, *Social Foundations,* pp. 449–453.

applies these concepts not only to the physical and the behavioral sciences but also to the social sciences as well as to the arts. In connection with the latter, he describes those who produce "representative" art, those who imitate nature as it "really is," as "the thing people," whereas those who focus on relationships and movement are described as "the force people." "The Thing artist," according to Rugg, "describes the shapes of the Things—earth, moon, gas, hammer, line, rocket, magnet, tuning fork, air. Most of the so-called 'art' of the world is of this type. . . . If it can be considered to be 'art' at all, it is the art of mechanism."[7] Expressive art, by contrast, gets to the significant relationships involved, "hence creative or expressional artists do not portray, describe, represent, photograph the surface contours of things; *they evoke the inner forces organizing, motivating, propelling life.*"[8] [Rugg's italics.] In another place he contrasts "thing artists" and "force artists" as follows:

> The thing painters paint the shape of the thing—man, woman, child, animal, house, landscape, vase of flowers, what-not. They represent the contours and dimensions as seen. They might better get a camera, for they are merely photographing objects—'taking a picture.' The force painters paint the relations that they sense between the things; that is the key to *movement, to action*. Paintings come *alive*; they move; and they move those dynamic observers who look at them with sensitive feeling.[9] [Rugg's italics.]

Rugg regards "movement" as the key to the expressive or creative process, and by movement he means the "total tensing adjustment of the body," with which the artist approaches his task. It will be recalled that he labels this tensile sense "feeling" or "gesture" and that at the end of his career he was attempting to articulate his concept of "a logic of the ges-

7. Rugg, *Foundations for American Education*, p. 439.
8. Ibid., p. 441.
9. Rugg and Withers, *Social Foundations*, p. 457.

ture," which he felt should become part of the educative process. Other implications for education may be drawn from his discussion of expressionism in art and, in fact, he lists many of the points just discussed as "esthetic concepts for education."[10] Moreover, he proposes that these concepts be utilized in the building of a "new school program."[11] Evidently he would have teachers foster self-expression in the school with an explicit expressionistic orientation, and this raises questions of legitimacy. It is one thing to argue for more emphasis on self-expression and creativity on the grounds that such emphases are likely to help develop certain desirable traits of character. It is quite another thing to suggest that a particular philosophy of art be adopted, within which creative activity should be encouraged. Rugg tends to present his aesthetic convictions as though they were self-evident, but this is plainly not the case. Against his expressionistic position, one could argue, for instance, that representative art aims neither to slavishly imitate, nor to distort beyond recognition that which is represented. Rather, it might be argued, the representative artist aims to *reflect* the object represented in order to express or to convey his insight or emotion. Thus, the argument might continue, imitation and distortion are never absolute. They are employed to varying degrees, depending on the artist's purpose.

This, of course, is only one of any number of positions that might be taken on the subject. The point is that aesthetics is a normative discipline and plausible reasons can be brought to bear in support of a variety of value judgments regarding the frame of reference within which the creative process should take place. One might question Rugg's approach, therefore, on the grounds that he attempts to impose a particular set of values to the exclusion of possible alternatives. I will discuss this issue in another context later in this chapter.

10. Rugg, *Foundations for American Eduation*, pp. 468–469.
11. Ibid., p. 433.

Schools of Living

Rugg refers to schools that foster the kinds of activities listed earlier as "schools of living" because he feels they provide an approximation of life as it is experienced outside the classroom. Like most progressive educators, he reacts strongly against the traditional classroom in which children are expected to passively assimilate subject matter parceled out by the teacher. Schools so organized, he argues, are mere schools of literacy and bare literacy is not enough. On the contrary, since the products of "education for literacy"—the literate rank and file, Rugg calls them—have simply memorized a number of isolated academic facts and have not been adequately informed about the world in which they live, they are ready dupes for the first clever demogogue who happens along. "Instead of constituting an informed thinking citizenry, cognizant of public questions and critically observant of the acts of their elected representatives," he argues, "the youths turned out from our schools are merely fit subjects for systematic propaganda."[12]

Rugg realizes, of course, that educators must devote a good deal of time and effort to the development of literacy, but he deplores what he regards as a tendency to emphasize literacy as an end in itself rather than as a tool for understanding contemporary society:

> A child will understand the industrial world around him, the family and the neighborhood, the community life, the causes of changes in the modern world, only when he has made them his own by reproducing them in the materials of his own experience. He shall not merely read descriptions of society and repeat the phrases and words of his elders in depicting it. His understanding of that society will develop only as he assimilates the outside world into his own nervous life through original re-creation.[13]

12. Rugg, *Great Technology*, p. 245.
13. Rugg and Shumaker, *Child-Centered School*, p. 150.

Rugg calls for a curriculum that will describe and interpret contemporary life on every level, from the local community to the international scene, a curriculum designed to develop sympathetic understanding of others, critical open-mindedness, and creative self-expression.[14] Thus the curriculum should be "culture-centered" in his view, that is, it must be designed from the characteristics, issues, and problems that exist in the total culture of which the school is a part.[15] The curriculum, then, must bridge the gap between the life of the school and the problems of contemporary civilization, a gap that in his opinion (as we saw in chapter 2) has been evident throughout the history of American education.

Rugg also lists the needs of children as a basis for curriculum design,[16] but his preoccupation with furnishing a description of society and highlighting its problems apparently prevents him from seeing the necessity for deciding which needs the curriculum should be built upon. This is hardly an unusual oversight. The notion of basing an educational program on the needs of youth is one frequently encountered in the literature on curriculum planning, but it is not always recognized that the very concept of "needs" is laden with ambiguities. There is little similarity, for example, between the basic need for food and such acquired needs as the yearning for a new car or the desire to understand geometry. Thus an initial distinction must be made between needs that are essential for survival and needs that stem from personal motivations and desires, for difficulties immediately arise when the latter are proposed as the basis of the curriculm.[17] Bode has called attention to two such difficulties: First, some way must be found to distinguish between "good" and "bad"

14. Ibid., pp. 7–9.
15. Rugg and Withers, *Social Foundations,* pp. 669–670. See also Rugg, *Foundations for American Education,* p. 653.
16. Rugg, *Foundations for American Education,* p. 654.
17. I am indebted here to Archambault for his analysis of needs. See Reginald D. Archambault, "The Concept of Need and Its Relation to Certain Aspects of Educational Theory," *Harvard Educational Review* 27 (Winter 1957):38–62.

desires. Second, some means must be provided for resolving conflicts between desires or deciding which of two conflicting desires should be given preference in the curriculum.[18]

Difficult questions arise, moreover, even when the more basic, organic needs are proposed as a partial basis for curriculum construction. To illustrate, are these basic needs the same for all people or do they vary according to cultural factors? Can "basic" needs be abstracted from the individual's personal goals and values? What if individual needs are in conflict with the needs of society?[19]

This brief listing, though by no means exhaustive, is perhaps indicative of the variety of problems that are encountered in connection with proposals to build the curriculum around the concept of needs. As already noted, Rugg fails to come to grips with these problems because he is more concerned with building a curriculum that will reflect the wider culture beyond the school. This concern leads him to focus particularly on the social studies curriculum, and in this connection he does provide a justification for his selection of content. We shall examine his selection process subsequently, but first it might prove instructive to let Rugg speak for himself with respect to the curriculum. As chairman of the National Society for the Study of Education committee responsible for the Society's *Twenty-Sixth Yearbook* (1927), Rugg made a rather eloquent statement in support of his position:

> Lacking a half-million dynamic teachers, are we not forced to put into our schools a dynamic curriculum? A curriculum which deals in a rich vivid manner with the modes of living of people all over the earth; which is full of throbbing anecdotes of human life? A curriculum which will set forth the crucial facts about the community in which people live; one which will interpret for them the chief features of the basic resources and industries upon

18. Boyd H. Bode, *Progressive Education at the Crossroads* (New York: Newson and Co., 1938), pp. 62–67.
19. Archambault, "Concept of Need," pp. 48ff.

which their lives depend in a fragile, interdependent civilization; one which will introduce them to the modes of living of other peoples? A curriculum which will enable pupils to visualize the problems set up by human migration; one which will provide them with an opportunity to study and think critically about the form of democratic government under which they are living and to compare it with the forms of government of other peoples? A curriculum which will not only inform, but will constantly have as its ideal the development of an attitude of sympathetic tolerance and of critical openmindedness? A curriculum which is built around a core of pupils' activities—studies of their home community, special reading and original investigation, a constantly growing stream of opportunities for participaton in open-forum discussion, debate, and exchange of ideas? A curriculum which deals courageously and intelligently with the issues of the cultural and industrial as well as the political history of their development? A curriculum which is constructed on a problem-solving organization, providing continuous practice in choosing between alternatives, in making decisions, in drawing generalizations? A curriculum consisting of a carefully graded organization of problems and exercises, one which recognizes the need for providing definite and systematic practice upon socially valuable skills? Finally, a curriculum which so makes use of dramatic episodic materials illustrating great humanitarian themes that by constant contact with it children grow in wise insights and attitudes and, constructively but critically, will be influenced to put their ideas sanely into action?[20]

The appendixes to this study show in some detail how Rugg transformed these ideas into concrete plans for curriculum reconstruction. The fact that these two charts are

20. Harold Rugg, "The School Curriculum and the Drama of American Life," in *Curriculum Making: Past and Present,* Twenty-Sixth Yearbook of the National Society for the Study of Education, pt. 1 (Bloomington, Ill.: Public School Publishing Co., 1927), pp. 7–8.

almost identical, though they appeared in books that were written almost a quarter of a century apart,[21] is an indication of the consistency of his thought over the years.

I have already stressed the importance to Rugg of a variety of activities and the full use of community resources in the life of the school. A glance at the charts reveals a number of other prominent features—broad units of study, flexible blocks of time, the "fusion" of subjects—many of which have been adopted in present-day schools. Rugg's curricular innovations were among his most significant contributions to educational theory and practice. Always a sensitive observer of new developments in the natural, social, and behavioral sciences, he was clearly in the vanguard of curriculum construction and years ahead of most of his contemporaries in this respect.

As the charts indicate, he lays particular stress on the importance of broad, integrated units of study. His target here is what he considers to be the artificial compartmentalization of the curriculum into segmented subjects, which in his view fail to reflect the interrelationships of the material to be learned. If students are to achieve a realistic conception of modern life, he insists, this practice must be dropped in favor of some plan for correlating or fusing subject-matter. Curriculum planners of a unit designed to provide understanding of the life of a given community, for example, would need to draw facts and concepts from a variety of subjects, including geography, economics, history, political science, and social psychology.[22] In Rugg's terms, these units of study "ramify ruthlessly across any conventional boundaries insofar as this is necessary to make available all meanings essential for understanding and all situations necessary to the vital, wholehearted expression of the student."[23]

21. Appendix 1 is reproduced from *American Life* (1936) and Appendix 2 from *Social Foundations* (1955).
22. Rugg, *American Life*, p. 334.
23. Ibid., p. 336.

The Role of the Social Studies

For Rugg, the social studies should bring children into contact with pressing contemporary social problems. Through these studies, he insists, children must be taught to think critically and to overcome the tendency to make impulsive judgments. He also warns teachers against allowing children to form chauvinistic attitudes. The pupil, he asserts, should be encouraged to take a reasonably critical attitude toward the civilization in which he lives, and he should cultivate a tolerant understanding of other races and nations. This includes an appreciation of the interdependence of nations in the modern world.[24]

Rugg's aim is to develop critical thinking in children by constantly confronting them with alternatives to persistent, unanswered questions.[25] Students, he contends, need practice in grasping social concepts and relationships and in forming valid generalizations; and this for Rugg implies a problem-solving approach, that is, an organization of the social studies around unsolved problems and issues. "Not the learning of *texts*," he argues, "but the solving of *problems* is what we need. Our materials must be *organized around issues, problems*—unanswered questions which the pupil recognizes as important and which he really strives to unravel."[26] [Rugg's italics.]

The problems he has in mind are, of course, the controversial social, economic, and political problems of the day. In his view,

there is no other way by which the democratic principle of consent can be carried on than the way of parliamentary

24. Harold Rugg and James Mendenhall, *Teacher's Guide for an Introduction to American Civilization* (Boston: Ginn & Company, 1929), pp. 49–50, 60, 101.
25. Harold Rugg, *Teacher's Guide for a History of American Civilization* (Boston: Ginn & Company, 1931), p. 5.
26. Harold Rugg, *The Social Studies*, Twenty-Second Yearbook of the National Society for the Study of Education, pt. 2 (Bloomington, Ill.: Public School Publishing Co., 1923), p. 20.

discussion of contemporary issues and problems. And this way must be applied to every phase of social life—to what goes on in the family, in the school, in the church, in the theatre, and in all the group and institutional activities of the people.[27] [Rugg's italics.]

In one of his later books he includes "the struggle over the ownership of property," racial conflict, and issues between religion and science among examples of controversial subjects that should be, but have not been, discussed in the schools.[28]

Rugg feels that one way to prepare children for intelligent civic participation is through a careful study of the immediate community. In the first three grades this study might take the form of activities such as field trips, dramatizations, or historical pageants. From the fourth to the sixth grade the work would begin to take on elements of criticism and appraisal. The work would be assigned in units and given a historical slant in order to provide the necessary sense of recurrence of important concepts. This approach, Rugg claims, should provide students with a wider perspective of the changing social groups around them and an understanding of the external organizational forms of community institutions.

The next level, the work of the junior and senior high schools, should explore beneath the surface of these outward forms to discover the underlying psychological factors that produce them. Studies should be made of how attitudes and opinions are formed and how personalities are molded by the pressure of social institutions. The culture would be appraised and evaluated at this level, and the school would examine ever more critically its problems and trends.[29]

These aims, ideals, and priorities were incorporated into Rugg's textbook series. Rugg felt that textbooks written about isolated subjects tended to be organized like reference works. "Social science textbooks," he writes, "are veritable ency-

27. Rugg, *American Life*, pp. 299–300.
28. Rugg, *Foundations for American Education*, pp. 674–683.
29. Rugg, *Culture and Education*, pp. 346–352.

clopedias. . . . They devote a half page to this and ten lines to that."[30] His own texts were designed to overcome this weakness by making liberal use of illustrations, narrative, and episodic material in bringing diverse subject matter to bear on particular problems. He felt that learning is greatly facilitated by the use of interesting, exciting readings; consequently, the dramatic episode was one of his favorite devices.

In keeping with these considerations, the material in the texts was organized around topics rather than into the usual divisions of subject matter. Each book utilized elements of history, geography, civics, and whatever else Rugg felt was needed to cover the particular topic under discussion. The books have been criticized for factual inaccuracies, oversimplification, and omission of significant material, as well as for a too-condensed treatment of long periods of history.[31] Although these criticisms are well documented, several studies have indicated, nonetheless, that pupils who used the Rugg textbooks compared favorably in achievement tests with those who used more conventional texts.[32] Moreover, the Rugg books did achieve the goals that Rugg had set for them, that is, to describe society to the best of the author's ability, to delineate a number of enduring social problems, to arrange the content in such a way as to force children to think critically about these problems—and to do all of this in a manner calculated to arouse and sustain the interest of the reader. In these respects, the books apparently won the admiration of most of the administrators, teachers, and pupils who used them.[33] Given these virtues and the scope of the undertaking (there were fourteen volumes in all, six of which were later

30. Rugg, NSSE Yearbook, 1923, Part 2, p. 18.
31. For a sampling see A. K. Loomis, reviews of *An Introduction to Problems of American Culture* and *Changing Governments and Changing Cultures* in *School Review* 40 (June 1932): 472–475; Edith P. Parker, review of *Changing Civilizations in the Modern World* in *School Review* 38 (December 1930): 790–793; and Burr W. Phillips, review of *Changing Governments and Changing Cultures* in *Elementary School Journal* 33 (January 1933): 797.
32. B. R. Buckingham, *The Rugg Course in the Classroom: The Junior High School Program* (Boston: Ginn & Company, 1935), pp. 69–72.
33. Ibid., pp. 67–68.

revised), the technical flaws—which, after all, could have been corrected had the series continued to be widely used—seem less serious in retrospect. In any case, the amazing amount of material covered in the Rugg books makes them a truly remarkable achievement in the history of American textbooks. Some forty years after publication they still come off rather well in comparison with many of the social studies textbooks of today.[34]

EDUCATIONAL ENDS AND MEANS

From the foregoing summary of his curriculum theory, it should be clear that Rugg has little patience with those who would minimize the importance of subject matter or the need for planning the curriculum in advance. In this connection he writes: "The issue is not 'subject matter' versus 'no subject matter.' It is really 'how much and what kinds of subject matter and how learned.' "[35] The criteria for the selection of instructional materials, he holds, are the capacities and interests of the children being taught *and* the data needed to study society. The latter should determine the general content of the curriculum, while the former will guide its organization and teaching strategies.[36] The teacher, then, should have at his disposal a general outline of content and activities with which to begin a given course of study; it is unrealistic, according to Rugg, to suppose, as some would have it, that the curriculum

34. An excellent treatment of the Rugg textbooks is provided by Virginia S. Wilson in "Harold Rugg's Social and Educational Philosophy as Reflected in His Textbook Series, 'Man and His Changing Society,' " (Ph.D. dissertation, Duke University, 1975). See also two informative accounts of the texts furnished by Elmer A. Winters, "Harold Rugg and Education for Social Reconstruction," chap. 3, and "Man and His Changing Society: The Textbooks of Harold Rugg," *History of Education Quarterly* 7 (Winter 1967): 493–514.

35. Rugg, *American Life*, pp. 343–344.

36. Harold Rugg, "Curriculum Making: Points of Emphasis," in *The Foundations of Curriculum Making*, NSSE Twenty-Sixth Yearbook, pt. 2 (Bloomington, Ill.: Public School Publishing Company, 1926), p. 153.

can be made "on the spot," out of the "spontaneous interests and activities of children."[37]

In another context he stresses the need for planning lessons in advance, while allowing for a limited amount of day-to-day, teacher-pupil planning within the general rubric of the course outline. Here he also recommends that parents and school administrators cooperate to some extent with teachers and pupils in the planning process.[38] All of this is, of course, consistent with his desire to bring school and community into closer contact with each other.

Rugg's Views Compared with Dewey's

Rugg's position with respect to planning and subject matter laid out in advance is closer to Dewey's than to the wing of the progressive group that followed, or at least claimed to follow, William H. Kilpatrick in the subject matter controversy.[39] In fact, Rugg's textbook series, with its organization of subject matter around contemporary problems and their historical antecedents, might be viewed as a practical implementation of Dewey's ideas concerning the indispensability of problem situations in activating the "habit" of intelligence. No attempt is here being made to establish direct lines of influence, however. Rather, the point to be made is simply that Rugg belongs with Dewey and the more conservative of the progressives regarding subject matter, and not with those who tended to disparage its importance.

If Rugg held views similar to Dewey's on this score, he nevertheless differed from Dewey regarding the aims of education. Rugg, following Randolph Bourne,[40] was dissatisfied

---

37. Ibid., p. 157.

38. Rugg, Foundations for American Education, pp. 659–661.

39. Although Kilpatrick's position on this issue was not as extreme as it is often depicted, he was willing to allow children's interests to determine more of the curriculum than were either Dewey or Rugg. See William H. Kilpatrick, Foundations of Method (New York: The Macmillan Co., 1925).

40. Bourne, "Twilight of Idols." (On p. 209 of Culture and Education Rugg points out, approvingly, that Bourne had criticized Dewey for subordinating vision to technique.)

with the open-endedness of Dewey's instrumentalism. With
Bourne, he felt the need for ultimate goals, to which the process of growth might be directed. Accordingly he disagrees
with Dewey's dictum that "since growth is the characteristic
of life, education is all one with growing; it has no end beyond itself."[41] More precisely Rugg goes part of the way with
Dewey, agreeing that education is growth and the reconstruction of experience, but he insists that it is growth with a particular end in view, namely, the "cultured person." In one
place the latter is described as a "creative craftsman," a person of individual integrity who is tolerant toward others and
constructively critical of social institutions.[42] Thus educational growth for Rugg is a continuous development toward a
definite goal, and the goal, or end in view, determines the
character of the school curriculum.

Principles of Selection

Rugg felt he had a scientific method for selecting content,
which he offered in opposition to what he regarded as the
"armchair" methods commonly followed by committees on
curriculum development. The setting for this dispute was provided in part by the report of the Second Committee of Eight
in 1921.[43] Rugg took the committee to task for relying on the
untested judgment of a handful of subject-matter specialists,
and for failing to provide an adequate philosophical basis for
the selection of content.[44]

His own method was to define important contemporary
problems and issues in the social, political, and economic
realms and then to develop discussion questions, generaliza-

41. Dewey, *Democracy and Education*, p. 62.
42. Rugg, *Culture and Education*, p. 297. For similar characterizations of the
cultured person, see *Child-Centered School*, pp. 8–9, and *Foundations for American
Education*, pp. 203–205.
43. Committee on History and Education for Citizenship appointed by the
American Historical Association, Joseph Schafer, chairman.
44. Harold Rugg, "How Shall We Reconstruct the Social Studies Curriculum?"
Historical Outlook 12 (May 1921): 184–189.

tions, and principles or concepts relating to the issues. The material was organized in accordance with what Rugg considered to be sound principles of learning, that is, it was organized into composite courses instead of into separate subjects. Further, the material was repeated from year to year in ascending order of complexity as children matured, and frequent use was made of episodic, narrative techniques in order to sustain interest and vitality. Finally, a variety of activities was designed as a vehicle for imparting subject matter. This methodology is essentially the one Rugg used in writing his texts. As a matter of fact, he was preparing the pamphlets that eventually became the textbooks at the time of the committee report.

Where did Rugg find the crucial issues and problems covered in the pamphlets? His procedure was to examine key writings chosen on the basis of recommendations made by a selected list of scholars who represented the various social sciences. These advisers were asked to name the books they would analyze if they were seeking information regarding the important problems of the day. From this and other leads (such as an examination of "scholarly" journals), Rugg and his associates compiled a list of some three hundred contemporary problems to be used as the heart of their curriculum.[45]

Now the obvious question at this point is, of course, in what sense, if any, may Rugg's method be regarded as scientific? Joseph Schafer, chairman of the Committee on History and Education for Citizenship, was prepared to deny that it was scientific in any sense. In an open letter to Rugg he wrote:

> You condemn "opinion" as a basis of curriculum making. What is the process you describe above if it is not a setting up of "opinion"—either your own or that of others chosen by you—as criteria for determining what is "vitally

45. J. Montgomery Gambrill, "Experimental Curriculum-Making in the Social Studies," *Historical Outlook* 14 (December 1923): 391–397. Rugg provides further descriptions of his methods in both *Culture and Education* and *That Men May Understand*.

important," "crucial," etc.? . . . Who are the "outstanding thinkers" and how do you select them for obviously you do select them? . . . if your investigator is a social reactionary he will collect opinions from a given group of 'prominent' men; if he is a liberal he will collect from a group largely or wholly distinct from the first, and if he is a radical he will collect from yet another group. . . . After all it is merely "opinion" camouflaged by the cant of a professed "scientific" investigation.[46]

Schafer was right, of course. A glance at Rugg's list of advisers reveals a conspicuous liberal strain, a strain which carries over into his pamphlets and textbooks and results in a very definite stance being adopted in relation to the problems considered.[47] Rugg could, and did, argue that he had sought out recognized authorities. Nonetheless the list is hardly exhaustive, and, as Schafer pointed out, a curriculum designer with a different point of view would no doubt have drawn upon an entirely different group. There has to be a value judgment made somewhere in the selection process. Once this is recognized, Rugg's method seems an eminently sensible one for achieving *his* desired objectives, namely to alert students to the fact that all is not well in the social order and to start them thinking critically about possible improvements. However, his questionable attempt to clothe his procedure in quasi-scientific attire raises doubts—despite his frequent protestations to the contrary—about his willingness to expose children to dissenting opinions. What is needed here is a candid admission of the value judgment being employed.

EDUCATIONAL FOUNDATIONS

Rugg's notion of building educational content around fundamental concepts eventually evolves into a conception of

46. Joseph Schafer and Harold Rugg, "The Methods and Aims of Committee Procedure: Open Letters from Dr. Schafer and Mr. Rugg," *Historical Outlook* 12 (October 1921): p. 248.
47. The list appears in Schafer and Rugg, ibid., p. 251.

foundations, upon which the entire educational program, from kindergarten through college, will rest. The design of such a program will require a scientific approach, but, according to Rugg, inasmuch as education has no body of primary concepts that pertain to it alone, it cannot become a full-fledged science in its own right. Education is, he feels, more of an art or technology based on the key concepts of other fields.[48]

In *Foundations for American Education* (1947), Rugg attempts to synthesize the key concepts of certain other disciplines which he thinks can be most useful in designing a structure for the modern school. He finds these disciplines to be sociology, esthetics, psychology, and ethics: "The central concepts of the Sociology and the Esthetics will govern the content of the program of studies; the concepts of the Psychology will determine the curriculum organization and teaching; the concepts of the Ethics will guide the climate of freedom and discipline and set the code of behavior for the life of the school."[49]

It is a little startling to note the absence of the natural sciences in this program, but Rugg grants the possibility of incorporating them into a fifth foundation in the future.[50] The quoted statement is somewhat misleading for it seems to imply that psychology and ethics merely provide the structure and general tone of the school. Actually this is not the case, since these areas serve a dual function in that they furnish content as well as determine the form of the overall program.[51] It is true, however, that the bulk of Rugg's subject matter does consist of basic concepts drawn from sociology, and of course much of his program consists of activities designed to provide experiences of a creative and appreciative nature. In this connection, it should be stressed that for Rugg sociology encompasses a number of fields: "(I use this compact term [sociology] throughout the book instead of the more

48. Rugg, *Foundations for American Education,* p. 803.
49. Ibid., p. 654.
50. Ibid., p. xiii.
51. Ibid., p. 655.

cumbersome enumeration of history, economics, political science, geography, and the other social sciences.)"[52]

In choosing his key concepts, issues, and problems from the four foundations, Rugg was faced once again with the task of justifying his selection process. By this time, possibly as a result of his earlier controversy with Schafer, he was sensitive enough to the charge of bias to perceive the need for the following disclaimer:

> There will be some who will say, 'Great though they are, every one of your men of the consensus is biased.' That is true, in the sense that no interpretation of human life is ever free of the bias of the critic's own frame of reference. My own final drawing up of the consensus stated in this book reflects my personal frame of reference. What I take from the trends and the scholars' interpretations must, in the last analysis, rest on *my* [Rugg's italics] judgment. . . . While it must of necessity be mine, I have gone to lengths to safeguard its consensus character.[53]

That Rugg's own biases do indeed intrude upon his selection of subject matter is evident from an examination of his recommendations for confronting students with the pressing social problems of the day. The following are representative of the kinds of problems he had in mind: "What is an economic system for?" "What are our available physical and human resources?" "What are the needs of the people?" "What standard of living has technology made possible?" "How can purchasing power be scientifically distributed?" "Is world planning possible in view of the fact that the means of production are privately owned?"[54]

Now the first thing to notice about these problems is that they involve a curious mixture of factual and valuative elements. The first question, for instance, clearly calls for a value

52. Ibid., pp. 26–27.
53. Ibid., p. 29.
54. Rugg, *American Life,* pp. 400–408.

judgment, and the last two depend on value judgments, namely that purchasing power should be "scientifically" distributed and that world planning is desirable. Yet Rugg combines these problems or questions with those that lend themselves to empirical determination without commenting on the distinction between the two categories. Furthermore, the key concepts he chooses for his curriculum are subject to similar criticism. A sampling of these includes the following:

1. "The stable, self-sufficient, and comparatively secure agrarian community of living has been transformed into the interdependent, unstable, insecure industrial community of a high standard of living."

2. "A second change is the loss of the worker's control over his product, his job, his share of the social income, and his craftsmanship. This control is now held by the middlemen manipulators of money and credit, hence the increasing dominance of promoters and financiers over the producers and creators."

3. "Third is competition on a national scale. Several great production plants . . . compete madly with one another in a tenuous world order, each utterly without central control and lacking central design which fits its production and distribution to the needs of its people."[55]

These concepts and the aforementioned problems are taken from one of Rugg's earlier works. The following concepts from the later *Foundations for American Education* are presented for comparison:

1. "Our industrial social order is a competitive system of pecuniary rivalry . . . a price system, with the money unit as the standard measure of efficiency and achievement." [Rugg's ellipses]

2. "The basic industries are large-scale, requiring large material equipment and financial support—all of which is held in private ownership and tends toward monopoly."[56]

55. Ibid., pp. 397–398.
56. Rugg, *Foundations for American Education*, p. 286.

As with his list of problems, an examination of Rugg's social studies concepts reveals a mixture of descriptive and valuative elements. Terms such as "unstable," "insecure," "manipulators," "lacking design," and "monopoly," are used pejoratively, and they clearly reflect Rugg's preferences. Here again one might argue that his suggested curriculum is designed not only to encourage critical inquiry by students but also to point them toward a specific social orientation. This is an issue that seems to arise frequently in connection with Rugg's writings and one that merits closer examination at this point.

The Indoctrination Issue

Given his desire to provide children with an objective description of our society—that is to say, a description of strengths and weaknesses, social justice and injustice—and his goal of equipping children with the cognitive tools to critically appraise social conditions for themselves, it seems clear that Rugg never deliberately attempts to indoctrinate children to his point of view. It is not so clear, however, that he is fully aware of how easy it is in dealing with the social studies to allow scholarship to lapse into partisanship and journalistic fervor. Thus there is some inconsistency between his stated objectives and his means of achieving them.

Specifically, his goal in regard to social, political, and economic issues is to develop in children the ability to make independent decisions based upon intelligently formed opinions. Blind acquiescence to a proposed course of action on the part of his students is not considered to be a legitimate aim. All the same, he does not feel that this position prevents him, or any teacher, from stating personal views on controversial questions.[57]

Now it might be argued that simply by virtue of his authority in the classroom the teacher imposes his own views

57. Rugg, American Life, pp. 297–302, 327.

upon his students merely by expressing them, and that complete neutrality is therefore impossible unless controversial issues are avoided altogether. Even then, the argument could be continued, the teacher is likely to reveal his biases on these issues indirectly by his day-to-day behavior.

There is a certain thrust to this argument, but it is not quite as clear-cut as it may appear on the surface. First of all a distinction must be made between "subjective" and "objective" neutrality. If a teacher decides for himself that he favors one side or the other of a controversial issue, then obviously he is not subjectively neutral on the subject. In this sense it can be maintained that neutrality is impossible once the choice has been made. It does not follow, however, that the teacher *must* reveal his bias in his classroom teaching and therefore forfeit his "objective" neutrality. Although it may be very difficult for the teacher to conceal his own views in practice, such concealment is not impossible, at least in principle.[58] Thus in treating controversial issues, some teachers set out to present all the available facts without revealing their own views. Their aim is, of course, to induce students to judge for themselves after due consideration of the relevant data.

On the other hand, those teachers who do feel that it is very difficult, if not impossible, to conceal their own biases usually prefer to state their preferences frankly, believing that there is a vast difference between imposing one's opinions on children and admitting one's preferences together with an exposition of opposing views. Rugg seems to take this latter position in that he recommends that the whole spectrum of political theory—democratic, fascist, communist, and socialist—be presented so that students may appraise each of them.[59]

This is probably as near as one can come to total objec-

58. For a related treatment of neutrality, to which I am indebted, see Robert H. Ennis, "The 'Impossibility' of Neutrality in Teaching," *Harvard Educational Review* 29 (Spring 1959): 128–136.
59. Rugg, *American Life*, p. 413.

tivity as far as the personal opinions of the teacher are concerned, but it may still fall short in that the teacher is likely to favor one position over another not only by stating his convictions, but also in his choice of textbooks and other teaching materials. The very structure of a social studies curriculum contains a built-in point of view to some extent because a choice must be made regarding the concepts to be taught. Further, the content finally selected consists of valuative as well as descriptive concepts. Thus it would seem that the teacher who wishes to be "objective" should be careful to distinguish between these two kinds of concepts and to inform his pupils which is which. But as I have noted, Rugg tends to blur the distinction in much of his work, with the result that his textbooks, together with his suggested social studies concepts and themes, reveal a proselytizing inclination in his selection of subject matter.

In Rugg's case, moreover, it seems legitimate to question just how far he is willing to go with his equal-time-for-other-views suggestion, notwithstanding his apparent belief that the facts themselves yield value judgments.[60] The conclusion he assumes students will draw from a study of competing ideologies is, of course, that society should be reconstructed along democratic, collectivist lines; but suppose, unlikely though it may seem, a significant number of students begin to draw other conclusions. Suppose, for example, they agree that society should be reconstructed, but on a communist or fascist model. It is doubtful that Rugg would be willing to accept this decision and continue to present opposing views impartially, for he sometimes speaks of building loyalty to democratic ideals and producing believers in "the democratic vista."[61] He also speaks of making a religion of democracy and creating a unifying democratic myth,[62] and it is difficult to

60. Rugg, *Foundations for American Education*, p. xi.
61. Rugg, *American Life*, pp. 265, 273.
62. Rugg, *Now Is the Moment*, pp. 215–216.

see how these wishes can be reconciled with his advice to follow the facts wherever they lead. It seems reasonable to ask, If you wish to create a unifying democratic myth, why gamble? Why not inculcate democratic values in the first place?

The upshot of all of this is a curious ambivalence in Rugg's conception of education for democracy. He advocates critical inquiry and wide-ranging, open discussion of social issues and public policy, yet he apparently has no qualms about using emotionally charged rhetorical devices to build commitment to democratic ideals. That one policy contravenes the other seems to have escaped his notice.

A Contemporary Criticism of Rugg

At this point it may be illuminating to consider a thoughtful criticism of Rugg's *Foundations for American Education* by Charles Brauner. In *American Educational Theory* Brauner Compares Rugg's *Foundations* with Dewey's *The Sources of a Science of Education* (1929) and finds that whereas Dewey's concept of basing practitioner training upon established research disciplines such as physics, physiology, sociology, psychology, and biology consisted of hard, factual content, Rugg, in introducing fields of study such as ethics and aesthetics, moved away from the quantitative, observation-centered sciences and toward a speculative, literary notion of the foundations. Moreover, Brauner's argument runs, even in the relatively respectable area of psychology, Rugg's emphasis is on the less well-established hypotheses of the discipline.[63]

Brauner further argues that Rugg's call for a foundations program that would synthesize information gathered in various disciplines, in order to build a sound theory of the nature of both man and society, places educators in the absurd posi-

63. Charles J. Brauner, *American Educational Theory* (Englewood Cliffs, N.J.: Prentice-Hall, 1964), pp. 198–211.

tion of speaking as experts in at least four disciplines when their training has rarely been such that they can qualify as experts in any one of the four fields.[64]

A third point of Brauner's is that Rugg and like-minded colleagues at Teachers College also went beyond Dewey's intent in providing the basis of a personal moral commitment. According to Brauner, Dewey was concerned with providing materials out of which personal beliefs could be constructed, but the Teachers College group went further and supplied certain materials in such a way that a particular social orientation would be the outcome.[65]

The end result of all this in Brauner's view is that Rugg and other supporters of the foundations outlook tended to drift away from disinterested scholarship toward editorial advocacy. Hence the foundations of education which Dewey had envisioned as the scientific underpinnings of educational theory eventually lapsed into a nonscholarly, moralistic doctrine.[66]

Brauner has drawn attention to some of the basic weaknesses of the foundations approach to the study of education. Critics of foundations programs have long been pointing out that interdisciplinary courses taught by nonspecialists are likely to result in a superficial, if not distorted, presentation of the material culled from the parent disciplines. There are those who argue, moreover, that the content usually included in foundations courses is part of general education and should be left to liberal arts departments. General education, so the argument continues, has little or no place in the professional training of practitioners.

This is a defensible position up to a point, but the assumption is that (1) students preparing for professional roles have had adequate training in the disciplines that bear on the practice of education and (2) they are capable of applying

64. Ibid., pp. 208–209.
65. Ibid., p. 199.
66. Ibid., p. 269.

relevant disciplinary content to educational problems. It is doubtful that either of these assumptions can be seriously defended in the majority of cases. What is needed is a way of applying the disciplines to certain persistent educational problems and concerns—not to provide "cookbook" solutions, but to furnish perspective from which the issues may be considered. As Harry Broudy puts it: "Foundational knowledge relates the school to other institutions and to the several intellectual disciplines. It displays educational problems in the midst of their multiform affiliations. Although foundational knowledge does not solve problems, it does prevent our being naive and provincial about them. It is the antidote to localism and narrow technicalism."[67] Thus foundational courses need not encroach upon the domain of the liberal arts or the behavioral and social sciences. They can and should be constructed so as to focus the insights and methodologies of the various disciplines upon the educational enterprise.

This discussion should be taken neither as a defense of Rugg's conception of the foundations nor as a criticism of Brauner's attack on Rugg. Brauner's argument is telling. The foundations as conceived by Rugg do seem to be the province of general rather than professional education, and Rugg does seem to be attempting to synthesize a wide assortment of disciplinary content for presentation in a somewhat journalistic fashion. But the function of foundations courses has frequently been misunderstood, both by proponents and critics of the foundations approach. Properly conceived, foundations courses can be developed so as to obviate the kinds of criticism (valid enough at present) offered by Brauner and others. It is not necessary, in other words, to throw out the baby with the bath water.

Further, although Brauner's criticism of Rugg's program of professional training is effective, it must be pointed out that

67. Harry S. Broudy, *The Scholars and the Public Schools* (Columbus: The College of Education, The Ohio State University, 1964), p. 53.

in this particular book Rugg wished to do more than simply provide the content for a professional course or courses. In *Foundations for American Education* he was also attempting to provide a comprehensive framework of aims, content, methods, and organization for schools below the college level. This distinction is important because obviously practitioners must seek guidelines in designing programs for these schools, and it would be difficult to defend the thesis that they should not draw upon fields such as ethics and aesthetics in addition to the "hard content" disciplines. Choices must be made, after all, and practitioners cannot simply stand by and wait for relatively undeveloped academic areas to achieve status equal to that of the more solidly established disciplines.

Thus it is quite possible to acknowledge the thrust of Brauner's criticism and still consider Rugg's recommendations as one set of viable alternatives available in developing a total school program. Viewed in this way, *Foundations for American Education* is both a thought-provoking personal philosophy of education and an excellent source of information for any number of themes in the history of progressive education.

6. SUMMARY AND APPRAISAL

IN RETROSPECT

In the previous chapters of this volume Rugg's thinking during a productive career that spanned forty years has been shown to be basically consistent. In reviewing his objectives and assessing his contribution to American educational theory, one almost has to start with Rugg's reformism. His plea is for a socially cooperative society marked by cultural achievement and appreciation. Essentially there are two pivotal elements in his plan for achieving this society: (1) social engineering in order to operate the economy more efficiently and to provide at least a passable standard of living for all; and (2) the fulfillment of individual capacities, particularly those related to creative self-expression, so that each individual may live a rich, full, and "cultured" life of personal integrity.

We saw in chapter 2 that Rugg was at least as concerned with individual self-realization as he was with the reconstruction of social machinery. Those critics who take him to task for stressing the importance of the state over the individual, or for neglecting the individual's spiritual needs, completely miss the mark in this respect. In fact a strong case can be made for the view that Rugg's social engineering was directed primarily toward creating an environment conducive to the development of individual talents and skills.

It is also worth noting, in this connection, that Rugg came closer than any progressive theorist other than John Dewey himself to reconciling the views of the child-centered and society-centered factions within the Progressive Education Association. These two groups—the one stressing creative individuality and the other social reform—were at odds with one another over association philosophy from the early thirties until the demise of the association in 1955; and if Rugg failed to achieve the desired intellectual synthesis due to theoretical difficulties discussed earlier, his efforts were nevertheless productive enough to merit the consideration of contemporary educators faced with conflicting advice from neoprogressive exponents of these two doctrines.

Rugg's dual emphasis on self-expression and social reconstruction is reflected in his charge to the school. On the one hand formal education should develop the pupil's appreciative capacities and practice him in a variety of creative endeavors; on the other, it should furnish a realistic description of society, pointing out weaknesses as well as strengths in existing social institutions. With regard to the latter, the assumption is, presumably, that when the student perceives contemporary society in this light and becomes aware of its shortcomings, he will rally to the call for social change. Rugg seems to believe that once he is furnished with the facts of the matter, the student will perceive the injustices inherent in the status quo and be moved to sanction social reconstruction along general collectivist lines. In other words, Rugg shares that faith common to many reformers that a forthright presentation of the facts is enough to elicit a demand for changes of a certain kind. Apparently he sees in the facts a self-evident necessity for social reconstruction.

This is an untenable position. Whether or not one decides to replace one set of conditions with another depends upon how one interprets the facts in light of one's system of values. It is quite possible, moreover, for a consideration of the facts to lead to a conflict between values held by a given individual, in which case his decision is in doubt. For example, an individual who values both equality and liberty might examine Rugg's facts, agree with him that they lead to inequalities in the distribution of economic benefits, and yet oppose any substantial changes on the grounds that such changes would lead to infringement of individual liberty. A person entertaining this point of view would be likely to hold that existing conditions, with all their imperfections, are better than the proposed alternatives and that it would be wrong therefore to tamper with the status quo. Rugg does not allow for such a clash of values because he neglects to distinguish adequately between descriptive and normative propositions. He seems to assume that moral questions are at bottom factual and therefore answerable by true statements that describe what course of action should be taken. As Isaiah Berlin has pointed out, it is an easy step from this position to the view that "since no true propositions can be inconsistent with one another, all the propositions which describe what should be done . . . must be compatible with one another. . . ."[1] Again, as Berlin has observed, however, "in life as normally lived, the ideals of one society and culture clash with those of another, and at times come into conflict within the moral experience of a single individual. . . ."[2]

The inference that Rugg seems to believe that the facts contain built-in norms is supported by his comment in another context that we must "conclude what the facts conclude."[3] The facts do not conclude anything, of course. They are just there to be interpreted by human observers, and we have just seen that when the interpretation involves alternative courses of action, the facts must be considered in relation to existing values. Furthermore, it is not altogether clear that Rugg is consistently willing to let the facts speak for themselves without his editorializing. As we saw in chapter 5, his attempt at objectivity and impartiality in the selection and organization of subject matter are undermined to some extent by his tendency to proselytize and by his failure to recognize the value judgments interspersed among his descriptive concepts.

This criticism is not intended to suggest that Rugg was

1. Isaiah Berlin, "Equality as an Ideal," in *Justice and Social Policy*, ed. Frederick A. Olafson (Englewood Cliffs, N.J.: Prentice-Hall, 1961), p. 143. (Originally published as "Equality" in the *Proceedings of the Aristotelian Society*, vol. 56, 1955–56 [London: Harrison & Sons, 1956].)
2. Ibid.
3. Rugg, *Foundations for American Education*, p. xi.

less than candid about his educational objectives or that he knowingly set out to impose his personal views on students; rather, it is intended to point out that some of the means he employed were not entirely consistent with his declared aims to provide children with the intellectual tools needed to form independent opinions on controversial issues and to develop personal standards of conduct. All the same, it must be emphasized again that there is no basis for the charges of those critics of Rugg who, during the controversy over his textbooks, accused him of attempting to subvert "the American way of life." The charge of subversion is ludicrous. It was frequently leveled at Rugg and his reconstructionist colleagues during the thirties and early forties, and it was, as Cremin has pointed out, "a sardonic commentary on a group that spent the best of its energies seeking to preserve that [American] way of life amidst the chaos of depression."[4]

As noted in chapter 2, Rugg never developed a comprehensive social philosophy. He was less concerned with theorizing about social and political ideals than with correcting what he considered to be immediate social and economic injustices and encouraging a greater concern for creativity in American culture. He attributed the injustices to a lack of design and control of our economic system and argued for increased planning in the production and distribution of goods, services, and purchasing power. Such planning would have to be carried out with the consent of the people, according to Rugg, or our democratic political institutions would be threatened. Here he gets into some difficulty, for it turns out that what he has in mind is the consent of an "intelligent minority" who will shape public opinion in order to elicit acceptance for the view that extensive social changes are necessary. Rugg writes about the need for popular consent and appeals to John Locke in his discussion, but his notion of an intellectual, consensus-building elite sounds almost Platonic. He would no doubt take strong issue with this judg-

4. Cremin, *Transformation of the School*, pp. 233–234.

ment because he probably did not recognize the elitist implications in his work. Nevertheless they are there and are
brought into sharp relief in the passages discussed in chapter
2.

In any case, Rugg sees education as the key to gaining
consent for social change. The prerequisite is an adequate
description of society to be provided for children in the formal
school setting and for adults in community discussion groups.
In this connection, Rugg had a rather curious notion that the
twentieth century was an unusually opportune time for synthesizing findings from the various disciplines into a concise
profile of contemporary American civilization. In the
foreword to *American Life and the School Curriculum,* he
writes: "I have attempted the . . . task of making a synthesis of
the principal strands of American culture. I am convinced that
while the great research tasks of the nineteenth century were
chiefly explorations in analysis, those of the twentieth century
will be enterprises in the building of new syntheses of knowledge."[5]

Although it is true that it is always desirable to integrate
knowledge from diverse fields into an instructive overview,
Rugg's claim that the task needs to be done now more than at
any other time is unconvincing. Surely we have not arrived at
a terminal point in the search for knowledge, at which we can
pause and put the pieces together with confidence in the
stability of the outcome. On the contrary, the so-called "explosion of knowledge" is clearly intensifying rather than
abating, and any synthesis made at this time is perhaps more
tentative than others that have been attempted in the past.
There is a very real danger, moreover, that an attempted synthesis of knowledge can result in a superficial hodgepodge of
concepts that might be more misleading than illuminating to
students. It will be recalled from chapter 5 that superficiality
was one of the criticisms leveled at Rugg's textbook series,
which was itself an effort to describe society.

5. Rugg, *American Life,* p. vi.

The problem here is how to supply adequate coverage of the material to be learned and at the same time to delve into it to some depth. It is conceivable that coverage in depth can be achieved only by virtue of a thorough grounding in the disciplines from which the "key" concepts are derived, in which case the objective should be to immerse students in the disciplines and make budding scholars of them. But this is probably an unattainable objective because of the obvious limitations of time, resources, and (in some cases) student ability. Besides, even if the goal of scholarship could be attained, most scholars find sufficient challenge in the task of mastering one discipline, without attempting to achieve competence in several related fields.

Given these limitations, Rugg's efforts to acquaint children with at least the major concepts of the various social sciences and to demonstrate how these areas of knowledge bear on contemporary problems of society make a good deal of sense. It seems resonable to hypothesize that a fusion of subject matter focused on problems of interest to students is likely to result in greater learning than a study of separate subject-matter fields in the abstract. To strive for a lasting "synthesis of the principal strands of American culture" in the process would seem to be too ambitious an undertaking, however.

For Rugg education is also a crucial factor in fostering creativity. It will be recalled that his conception of the "great new epoch" includes the development of "multitudes of individuals," that is, "a society of men and women each of whom is developed to his very highest potential stature."[6] We saw in chapter 2 that Rugg thinks it is through creative activity, especially as manifested in the arts, that persons develop integrity and attain individuality. Further, he thinks that a society of creative individuals will be characterized by good will and cooperation as opposed to the antisocial competition he finds prevalent in society at present. In challenging these

6. Ibid., p. 267.

claims, I noted that although creative self-expression may sometimes have desirable effects on character, there is no empirical evidence to suggest that this is invariably the case. Nor is there any logical contradiction in attributing both creativity and a lack of integrity to one and the same individual.

Rugg's high regard for creative activity naturally leads him to recommend a substantial extension of art instruction in the schools, and as we observed in chapter 5, he makes a number of sensible recommendations to facilitate self-expression in the school setting. He also tends to advance an expressionistic orientation while giving short shrift to competing philosophies of art. On the whole, nonetheless, he makes a positive contribution in calling attention to a much-neglected area of the curriculum and in offering a number of sound practical suggestions for filling the void.

It is when Rugg attempts to link creativity with "the artist's way of knowing" that he encounters theoretical difficulties and his mandate to the schools becomes unclear. He believes that in addition to the generally accepted ways of acquiring knowledge—sensation, observation, experimental inquiry, and thought processes—there is an "intuitive" way of knowing by "feeling," which is capable of providing insights that are certain. A number of problems in this position were pointed out in chapter 4, among them that Rugg had been unable to furnish a convincing operational account of exactly what "feeling" is once it is dissociated from sensation, emotion, and thought. In the last analysis Rugg seems to equate "feeling" with "total bodily gesture" and the latter with the act of knowing. This view is objectionable on two counts: (1) it reduces thoughts or ideas to their motor determinants, and (2) it is an instance of what Gilbert Ryle has called a category mistake. That is to say, the view in question confuses an activity (bodily gesture) with an achievement (knowledge).

Given these problems, it is difficult to derive educational implications from Rugg's epistemological and psychological views. The difficulty becomes particularly evident when we attempt to determine how his recommendation for a "logic of the gesture" might be implemented, or how the occurrence of the "flash of insight" might be facilitated.

CHARACTERISTICS OF RUGG'S WORK

Rugg's overoptimistic tendencies were briefly alluded to in chapter 2. This quixotic strain was no passing stage in his thought; if anything it grew more pronounced in his later writings, particularly in *The Teacher of Teachers* (1952), where he conceives of those who train teachers as cultural legislators who will set the tone for society at large. Similarly, his expectations regarding the appearance of "school-centered communities" and the extent to which the "intelligent minority" would respond to his recommendations for an intricate network of planning agencies were somewhat unrealistic on occasion.

Another slightly vexing characteristic of Rugg's work is a penchant for repetition from one book to another which is striking. He seemed to feel that in every major book he needed to preface his proposals with a long account of industrial and educational history, and this practice makes several of his works unnecessarily long and tiresome. His proposals, too, tend to be repetitious, but this inclination is understandable in view of the fact that he continued to regard their adoption as the only alternative to social chaos.

Rugg's eclectic style has been mentioned at various points in this study. Like most of us, perhaps, he hated to let go of what seemed to be a good idea even when it conflicted with another idea that he wished to adopt. For example, he attempts to combine a "tough-minded" empiricism with a "tender-minded," somewhat romantic idealism. He also combines an intuitive theory of knowledge with a functional theory of mind, which is a rather unusual merger. In *Foun-*

dations, his psychological precepts are drawn from no fewer than nine competing psychologies,[7] and in *Imagination,* he frequently appeals to a bewildering array of authorities in support of his arguments.[8] The result is sometimes a consensus on such a broad scale that little more than agreement about truisms emerges. Further, the important differences in the views of those to whom he appeals are often overlooked. Although his eclectic approach certainly rules out any traces of parochialism in his work, it also results in many inconsistencies and internal tensions.

Still another example of Rugg's ample tolerance for conflicting ideas entertained concurrently is evident in his prescriptions for social reconstruction. There is at least a tension between his notions of creative individualism and social engineering. The independent, autonomous individuals that he sees emerging from his system of education might well find the prospect of a planned society repugnant. Perhaps this tension can be fairly easily endured, but it is at least worthy of some concern and comment, and the fact that Rugg fails to provide any reassurance is just one more indication that as a rule he is not overly alert to potential areas of conflict in his thinking.

RUGG'S CONTRIBUTIONS TO EDUCATIONAL THEORY

Rugg saw his role as one of synthesizing for educational consumption the findings of scholars working at the boundaries of knowledge in their respective disciplines. He does offer some theoretical contributions of his own with his efforts to explain creativity and the artist's "intuitive way of knowing," but even here he devotes most of his energy to the task of bringing together the ideas of others. In the performance of

7. Rugg, *Foundations for American Education,* p. 123.
8. Rugg, *Imagination,* passim.

this task, Rugg's display of erudition is impressive. He had a remarkable capacity for absorbing and retaining the essential concepts of a variety of disciplines. Had he chosen to channel his ability into one field, he might have been an outstanding historian, sociologist, or psychologist.

He was mainly interested in education, however, and in this connection he was extremely sensitive to new developments. For example, he anticipated the current intense interest in creativity long before it developed. He was, moreover, always in close touch with such aspects of progressive education as the measurement movement and the attempt to create a science of education, child psychology and the related emphasis on child-centered education, and social reform featuring the school as an agent of social change.

A substantial part of this study has been devoted to pointing out difficulties in Rugg's treatment of many of these topics, but these difficulties should not be permitted to conceal his accomplishments. It has often been claimed, and with considerable justification, that Rugg's work touched more significant areas of progressive education than that of nearly anyone connected with the movement. As noted earlier, he made important contributions to the field of educational statistics (his *Statistical Methods Applied to Education,* 1917, for example, became a standard in the field),[9] and he was a gifted innovator in the area of curriculum development. In fact, his "broad-fields" approach to building courses around the fundamental concepts and themes of several disciplines was apparently the first of its kind.[10] He was also a keen critic of traditional educational practices; indeed, his suggestions for change were among the most imaginative put forth by his generation of educators. Further, his social studies textbook series was one of the outstanding educational efforts of the twenties and thirties; had he never accomplished anything

9. Carleton Washburne, "Harold Rugg and the New Education," *Educational Theory* 10 (July 1960):180.

10. B. Othanel Smith, William O. Stanley, and J. Harlan Shores, *Fundamentals of Curriculum Development* (Yonkers-on-Hudson, N.Y.: World Book Co., 1950), p. 406.

else, this achievement by itself would have sufficed to insure his niche in the history of progressive education. Rugg was, moreover, a talented synthesizer of current developments in a variety of disciplines. Several of his books, notably *Foundations for American Education* (1947) and *Imagination* (1963), are vast storehouses of information as well as valuable secondary sources for researchers interested in topics on the social and behavioral sciences and problems in the field of education. Finally, his suggestions for establishing closer ties between school and community, for viewing the school as only one among several educative agencies in the community, and for regarding education as a lifelong process taking place in a "school-centered community" anticipated a number of the innovative educational proposals of the sixties and seventies. I will return to these suggestions later in the chapter.

RUGG'S INFLUENCE

There is no question that Rugg, through his personal force and practical educational accomplishments, must be regarded as one of the most important figures of the progressive era. It is difficult to assess his lasting influence on education and social reform, however, because of the paucity of evidence available for examination. Since thousands of adults and millions of children read his articles and books, he must have had some impact, but the extent of this impact is almost impossible to measure because of the lack of supporting evidence; no disciples have declared themselves—not, at any rate, in print. The evidence is particularly tenuous with regard to Rugg's influence on the social scene beyond the school. Zeitlin reports that *The Social Frontier* had little effect on New Deal policies.[11] Since Rugg's articles for that particular journal are

11. Cremin, *Transformation of the School*, p. 233, citing Harry Zeitlin, "Federal Relations in American Education, 1933–1944: A Study of New Deal Efforts and Innovations" (doctoral dissertation, Columbia University, 1958).

representative of his overall social philosophy, it seems reasonable to infer that his books did not influence the Roosevelt administration either. At least there is no evidence of such influence. This is hardly surprising in view of Roosevelt's well-known preference for piecemeal, "on-the-spot" social engineering as opposed to long-range planning. Nor is there any indication that Rugg's writings have significantly affected public policy since the New Deal era. It is probably true that the cumulative writings of liberal professors have contributed somewhat to the passage of welfare legislation, but even this joint contribution is very difficult to measure apart from all the other technological, political, and economic forces that have led to actual social change.

On the educational scene Rugg seems to have exerted considerable influence on the field of curriculum construction. The extent of this influence is difficult to determine precisely, however, because it is not always acknowledged by curriculum builders who apparently draw on his ideas. This may be because these ideas have filtered down through two or three generations of curriculum theorists since Rugg formulated them in the early twenties, and undoubtedly they have been modified in the process. At any rate, he has, as we have seen, been credited with developing the "theme approach" to broad-fields courses, and clearly he pioneered in formulating systematic techniques for selecting course materials.[12] Consequently he had considerable influence on the development of a number of state programs in the social studies.[13] Finally, he clearly had a hand in expanding the school curriculum to include discussion of contemporary social and political issues (even though the consideration of such issues has fallen short of his expectations).

Judged on the basis of the limited evidence available, and pending future developments, Rugg's long-range influence on education apart from the area of curriculum con-

12. B. Othanel Smith, "Harold Ordway Rugg, 1886–1960," *Educational Theory* 10 (July 1960): 176.

13. Winters, "Harold Rugg and Education for Social Reconstruction," p. 240.

struction seems to have been slight. His network of forums, panels, study groups, and councils never was organized, there has been no general acceptance of his educational foundations, and public schools deal with controversial issues only as long as they do not become too controversial. With respect to the latter, the areas that Rugg designated as "neglected"—sex education, issues regarding the ownership of property, racial conflict, the study of religions—continue to be regarded as "off limits" in many communities.

Similarly the schools' provision for creative expression in the arts is generally rather modest. More often than not, the policy has been to devote a regimented hour or so per week to art instruction and to regard the development of artistic talent as a "frill" to be added only if and when the more "practical" subjects have been insured a place in the curriculum.[14] That this attitude has been reflected in our society at large has been brought out vividly in Peter Blake's *God's Own Junkyard.*[15] Judging from Blake's photographs, it would appear that few Americans have responded to Rugg's call for a "cultured" society, deeply concerned with aesthetic appreciation and creative activity. In recent years, to be sure, educators have become more sensitive to criticism directed at their less-than-enthusiastic efforts to secure a place for the arts in the school curriculum. It is unlikely, however, that this phenomenon is due in any direct sense to the efforts of Rugg and his progressive colleagues. Rather, it appears to be the result of a more recent shift in emphasis, in some quarters, from the cognitive, to the affective growth of students, a shift brought on in part by a negative reaction in the 1960s to the rigorous academic programs developed in the wake of Sputnik 1.

As for the discussion of controversial issues, the history of the Rugg textbooks provides ample evidence of the opposi-

14. Robert C. Osborn, "Art Gets the Tag End of Friday," *American Education* 1 (February 1965): 5–7.

15. Peter Blake, *God's Own Junkyard: The Planned Deterioration of America's Landscape* (New York: Holt, Rinehart & Winston, 1964).

tion that any such effort is likely to encounter. If Rugg's program for open discussion of controversial issues is to be introduced into the schools, it must be condoned by adults who have seldom been exposed to this kind of education themselves and who therefore have little frame of reference for evaluating the program. On the contrary, most adults remember school as the place where values acquired in the home and in the immediate community were reinforced and where conflicting views were given scant attention, if they were considered at all. They see no reason why this policy should be changed or even challenged. Given this prevailing attitude, perhaps the wonder is not that Rugg's textbooks literally went up in smoke in at least one place but that he got his books into the schools at all.[16]

The situation does not appear to have improved much in the years since the furor over the Rugg books. The self-appointed censors still stand ready to denounce and exorcise any materials that they regard as subversive. In 1959, to cite just one instance, the Daughters of the American Revolution examined 220 textbooks in all fields and found 170 of them to be "un-American."[17] As a matter of fact, it seems almost the rule rather than the exception that each new school year is marked by yet another textbook controversy. In 1973, for example, Kurt Vonnegut's *Slaughterhouse-Five* and James Dickey's *Deliverance* were burned in the school furnace in Drake, North Dakota, and during the school year 1974–75 people in Kanawha County, West Virginia, were actually shooting at one another because of the approval by the board of education of writings by Allen Ginsburg, Malcolm X, Dick Gregory, and Eldridge Cleaver, among others.

16. Of course the pamphlets from which the books evolved had already been used experimentally in a number of schools without evoking anything resembling the later storm of protest directed against Rugg. Given this fact together with the enthusiasm with which teachers had received the pamphlets, the publisher, Ginn & Company, apparently did not anticipate the attacks that ensued around 1940. (Conversation with Henry Halvorson, editor-in-chief, Ginn & Company, July 1966.)

17. Nelson and Roberts, *Censors and the Schools,* p. 5.

In addition to traditional "watch dog" groups such as the DAR and the American Legion, a number of new organizations have sprung up in recent years, including one that referred to itself as the National Indignation Convention![18] The pressure on textbook publishers exerted by these groups should not be underestimated. For competitive reasons, publishers find it to their advantage to skirt controversial issues.[19] The result, of course, is a procession of innocuous textbooks that agitate neither the sensibilities of the censors nor the intellects of the children who use them.

It might be argued that the recent trend toward offering some instruction about communism in the public schools augurs well for a change in attitude regarding controversial topics. But here again a closer look reveals that the treatment accorded the subject is usually more in the nature of a propaganda campaign than an objective account of the nature of communist theory and practice designed to foster understanding. Frequently, the objective of presenting communism as a "threat to the free world" or as a "philosophy of enslavement" is built right into the course outline. In many cases, as a matter of fact, such objectives are explicitly stated in policy recommendations put out by state boards of education.[20] One fears that this sort of indoctrination is the rule rather than the exception in these courses throughout the country.

The extent of Rugg's influence among teacher training institutions is also questionable. The foundations notion had been in the wind for several years and though a number of insitutions had launched foundations programs by 1950, it is rather doubtful that these programs were influenced directly by Rugg's writings. Brauner seems to think that Rugg did exert considerable influence on some of these programs, especially the one developed at Illinois. He writes:

18. Ibid., p. 22.
19. Ibid., pp. 178–190.
20. Roland F. Gray, "Teaching About Communism: A Survey of Objectives," *Social Education* 28 (February 1964): 72.

A scholarly and extensive fulfillment of Rugg's idea of a foundation program was carried out by the largely Columbia-trained foundation staff of the University of Illinois. In 1947, the year of Rugg's publication, the College of Education at the University of Illinois began a reorganizational study of their graduate program. Three years later, it put many of Rugg's suggestions to work.[21]

But there does not appear to be any evidence available in print to indicate that the architects of this program consciously referred to Rugg's ideas when they designed it. On the other hand, they no doubt drew upon their experience with Education 200-F at Teachers College, and Rugg had contributed heavily to the development of that course. He seems therefore to have exerted at least an indirect influence on the highly regarded and widely emulated Illinois program.

Rugg's influence, if any, on later reconstructionists is another moot point. One obstacle to assessment in this respect is the fact that reconstructionists, like existentialists, often object to the label. The outstanding exception to this generalization is Theodore Brameld, who is widely regarded as the leading reconstructionist theorist of the day. Rugg probably had little influence on Brameld's philosophical development, but there are a number of common themes in their writings on education. Since Brameld greatly admired and respected Rugg,[22] it is not unreasonable to suppose that Rugg's reconstructionism was incorporated, at least to some extent, into Brameld's own thinking in this area.

RUGG'S RELEVANCE TO CURRENT ISSUES

Does the America that Rugg worried about and prescribed for still exist, or has it changed so much that his writings are now

21. Brauner, *American Educational Theory*, pp. 211–212.
22. Letter from Theodore Brameld, June 8, 1966.

hopelessly dated? It could be argued, for instance, that Rugg's work was a response to a specific set of economic problems that became particularly evident during the Depression, and that his view that the social, political, economic, and cultural life of the nation was passing through a dangerous period of crisis is no longer pertinent. A criticism of this genre has in fact been directed at Dewey and his followers (among whom Rugg can be included in this context) by Frederic Lilge, who writes:

> The particular economic problems of the thirties to which Dewey and his followers responded are no longer in the center of attention. The reason is not that they were solved by the socialist reconstruction recommended by the philosophers, but that rapid technological progress, greatly stimulated by the last war, and an expanding although not basically revised economy have provided rising incomes and continued upward social mobility. As for inflation, automation, and other problems of today, few people look to a socialized economy for their solution. . . . The traditions and institutions which Dewey had regarded as weakening and frustrating the realization of a democratic society continue to exist without causing the same anxiety.[23]

A similar critique of Dewey in particular and the progressives in general has been offered by Kimball and McClellan, who hold that the progressives were attempting to preserve the values of an earlier agrarian culture in a new society undergoing tremendous change because of rapid industrialization and urbanization.[24] They go on to argue persuasively that since the transformation has now been completed, it makes little sense to attempt to salvage the values and attitudes of an obsolete past. The new America, Kimball and

23. Frederic Lilge, "The Vain Quest for Unity: John Dewey's Social and Educational Thought in Retrospect," in *Dewey on Education: Appraisals,* ed. Reginald D. Archambault (New York: Random House, 1966), p. 64.
24. Solon T. Kimball and James D. McClellan, Jr., *Education and the New America* (New York: Random House, 1962), p. 81.

McClellan insist, is one marked by huge corporate structures, one in which opportunity rests not in the small, local community but rather in the new bureaucratic supercorporation, whether public or private, and that the style of life within these large units is a far different kind of existence from that experienced in the simpler family-community life characteristic of the earlier America.[25]

The school, so the argument continues, should recognize the characteristics of the new America by facilitating the adjustment of youngsters to life within and among the colossal superstructures of modern American society, and this is best accomplished by building an intellectual commitment (as opposed to an emotional one) to the complex reality that is contemporary American society. This type of commitment is best achieved, moreover, through a rigorous study of the various disciplines. The capacity for dispassionate, critical analysis is, then, the prerequisite for commitment in and to the new America.[26]

One of the important points that both Lilge and Kimball and McClellan attempt to establish is that even if the progressives' response to industrial and technological development was well taken at one time, their suggestions for reform are no longer viable. According to these critics of the progressives, communal control of giant industry is no longer regarded by most informed observers as a realistic solution to present economic problems. The privately controlled (in large part), corporate society is here to stay, and the discussion of social and economic problems must be carried on against the background of this hard fact of life.

Whether these arguments are valid or not is highly debatable. Certainly the face of America has changed in forty years,[27] and no doubt some of the social criticism voiced by

25. Ibid., pp. 115–134, 183–215.
26. Ibid., pp. 279–304.
27. For that matter, it has changed considerably since these critiques were written in the late 1950s and early sixties, and the writers might well view the situation somewhat differently at present.

Dewey, Rugg, and others of their persuasion now seems dated. This does not mean, however, that their overall analysis of American society is no longer applicable. Nor is it obvious that private interests are even now so firmly in control of our corporate society that their dislodgment is unthinkable. In fact, it could be argued to the contrary that much of the social legislation enacted during and since the Great Depression, together with the consciousness-raising efforts of the New Left over the last decade or so, has moved the country a step closer to the sort of collective control desired by Dewey, Rugg, and others. As Norman Thomas had pointed out for years, "socialistic planks" have a way of eventually finding places for themselves in the platforms of our major political parties.

Much more could be said on both sides of this issue, but even if it could be shown that Dewey's and Rugg's political and economic views were obsolete (which is unlikely), much of their diagnosis of social ills would remain as topical now as it was during the thirties and before. We still hear a great deal about economic injustice, social fragmentation and isolation, group conflict, inequality of opportunity, disregard for human dignity, and cultural barrenness, to mention but a few problems that continue to resist solution. Both Dewey and Rugg dealt rather extensively with these themes, most of which transcend a relatively simple economic and political analysis. They were men of multiple interests, whose thought ranged over a wide variety of fields and freely crossed disciplinary boundaries. The mere fact, therefore, that a changing technology has introduced a host of new conditions and problems should not lead us to conclude that the march of time has left their work behind. All of this is rather obvious with regard to Dewey, but it needs to be pointed out with respect to Rugg, since his work is less well known.

It was noted in an earlier section of this chapter that many of Rugg's views regarding the curriculum, instruction in the arts, and, in fact, the life of the school as a whole, together with the school's relation to the surrounding community, are still worthy of serious consideration. That his social thought has received its share of criticism in this study should not obscure the merit in his notion of developing and coordinating a network of planning boards and councils, consisting of representatives of business, labor, government, and the general public, to deal with pressing social problems. Surely such agencies are desirable if the practical problems of launching and maintaining them can be solved. Similarly, his plea for more creative activity and more appreciation of cultural pursuits is certainly timely in a society where developing technology and automation are leading inevitably to increases in available leisure time. And again, his idea for closing the gap between school and society (a gap that still renders formal education virtually meaningless for thousands of youngsters if the school dropout rate is any indication) by making education the responsibility of the entire community deserves more consideration than it has thus far received from educators. If the school has little significance for students because it is isolated from their everyday problems and concerns, it makes sense to broaden our conception of education by viewing the entire community—and beyond, if feasible—as part of the setting in which the process of education takes place. Thus the present formal school might be conceived as a "classroom" (in a sense) within the larger school, which would entail the entire community. This is an idea promising enough to warrant a trial. Unfortunately, it seems for the most part to have lain dormant since Rugg proposed it nearly half a century ago. Occasionally one sees it reflected in the educational literature,[28] however, and indeed a very similar idea is currently being implemented in the form of the Parkway Program in Philadelphia.[29] Here again, Rugg seems to have an-

28. See, for example, Herbert A. Thelan, *Education and the Human Quest* (New York: Harper & Brothers, 1960), pp. 188–209. Also, Fred M. Newmann and Donald Oliver, "Education and Community," *Harvard Educational Review* 37 (Winter 1967): 61–106.

29. Donald William Cox, *The City as a Schoolhouse: The Story of the Parkway Program* (Valley Forge, Pa.: Judson Press, 1972).

ticipated developments that would occur a generation or more later. In short, then, we must conclude that much of Rugg's work—difficulties therein notwithstanding—has in fact retained its relevance for the concerns of the present.

THE SCHOOL AND SOCIAL CHANGE

Rugg's career provides an interesting case study to ponder in connection with the old question of whether or not the school can be effectively utilized as an agent of social change. This question was the locus for much spirited controversy during the 1930s. On the one side were Rugg and his colleagues, who felt that the school could and should stand in the vanguard of social change; on the other, stood their critics, who were of the opinion that the school should merely reflect the dominant values of the society at large and transmit these values to the young.

For a while the debate between the reconstructionists and their opponents occupied considerable space in the educational journals, and an examination of the literature reveals a surprising amount of support from "the establishment" for the reconstructionist view. For example, the United States commissioner of education wrote, "Most of us are convinced that our depression-ridden, war-threatened world needs *some* drastic reorganization."[30] The National Education Association's Department of Superintendence passed a resolution deploring special privilege and selfishness.[31] A New York superintendent of schools called the old order sick and forecast its demise.[32] A Delaware superintendent said that projected change in the social order should be discussed freely.[33]

30. J. W. Studebaker, "Safeguarding Democracy Through Adult Civic Education," U.S. Office of Education *Bulletin No. 6*, 1936, p. 1.

31. Belmont Farley, "The Superintendents at St. Louis," *School and Society* 43 (14 March 1936): 354.

32. Frederick Bair, "A Social Philosophy of Education Challenges the Teacher," *New York State Education* 24 (October 1936): 26–27.

33. Samuel Burr, "Democracy Can Bear Comparisons," *Journal of Education* 118 (17 June 1935): 329–330.

A university president hailed the new spirit and the willingness to build a better society.[34] And a school principal called for dynamic schools to regenerate society.[35] Of course there was considerable opposition too, but that so many educators were willing to speak out for the employment of schools as agents of social reform was noteworthy. There was a sense of excitement, a spirit of adventure in the air.

Yet despite all the talk very little was done to put reconstructionist proposals into practice. The schools never did embark on any concerted effort to reconstruct society, and the final issue of *Frontiers of Democracy* (formerly *The Social Frontier*) carried an article in which Theodore Brameld ruefully considered the possibility that the conservatives were right after all, that perhaps the schools were destined to follow rather than lead.[36] From that time until the late sixties the whole question received relatively little attention, but in recent years it has once again emerged as an issue deemed worthy of serious consideration.

Rugg, with his textbook series, was an exception to the rule that professor-reformers fail to get their programs into the schools. On the other hand, the short-lived success of the series suggests that his strategy—which was to defy vested interests by familiarizing children with controversial issues and calling attention to society's deficiencies and problems as he perceived them—may have been doomed from the start. The fate of his textbooks lends support to the argument that the public schools are no place to attempt to teach children to think on Rugg's terms, since these schools are not expected to challenge existing conditions. The comments of two astute observers of the social scene are relevant here. In a review of Rugg's *Culture and Education* John Chamberlain wrote,

34. Walter Hullihen, "A Further Obligation to the Social Order," in *Proceedings of the National Association of State Universities* (n.p., 1933), p. 55.

35. Truman Reed, "Delusions of Grandeur," *Junior-Senior High School Clearing House* 7 (January 1933): 266.

36. Theodore Brameld, "Is the Conservative Right?" *Frontiers of Democracy* 10 (December 1943): 93–94.

He [Rugg] hopes for the salvation of democracy through primary and secondary education, and does not see that this education can be no more than a reflex of the very political situation . . . that he sincerely deplores. Dr. Rugg ought to be the first to know that the stream of mass education can rise no higher than its source in political representation; the school board is of a piece with plutocratic control in city hall and legislature. Certain endowed schools, no doubt, might be able to put Dr. Rugg's theories into very frutiful practice; but regeneration of the body politic as a whole must come, we feel, from some source outside of the public school.[37]

In another review of the same book Reinhold Niebuhr called Rugg's assumption that the school could reform society in the face of resistance from the privileged and the unenlightened a naive, romantic hope. Niebuhr argued that social change comes about largely as the result of pressure exerted by "out groups" rather than through education.[38]

It may be, then, that Rugg's method is too direct, too much a threat to accepted values. In the long run Dewey's approach may be more promising. Dewey sought to "institutionalize" intelligent, critical thinking in the schools by making the scientific or experimental method the model for problem-solving within the school context. Dewey's notion, it seems, was that if the methods, habits, and attitudes typical of scientific inquiry were widely utilized in school, they would carry over into adult life and be effectively employed in solving social problems and formulating moral ends.[39] Of course Rugg agreed pretty much with Dewey here. The difference between them was one of degree rather than kind. Like Dewey, Rugg wanted the school to foster critical intelligence,

37. John Chamberlain, review of *Culture and Education in America* in *Nation* 133 (7 October 1931): 368.

38. Reinhold Niebuhr, review of *Culture and Education* in *World Tomorrow* 14 (December 1931): 407.

39. Dewey, *Democracy and Education*, pp. 115, 192. This view also finds expression in most of Dewey's other major works on education and related topics.

and like Rugg, Dewey wanted the school to align itself with the "newer scientific, technological, and cultural forces that are producing change in the old order."[40] Regarding the school as an agent of social change, Dewey argued that although schools do reflect the existing social order, social conditions are always changing. The changes, moreover, are in different directions, and the school, by choosing to follow in one of these directions, has a hand in shaping future social conditions.[41]

Perhaps the real difference between Dewey and Rugg is one of emphasis, with Dewey coming down harder on scientific inquiry and Rugg laying greater stress on pointing out existing social ills. Thus Dewey's approach is probably less abrasive than Rugg's to the community at large. Rather than openly challenging community biases it exerts a more subtle influence by advancing a spirit of rationality that is incompatible with the "unexamined life," both individual and social.

To be sure, even Dewey's approach cannot avoid clashing with community orthodoxies altogether. Somewhere along the way, in the application of critical intelligence to the study of society, it is bound to touch upon sensitive areas. The only alternative would be to confine this approach to the natural sciences and depend on some kind of transfer of training to carry it over to social concerns, and this seems unlikely. Natural scientists, too, can be uninformed and biased with regard to social problems. It was partly his awareness of this problem that led Rugg to stress the importance of adult education. His aim was to establish adult study groups in which social issues would be discussed freely, and then to obtain a mandate from the adults to study the same issues in the schools. As we saw earlier, he neither got his study groups organized nor secured his mandate.

Rugg failed to win public support for his views partly

40. John Dewey, "Education and Social Change," *Social Frontier* 3 (May 1937): 236.
41. Ibid., pp. 235–238.

because many of his proposals were at marked variance to the values, attitudes, and beliefs held by influential segments of the society he wished to make over. This may be another indication that the more detached, "scientific" approach attributed to Dewey above is more likely to succeed. All the same, neither approach, as already pointed out, is free from the risk of incurring public opposition. Actually there is a vicious circle involved. In order to achieve social reform, we must alert children to social problems, but then we need the support of adults who frequently fear the open discussion of such issues. Although there is no simple solution to this problem, it is probably easier to break the circle using Dewey's "scientific" approach than it is to fling down the gauntlet as Rugg did. Dewey's recommendation has a mandate of sorts at the outset. Given the general public's respect for scientific achievement together with both the popular desire to compete with other nations for scientific breakthroughs and the need to prepare people for intelligent citizenship in an era of advanced technology and automation, it is difficult for members of the community to question an emphasis on the methods of science. This may hold true even when people find the application of scientific rationality to ethical and political issues disconcerting to some extent.

With this opening wedge it may be possible gradually to extend the use of free and open inquiry to social and moral problems to a degree that has been improbable in the past. Accordingly, the school may thereby aid in developing attitudes, dispositions, and insights that will eventually render the community more receptive to critical dialogue regarding proposals for social improvement. In this manner the school may yet play a small part, indirectly at least, in the solution of social problems. If so, it is likely that those who achieve this success will have profited from the experiences of reformers like Harold Rugg who pioneered in the effort to establish the school as an agent of social change.

A NEXT-STEP JUNIOR-SENIOR-HIGH-SCHOOL PROGRAM

I. The Life of the School as a Whole: the Heart of the Curriculum

Practicing competitive individuals in social co-operation through the school assembly and council, class councils and committees, the newspaper and magazine, the court, athletic, literary, dramatic, and scientific organizations, etc. The co-operative participation of students in the group activities of the school develops social techniques — for example, organizing people, taking part in open-forum discussion, planning excursions, and the like. These are not extracurricular; they are the crux of the curriculum.

GRADES: VII, VIII, IX	X	XI, XII

II. Body Education

TIME: 1 hour daily. **GRADES:** VII-XII

1. Participation in intramural outdoor and indoor games — tennis, baseball, football, basketball, etc.
2. Use of the modern dance and its integration with literature, dramatics, pageantry, etc.
3. Integration of the foregoing with the scientific data of body engineering, also with work of VI, "The Study of Personality and Human Behavior."

III. The Study of Man and His Changing Society—the New Social Science

TIME: 1 to 1½ hours daily each year. **GRADES:** VII-XII

GRADES: VII, VIII, IX	X	XI, XII
A. INTRODUCTION TO AMERICAN CIVILIZATION AND CULTURE. An integration of all factors necessary for intelligent understanding and participation. 1. Contemporary. 2. Historical. { a. Economic life. b. Government. c. Social and aesthetic life. Including geographical and psychological factors. B. INTRODUCTION TO 12 OR 15 KEY CIVILIZATIONS AND CULTURES OF THE MODERN WORLD 1. *Changing Industrial:* Great Britain, France, Germany, Japan, and their empires. 2. *Changing Agricultural:* Russia, China, Japan, India, Near East, Mexico and other Latin-American examples. 3. *Simple Types:* For example, island types (Samoa), desert or steppe types, central-African types.	A World View of the Development of Civilizations and Cultures (World history, Social anthropology, etc.)	A Critical Study of Problems and Issues of Our Changing American Civilization (Economic, political, social, cultural)

TIME: 1 to 1½ hours daily. **GRADES:** VII–XII	**IV.** *Introduction to Creative and Appreciative Arts* 1. Reading, observation, listening to and critical discussion of poetry, fiction, novels, **plays, music, painting,** sculpture, and architecture. 2. Excursions to galleries and museums, concerts, theaters, etc., including in upper years **a** world history of literature and the other fine arts. Closely integrated with "A World View of the Development of Civilizations and Cultures."
TIME: 1 hour daily. **GRADES:** VII–XII	**V.** *Creative Work Period (individual and group creative activity)* 1. Teachers and rooms available in all the arts and sciences at stated intervals; library and reading rooms, laboratories, art and music studios, shops, theater, student periodicals, offices, club rooms, etc. 2. All activity voluntary; carried on in individual or group "projects" or "research units."
TIME: 1 hour daily. **GRADES:** VII–XII	**VI. A.** *Introduction to the Physical and Natural World* An integration of all factors necessary for intelligent understanding and appreciation of concepts and laws.	**VI. B.** *The Study of Personality and Human Behavior* A critical study of personality and conduct. 1. Bodily factors — health, diet, **understanding of** disease, etc. 2. **Psychological factors — attitudes, beliefs, stereo-types, personal relations, mental hygiene, etc.** 3. **Sex factors.**
TIME: 2–3 hours per week. **GRADES:** VII–IX	**VII.** *General Mathematics* Needed technique and concepts.	
	VIII. *Foreign Language* Optional offering in modern foreign language or in Latin for small **selected** groups. **No student to take a** modern language for less than four years.
	Special remedial periods to be provided each week for individuals needing it.
	All work (except mathematical and other techniques) to be organized in the form of projects or units-of-study.

Source. From Harold Rugg, *American Life and the School Curriculum: Next Steps Toward Schools of Living* (Boston: Ginn & Company, 1936), pp. 354–355. Reprinted by permission.

APPENDIX 2

THE LIFE OF THE SCHOOL AS A WHOLE

The school assembly and council, class councils and committees, the newspaper and magazine, the court, athletic, literary, dramatic, and scientific organizations, and so on. The cooperative participation of students in these group activities of the school develops social techniques—for example, organizing people, taking part in open forum discussion, planning excursions, and so on.

ORGANIZATION OF THE CURRICULUM

Grade 7	Grade 8	Grade 9	Grade 10	Grade 11	Grade 12
A. Introduction to American Civilization and Culture An integration of all factors necessary for intelligent understanding and participation. 1. Contemporary. 2. Historical. Economic life, government, and social and esthetic life, including geographic and psychological factors. *B. Introduction of 12 to 15 Key Civilizations and Cultures of the Modern World* 1. Changing Industrial: Great Britain, France, Germany, Japan, and their empires. 2. Changing Agricultural: Russia, China, India, the Near East, Mexico, and other Latin American examples. 3. Simple Types: Island types (e.g., Samoa); desert or steppe types; central African types.			*A World View of the Development of Civilizations and Cultures* World History, Social Anthropology, etc.	*A Critical Study of Problems and Issues of Our Changing American Civilization* Economic, Political, Social, Esthetic.	

Introduction to the Physical and Natural World: An integration of all factors necessary for intelligent understanding and appreciation of concepts and laws.

Source. From Harold Rugg and William Withers, *Social Foundations of Education* (New York: Prentice-Hall, 1955), pp. 677–678. Reprinted by permission.

The Study of Personality and Human Behavior
A critical study of personality and conduct.
  1. Bodily factors: health, diet, understanding of disease, etc.
  2. Psychological factors: attitudes, beliefs, stereotypes,
      personal relations, mental hygiene, etc.
  3. Sex factors.

Introduction to the Creative and Appreciative Life
1. Reading, observation, listening and critical discussion of poetry, fiction, novels, plays, music, painting, sculpture and architecture.
2. Excursions to galleries, museums, concerts and theatres, etc. Including in upper years a World History of Literature and the other fine arts. (Closely integrated with "World View of Development of Civilization and Culture.")

Creative Work Period (Individual and group creative activity)
Teachers and rooms available in all arts and sciences at stated intervals; library and reading rooms, laboratories, art and music studios, shops, theatre, student periodicals, offices, club rooms, etc.
All activity voluntary; carried on in individual or group "projects" or "research units."

Body Education
(a) Participation in intra-mural, outdoor and indoor games—tennis, baseball, football, basketball, etc.
(b) Use of the dance and integration with literature, dramatics, pageantry, etc.

General Mathematics Needed technique and concepts	*Advanced Mathematics and Science Study* for selected students specializing in any of the sciences

Foreign Language
Optional offering in modern foreign language and in Latin for small selected groups. No student to take a modern language for less than four years.
Special remedial periods to be provided each week for individuals needing it.

All Work (Except mathematical and other techniques)
To be organized in problem form of "projects" or "units of work."

BIBLIOGRAPHY

PRIMARY SOURCES

Books and Pamphlets by Rugg

*America's March Toward Democracy. Rev. of A History of American Government and Culture. Boston: Ginn & Company, 1937.

American Life and the School Curriculum: Next Steps Toward Schools of Living. Boston: Ginn & Company, 1936.

Building a Science of Society for the Schools. Boston: Ginn & Company, 1934.

*Changing Civilizations in the Modern World: A Textbook in World Geography with Historical Backgrounds. Boston: Ginn & Company, 1930.

*Changing Countries and Changing Peoples. Rev. of Changing Civilizations in the Modern World. Boston: Ginn & Company, 1938.

*Changing Governments and Changing Cultures, Democracy Versus Dictatorship: The World Struggle. Boston: Ginn & Company, 1937.

*Changing Governments and Changing Cultures: The World's March Toward Democracy. Boston: Ginn & Company, 1932.

*Citizenship and Civic Affairs. Boston: Ginn & Company, 1940.

*The Conquest of America. Rev. of A History of American Civilization. Boston: Ginn & Company, 1937.

Culture and Education in America. New York: Harcourt, Brace & Co., 1931.

(ed.). Democracy and the Curriculum: The Life and Program of the American School. The Third Yearbook of the John Dewey Society. New York: D. Appleton-Century Co., 1939.

*Part of Rugg's textbook series, Man and His Changing Society.

The Experimental Determination of Mental Discipline in School Studies. Baltimore: Warwick and York, 1916.

Foundations for American Education. Yonkers-on-Hudson, N.Y.: World Book Co., 1947.

The Great Technology: Social Chaos and the Public Mind. New York: John Day Co., 1933.

*A History of American Civilization: Economic and Social. Boston: Ginn & Company, 1930.

*A History of American Government and Culture: America's March Toward Democracy. Boston: Ginn & Company, 1931.

Imagination. Foreword and editorial comments by Kenneth D. Benne. New York: Harper & Row, Publishers, 1963.

*An Introduction to American Civilization: A Study of Economic Life in the United States. Boston: Ginn & Company, 1929.

*An Introduction to Problems of American Culture. Boston: Ginn & Company, 1931.

Now Is the Moment. New York: Duell, Sloan and Pearce, 1943.

*Our Country and Our People. Rev. of An Introduction to American Civilization. Boston: Ginn & Company, 1938.

A Primer of Graphics and Statistics. Boston: Houghton Mifflin Company, 1925.

The Psychology of the Elementary School Subjects. n.p., 1926.

(ed.). Readings in the Foundations of Education. 2 vols. New York: Teachers College, Columbia University, 1941.

Statistical Methods Applied to Education. Boston: Houghton Mifflin Company, 1917.

The Teacher of Teachers: Frontiers of Theory and Practice in Teacher Education. New York: Harper & Brothers, 1952.

Teacher's Guide for Changing Governments and Changing Cultures. Boston: Ginn & Company, 1932.

Teacher's Guide for A History of American Civilization: Economic and Social. Boston: Ginn & Company, 1931.

Teacher's Guide for A History of American Government and Culture. Boston: Ginn & Company, 1931.

Teacher's Guide for An Introduction to Problems of American Culture. Boston: Ginn & Company, 1932.

That Men May Understand: An American in the Long Armistice. New York: Doubleday, Doran & Company, 1941.

*Part of Rugg's textbook series, Man and His Changing Society.

with Bagley, W. C. *The Content of American History As Taught in the Seventh and Eighth Grades.* Urbana: University of Illinois, 1916.

with Brooks, Marian. *The Teacher in School and Society: An Introduction to Education.* Yonkers-on-Hudson, N.Y.: World Book Co., 1950.

with Clark, John R. *Fundamentals of High School Mathematics.* Yonkers-on-Hudson, N.Y.: World Book Co., 1919.

_____. *Scientific Method in the Reconstruction of Ninth Grade Mathematics.* Chicago: University of Chicago Press, 1918.

with Frank, Waldo; Mumford, Lewis; Norman, Dorothy; and Rosenfeld, Paul, eds. *America and Alfred Stieglitz: A Collective Portrait.* New York: Doubleday, Doran & Company, 1934.

with Hockett, John. *Objective Studies in Map Location.* New York: The Lincoln School of Teachers College, 1925.

*with Krueger, Louise. *The Building of America.* Boston: Ginn & Company, 1936.

_____. *The Building of America Workbook.* Boston: Ginn & Company, 1936.

*_____. *Communities of Men.* Boston: Ginn & Company, 1936.

_____. *Communities of Men Workbook.* Boston: Ginn & Company, 1936.

*_____. *The First Book of the Earth.* Boston: Ginn & Company, 1936.

_____. *The First Book of the Earth Workbook.* Boston: Ginn & Company, 1936.

*_____. *Man at Work: His Arts and Crafts.* Boston: Ginn & Company, 1937.

*_____. *Man at Work: His Industries.* Boston: Ginn & Company, 1937.

*_____. *Mankind Throughout the Ages.* Boston: Ginn & Company, 1938.

*_____. *Nature Peoples.* Boston: Ginn & Company, 1936.

_____. *Nature Peoples Workbook.* Boston: Ginn & Company, 1936.

*_____. *Peoples and Countries.* Boston: Ginn & Company, 1936.

_____. *Peoples and Countries Workbook.* Boston: Ginn & Company, 1937.

*Part of Rugg's textbook series, *Man and His Changing Society.*

_____. *The Social Studies in the Elementary School: A Tentative "Course of Study."* n.p., n.d.

with Krueger, Marvin. *Social Reconstruction: Study Guide for Group and Class Discussion.* New York: John Day Co., 1933.

_____. *Study Guide to National Recovery: An Introduction to Economic Problems.* New York: John Day Co., 1933.

with Mendenhall, James E. *Pupil's Workbook to Accompany Changing Civilizations in the Modern World.* Boston: Ginn & Company, 1930.

_____. *Pupil's Workbook to Accompany An Introduction to American Civilization.* Boston: Ginn & Company, 1929.

_____. *Pupil's Workbook of Directed Study to Accompany Changing Governments and Changing Cultures.* Boston: Ginn & Company, 1937.

_____. *Pupil's Workbook of Directed Study to Accompany Citizenship and Civic Affairs.* Boston: Ginn & Company, 1940.

_____. *Pupil's Workbook of Directed Study to Accompany A History of American Civilization.* Boston: Ginn & Company, 1930.

_____. *Pupil's Workbook of Directed Study to Accompany An Introduction to Problems of American Culture.* Boston: Ginn & Company, 1931.

_____. *Teacher's Guide for Changing Civilizations in the Modern World.* Boston: Ginn & Company, 1930.

_____. *Teacher's Guide for An Introduction to American Civilization.* Boston: Ginn & Company, 1929.

with Rugg, Earle, and Schweppe, Emma. *America and Her Immigrants.* The Social Science Pamphlets. New York: The Lincoln School, 1922.

_____. *America's March Toward Democracy.* The Social Science Pamphlets. New York: The Lincoln School, 1922.

_____. *Explorers and Settlers Westward Bound.* The Social Science Pamphlets. New York: The Lincoln School, 1924.

_____. *How Nations Live Together.* The Social Science Pamphlets. New York: The Lincoln School, 1922.

_____. *Industries and Trade Which Bind Nations Together.* The Social Science Pamphlets. New York: The Lincoln School, 1924.

_____. *The Mechanical Conquest of America.* The Social Science Pamphlets. New York: The Lincoln School, 1922.

_____. *Resources and Industries in a Machine World.* The Social Science Pamphlets. New York: The Lincoln School, 1922.

with Shumaker, Ann. *The Child-Centered School: An Appraisal of the New Education.* Yonkers-on-Hudson, N.Y.: World Book Co., 1928.

with Withers, William. *Social Foundations of Education.* Englewood Cliffs, N.J.: Prentice-Hall, 1955.

with Woods, Elizabeth G.; Schweppe, Emma; and Hockett, John A. *America's March Toward Democracy,* pt. 1. The Social Science Pamphlets. New York: The Lincoln School, 1926.

_____. *America's March Toward Democracy,* pt. 2. The Social Science Pamphlets. New York: The Lincoln School, 1926.

_____. *The Mechanical Conquest of America.* The Social Science Pamphlets. New York: The Lincoln School, 1926.

_____. *Problems of American Government.* The Social Science Pamphlets. New York: The Lincoln School, 1926.

_____. *Problems of American Industry and Business.* The Social Science Pamphlets. New York: The Lincoln School, 1926.

Articles by Rugg

"After Three Decades of Scientific Method in Education." *Teachers College Record* 36 (November 1934): 111–122.

"After Two Years of the New Deal: What?" *Scholastic* 26 (9 March 1935): 15–16f.

"America's Effort of Reason and Adventure of Beauty." *Progressive Education* 8 (May 1931): 367–375.

"America and the War: Will We Stay Out?" *Scholastic* 35 (6 November 1939): 155–175.

"American Culture and the Reconstruction of the School Curriculum." In *Proceedings* of the National Education Association, vol. 65. Washington, D.C.: The Association, 1927. Pp. 771–776.

"The American Experimental School." *Teachers College Record* 30 (February 1929): 407–424.

"The American Mind and the 'Class' Problem." *Social Frontier* 2 (February 1936): 138–142.

"The American Scholar Faces a Social Crisis." *Social Frontier* 1 (March 1935): 10–13.

"The American Way of Progress." *Scholastic* 26 (13 April 1935): 11–12.

"American Youth in a World at War." *Scholastic* 25 (9 October 1939): 15s–17s.

"Art and the Artist in American Life and Education." In *Readings in the Foundations of Education,* vol. 2, edited by Harold Rugg. New York: Teachers College, Columbia University, 1941.

"Art During the Building of America." *Scholastic* 30 (3 April 1937): 10–11, 24.

"The Artist and the Great Transition." In *America and Alfred Stieglitz: A Collective Portrait,* edited by Waldo Frank, Lewis Mumford, Dorothy Norman, Paul Rosenfeld, and Harold Rugg. New York: Doubleday, Doran & Company, 1934.

"Australia—World's Social Laboratory." *Scholastic* 31 (13 November 1937): 25s–28s.

"Automation—Imperatives for Educational Theory." *Educational Theory* 8 (April 1958): 1–11.

"A Brave New World." *Scholastic* 38 (19 May 1941): 11–12.

"Britain's Stake in Mussolini's War." *Scholastic* 27 (16 November 1935): 14–15.

"Brother, Can You Spare a Dime?" *Scholastic* 27 (28 September 1935): 12–13.

"Can America Keep Out of War?" *Scholastic* 28 (28 March 1936): 15–16, 27.

"The Constitution and the New Epoch." *Scholastic* 24 (14 April 1934): 16–17.

"Cooperative Production and Consumption." *Scholastic* 28 (2 May 1936): 12–13, 27.

"Creative America: Can She Begin Again?" *Frontiers of Democracy* 6 (October 1939): 9–11.

"Creative America Today." *Scholastic* 34 (20 May 1939): 13s–15s.

"The Creative Artist in Industrial America." *Scholastic* 30 (24 April 1937): 17–18, 24.

"The Creative Imagination: Imperatives for Educational Theory." In *Proceedings of the Sixteenth Annual Meeting* of the Philosophy of Education Society. Lawrence, Kans.: University of Kansas Press, 1960.

"The Curriculum in the Child-Centered School." In *Education for Complete Living,* Proceedings of the New Education Fellowship.

Melbourne: Australian Council for Educational Research, 1937.
Pp. 338–343.

"Curriculum-Design in the Social Sciences: What I Believe . . ." In
The Future of the Social Studies, edited by James A. Michener.
Cambridge, Mass.: The National Council for the Social Studies,
1939.

"Curriculum-Making in Laboratory Schools." In *The Foundations
and Technique of Curriculum-Construction.* Twenty-sixth Yearbook of the National Society for the Study of Education, pt. 1.
Bloomington, Ill.: Public School Publishing Co., 1926.

"Curriculum-Making: Points of Emphasis." In *The Foundations and
Technique of Curriculum-Construction.* Twenty-sixth Yearbook
of the National Society for the Study of Education, pt. 2.
Bloomington, Ill.: Public School Publishing Co., 1926.

"Curriculum-Making and the Scientific Study of Education Since
1910." In *The Foundations and Technique of Curriculum-
Construction.* Twenty-sixth Yearbook of the National Society for
the Study of Education, pt. 1. Bloomington, Ill.: Public School
Publishing Co., 1926.

"Curriculum Making: What Shall Constitute the Procedure of
National Committees?" *Journal of Educational Psychology* 15
(January 1924): 23–42.

"The Dance and the Theatre in America." *Scholastic* 30 (29 May
1937): 7–8, 23.

"Democracy in Action: The American Way." *Scholastic* 29 (23
January 1937): 16–17, 26.

"Democracy, Indoctrination, and Controversial Issues in the
Schools." In *Education for Complete Living,* Proceedings of the
New Education Fellowship. Melbourne: Australian Council for
Educational Research, 1937. Pp. 170–177.

"Democracy vs. Dictatorship." *Scholastic* 29 (5 December 1936):
12–13, 17.

"Depression or New Epoch: The Arguments for Each View." In
Readings in the Foundations of Education, vol. 1, edited by
Harold Rugg. New York: Teachers College, Columbia University,
1941.

"Dewey and His Contemporaries: The Frontiers of Educational
Thought in the Early 1900's." *Indiana University School of
Education Bulletin* 36 (January 1960): 1–14.

"The Dictator and the Sideshow." *Scholastic* 27 (19 October 1935): 13–14.

"Discussion of Professor Bode's Paper." *Teachers College Record* 30 (December 1928): 192–199.

"Do the Social Studies Prepare Pupils Adequately for Life Activities?" In *The Social Studies in the Elementary and Secondary School*. Twenty-second Yearbook of the National Society for the Study of Education, pt. 2. Bloomington, Ill.: Public School Publishing Co., 1922.

"Education and the Great Transition." *New Era* 15 (September 1934): 166–171.

"Education and International Understanding." *Progressive Education* 8 (April 1931): 294–302.

"Education and Social Hysteria." *Teachers College Record* 42 (March 1941): 493–505.

"Education and Social Progress in the 'New' Industrial-Democratic Countries." In *Modern Trends in Education*, Proceedings of the New Education Fellowship, 1937. Wellington, New Zealand: Whitcombe & Tombs, 1938. Pp. 30–42.

"Educational Planning for Post-War Reconstruction." *Frontiers of Democracy* 9 (April-May 1943): 217–223, 246–254.

"The Educator in the Great Transition." *Teachers College Record* 37 (November 1935): 111–118.

"The Educator and the Scientific Study of Society." *Progressive Education* 11 (January-February 1934): 3–5.

"Educators Join Forces to Fight World-Wide Ills." *Teachers College Record* 33 (April 1932): 648–649.

"Four Walls and a Roof." *Scholastic* 34 (4 March 1939): 13s–15s, 18s.

"Francis Wayland Parker and His Schools." In *Education and Philosophy*. Yearbook of Education. London: Evans Brothers, 1957.

"Gambling vs. Investing." *Scholastic* 25 (19 January 1935): 15–16f.

"Government and the Arts." *Scholastic* 30 (20 February 1937): 17–19.

"Government by Statesmen or by Politicians." *Scholastic* 28 (22 February 1936): 14–15, 31.

"How to Keep in Touch with the Quantitative Literature of Education." *Elementary School Journal* 18 (December 1917): 301–310.

"How Shall We Reconstruct the Social Studies Curriculum?" *Historical Outlook* 12 (May 1921): 184–189.

"Immediate Proposals." *Social Frontier* 3 (October 1936): 15.

"Imperial Germany vs. Imperial Britain." *Scholastic* 32 (28 May 1938): 25s–27s.

"Improvising in a Divided World." *Child Study* 25 (Summer 1948): 79.

"International Cooperation or New Style Imperialism?" *Scholastic* 27 (7 December 1935): 13–14, 20.

"Introduction." In *Readings in the Foundations of Education,* vol. 2, edited by Harold Rugg. New York: Teachers College, Columbia University, 1941.

"Is Nordic Superiority a Myth? *Scholastic* 25 (8 December 1934): 13–14.

"Is Our Constitution Obsolete?" *Scholastic* 24 (10 March 1934): 13–14.

"Is the Rating of Human Character Practicable?" *Journal of Educational Psychology* 12 (November and December 1921): 425–438, 485–501; 13 (January and February 1922): 30–42, 81–93.

"Japan, Over-Lord of Eastern Asia." *Scholastic* 27 (25 January 1936): 15–17.

"Laurin Zilliacus: World Citizen and Beloved Friend (1895–1959)." *New Era* 40 (December 1959): 239–240.

"Let's Tend Our Own Garden." *Scholastic* 35 (11 December 1939): 16s–17s, 20s.

"Liberty in the Power Age." *Scholastic* 25 (3 November 1934): 15–16.

"Lost, $287,000,000,000." *Scholastic* 26 (16 February 1935): 15–16.

"Man as Master of the Creative Act." In *Readings in the Foundations of Education,* vol. 2, edited by Harold Rugg. New York: Teachers College, Columbia University, 1941.

"The Measure of the New Education: As Shown by the Sixth World Conference." *New Era* 13 (September 1932): 247–250.

"Needed Changes in the Committee Procedure of Reconstructing the Social Studies." *Elementary School Journal* 21 (May 1921): 688–702.

"A New Climate of Opinion." *Survey Graphic* 22 (March 1933): 162–175f.

"New Dangers to Democracy." *Scholastic* 24 (19 May 1934): 17–18.

"The New Deal at the Cross-Roads." *Scholastic* 26 (23 March 1935): 15–17.

"The New Education." *Educational Review* 24 (July 1932): 217–221.

"New Frontiers in Industry." *Scholastic* 36 (20 May 1940): 11–13.

"A New Master in Europe?" *Scholastic* 33 (5 November 1938): 7–8, 34.

"The New Psychology and the Child-Centered School." In *Modern Trends in Education,* Proceedings of the New Education Fellowship, 1937. Wellington, New Zealand: Whitcombe & Tombs, 1938. Pp. 128–142.

"New Regions for Old: America Rebuilds." *Scholastic* 36 (26 February 1940): 11–13.

"New Worlds for Children." *School and Community* 16 (January 1930): 31 f.

"New Zealand: An Experiment in Democracy." *Scholastic* 31 (2 October 1937): 12–14.

"1941: Whose Year?" *Scholastic* 38 (17 February 1941): 11–13.

"Our Battle vs. Mein Kampf!" *Scholastic* 33 (10 December 1938): 26s–28s.

"A People's Government in Britain." *Scholastic* 38 (28 April 1941): 13–15.

"The Politicians and the Cost of the Government." *Scholastic* 28 (7 March 1936): 14–15, 25.

"Politics in a Presidential Year." *Scholastic* 28 (16 May 1936): 14–15, 28.

"A Preface to the Reconstruction of the American School Curriculum." *Teachers College Record* 27 (March 1926): 600–616.

"A Preface to a Theory for the New Individualism." *Teachers College Record* 32 (May 1931): 705–718.

"The Present Status of the Science of Education." In *Proceedings* of the National Education Association, vol. 72. Washington, D.C.: The Association, 1934. Pp. 235–237.

"Problems of a Changing Population." *Scholastic* 33 (8 October 1938): 25s–27s.

"Problems of Contemporary Life As the Basis for Curriculum-Making in the Social Studies." In *The Social Studies in the Elementary and Secondary School.* Twenty-second Yearbook of the National Society for the Study of Education, pt. 2. Bloomington, Ill.: Public School Publishing Co., 1923.

Progressive Education after 20 Years. Booklet No. 8 (Progressive Education Booklets). Columbus, Ohio: American Education Press, 1938. Pp. 5–19.

"Progressive Education—Which Way?" *Progressive Education* 25 (February 1948): 35–37, 45–46, 52–53.

"Propaganda and the Intelligent World Citizen." *Scholastic* 31 (11 December 1937): 25s–27s.

"A Proposed Statement of Policy for Progressive Education." *Progressive Education* 31 (November 1953): 33–40, 43.

"Psychologies of 1929." *New Era* 10 (October 1929): 210–212.

"Rating Scales for Pupils' Dynamic Qualities: Standardizing Methods of Judging Human Character." *School Review* 28 (May 1920): 337–349.

" 'Recession'—From What?" *Scholastic* 32 (12 February 1938): 25s, 28s.

"Reconstruction of the American School Curriculum." *New Era* 10 (April 1929): 81–84.

"Recovery via Engineering or Politics?" *Scholastic* 24 (17 February 1934): 13–14.

"Rivets and the Rebuilding of America." *Scholastic* 36 (25 March 1940): 11–13.

"The Role of Form . . . Order . . . Movement . . . Unity." In *Readings in the Foundations of Education,* vol. 2, edited by Harold Rugg. New York: Teachers College, Columbia University, 1941.

"The Roosevelt Government and the Great Depression." *Scholastic* 32 (26 February 1938): 25s–28s.

"The Roosevelt Government and Social Reconstruction." *Scholastic* 32 (12 March 1938): 25s–28s.

"The School Curriculum and the Drama of American Life." In *The Foundations and Technique of Curriculum-Construction.* Twenty-sixth Yearbook of the National Society for the Study of Education, pt. 1. Bloomington, Ill.: Public School Publishing Co., 1926.

"The School Curriculum 1825–1890." In *The Foundations and Technique of Curriculum-Construction.* Twenty-sixth Yearbook of the National Society for the Sudy of Education, pt. 1. Bloomington, Ill.: Public School Publishing Co., 1926.

"Schools of Creative Life . . . Unfinished Business in Education." *National Elementary Principal* 36 (May 1957): 12–15.

"Self-Cultivation and the Creative Act: Issues and Criteria." *Journal of Educational Psychology* 22 (April 1931): 241–254.

"Self-Improvement of Teachers Through Self-Rating." *Elementary School Journal* 20 (May 1920): 670–684.

"Shall We Study Economic-Social Problems in the Schools?" In *Official Report* of the Department of Superintendence, National Education Association. Washington, D.C.: The Association, 1935. Pp. 257–261.

"Social Reconstruction Through Education." *Progressive Education* 10 (January 1933); 11–18.

"South Africa, A Land of Violent Extremes." *Scholastic* 25 (13 October 1934): 15–17.

"Statistical Methods Applied to Educational Testing." In *The Nature, History, and General Principles of Intelligence Testing.* Twenty-first Yearbook of the National Society for the Study of Education, pt. 1. Bloomington, Ill.: Public School Publishing Co., 1923.

"The Story of the Arts of the Theatre." *Scholastic* 30 (22 May 1937): 8–9.

"A Study in Censorship: Good Concepts and Bad Words." *Social Education* 5 (March 1941): 176–181.

"Summary of the Literature of Public School Costs and Business Management." *Elementary School Journal* 17 (April 1917): 591–602.

"Surveying the Farm Problem." *Scholastic* 33 (7 January 1939): 15s–17s; 34 (4 February 1939): 15s–17s.

"The Sustained-Yield Principle: Can America Put Back What It Takes Out?" *Scholastic* 35 (22 January 1940): 13s–15s.

"The Swing of the Political Pendulum." *Scholastic* 29 (17 October 1936): 13–14, 22.

"T.V.A.—A Social Laboratory for the Nation." *Scholastic* 34 (22 April 1939): 13s–15s, 18s.

"Taking Stock of the New Deal." *Scholastic* 26 (2 March 1935): 13–14.

"The Teacher of Teachers: A Preface to Appraisal." *Journal of Teacher Education* 2 (March 1951): 3–8.

"Teachers' Marks and the Reconstruction of the Marking System." *Elementary School Journal* 18 (May 1918): 701–719.

"Teaching the Social Studies in the Grades." *Wisconsin Journal of Education* 62 (February 1930): 267–268.

"The Technological Achievements of the Europeans before the Industrial Revolution." In *Readings in the Foundations of Education,* vol. 1, edited by Harold Rugg. New York: Teachers College, Columbia University, 1941.

"This Has Happened Before." *Frontiers of Democracy* 7 (January 1941): 105–108.

"Three Decades of Mental Discipline: Curriculum-Making Via National Committees." In *The Foundations and Technique of Curriculum-Construction.* Twenty-sixth Yearbook of the National Society for the Study of Education, pt. 1. Bloomington, Ill.: Public School Publishing Co., 1926.

"Three Stages in the Art of a People . . . and in the Development of the Artist." In *Readings in the Foundations of Education,* vol. 2, edited by Harold Rugg. New York: Teachers College, Columbia University, 1941.

"Total War and Total Defense." *Scholastic* 37 (11 November 1940): 9–11.

"The War and American Public Opinion." *Scholastic* 38 (17 March 1941): 11–13.

"The War Education of Adults: Four Open Letters." *Frontiers of Democracy* 9 (December 1942): 75–81.

"We Accept in Principle But Reject in Practice—Is This Leadership?" *Frontiers of Democracy* 10 (December 1943): 71–72.

"What Are the Issues? The 1942 Balance-Sheet of Plans for the Post-War World." *Frontiers of Democracy* 9 (January 1943): 101–108.

"What Is Credit-for-Quality?" *Elementary School Journal* 19 (April 1919): 634–644.

"What Problems of International Relations Must Teachers Face?" *Progressive Education* 14 (December 1937): 614–617.

"What Shall We Teach Our Youth About Economic Life in America?" *Educational Outlook* 19 (May 1945): 158–168.

"What Should Be Taught About Advertising in a Consumer Course?" *Educational Trends* 8 (May 1940): 17–20.

"White and Black in Africa." *Scholastic* 25 (20 October 1934): 14–15f.

"Who Are the Superior People?" *Scholastic* 25 (15 December 1934): 15–16f.

"The William H. Kilpatrick Day—Eightieth Birthday Celebration." *Progressive Education* 29 (February 1952): 153–155.

"The World-Wide Struggle Over Ownership and Government." *Scholastic* 29 (14 November 1936): 3–4, 26.

"The Year of Decision 1943–1944: The People Must Make Up Their Minds." *Frontiers of Democracy* 10 (October 1943): 3–5.

With Chapman, I. I. "Our Social Economic Situation and the New Education." In *Official Report* of the Department of Superintendence, National Education Association. Washington, D.C.: The Association, 1934. Pp. 201–202.

With Clark, John Roscoe. "A Cooperative Investigation in the Testings and Experimental Teaching of First-Year Algebra." *School Review* 25 (May 1917): 346–349.

————. "The Improvement of Ability in the Use of the Formal Operations of Algebra by Means of Formal Practice Exercises." *School Review* 25 (October 1917): 546–554.

————. "Standardized Tests and the Improvement of Teaching in First-Year Algebra." *School Review* 25 (17 February 1917): 113–132; 25 (March 1917): 196–213.

With Counts, George S. "A Critical Appraisal of Current Methods of Curriculum-Making." In *The Foundations and Technique of Curriculum-Construction.* Twenty-sixth Yearbook of the National Society for the Study of Education, pt. 1. Bloomington, Ill.: Public School Publishing Co., 1926.

With Krueger, Louise, and Sondergard, Arensa. "A Study of the Language of Kindergarten Children." *Journal of Educational Psychology* 20 (January 1929): 1–18.

With Rugg, Earle, and Schweppe, Emma. "A Proposed Social Science Course for the Junior High School." In *The Social Studies in the Elementary and Secondary School.* Twenty-second Yearbook of the National Society for the Study of Education, pt. 2. Bloomington, Ill.: Public School Publishing Co., 1923.

With Schafer, Joseph. "The Methods and Aims of Committee Procedure: Open Letters from Dr. Schafer and Mr. Rugg." *Historical Outlook* 12 (October 1921): 247–252.

SECONDARY SOURCES

Reviews of Rugg's Books

Adler, Mortimer J. Review of *American Life and the School Curriculum. Commonweal* 29 (17 March 1939): 581–583.

Allen, Charles F. Review of *A History of American Civilization, Economic and Social. School Review* 38 (December 1930): 793–795.

Almack, John C. Review of *Culture and Education in America. School Review* 39 (December 1931): 788.

Anderson, Howard R. Review of *An Introduction to Problems of American Culture. Elementary School Journal* 32 (June 1932): 797–799.

Aquinice, Sister Mary, O.P. Review of *Social Foundations of Education. American Catholic Sociological Review* 17 (June 1956): 164–165.

Barnes, Harry Elmer. Review of *The Great Technology. American Journal of Sociology* 39 (January 1934): 551–552.

Bass, Altha Leah. Review of *The Child-Centered School. Survey* 61 (15 March 1929): 816.

Boyd, David. Review of *The Great Technology. Christian Century* 50 (1 November 1933): 1377–1378.

Boynton, Percy H. Review of *Culture and Education in America. New Republic* 69 (18 November 1931): 23.

Brameld, Theodore. Review of *Foundations for American Education. Progressive Education* 25 (May 1948): 141.

Brickman, William W. Review of *Foundations for American Education. School and Society* 66 (29 November 1947): 426.

Brown, Kenneth Irving. Review of *That Men May Understand. Christian Century* 58 (9 July 1941): 885–886.

Buchanan, John. Review of *That Men May Understand. Living Age* 360 (May 1941): 295–296.

Burton, William H. Review of *The Teacher of Teachers. School Review* 61 (January 1953): 54–55.

Cartwright, William S. Review of *The Teacher of Teachers. Annals of the American Academy of Political and Social Science* 286 (March 1953): 214–215.

Chamberlain, John. Review of *Culture and Education in America. Nation* 133 (7 October 1931): 368.

Davis, Grace. Review of *Changing Countries and Changing Peoples* and *Our Country and Our People. Social Studies* 30 (January 1939): 45–46.

Dearborn, Ned H. Review of *That Men May Understand. Survey Graphic* 30 (May 1941): 310.

Decharms, Richard. Review of *Imagination*. *Harvard Educational Review* 33 (Fall 1963): 555–558.

Dennis, Lawrence. Review of *The Great Technology*. *Saturday Review of Literature* 9 (27 May 1933): 615.

De Rosis, Louis. Review of *Imagination*. *Library Journal* 88 (1 June 1963): 2264.

Dexter, Byron. Review of *That Men May Understand*. *New Republic* 105 (14 July 1941): 61–62.

Duffus, R. L. Review of *Culture and Education in America*. *New York Times,* 21 June 1931, sec. 4, p. 13.

Ellis, Elmer. Review of *A History of American Government and Culture*. *School Review* 39 (June 1931): 475–476.

Gotesky, Rubin. Review of *That Men May Understand*. *Saturday Review of Literature* 24 (7 June 1941): 14.

Gould, Kenneth M. Review of the Junior High School Books in *Man and His Changing Society*. *Progressive Education* 9 (May 1932): 400–402.

Horn, Ernest. Review of *The Child-Centered School*. *Elementary School Journal* 29 (March 1929): 547–551.

Irwin, John. Review of *Social Reconstruction*. *Christian Century* 51 (7 February 1934): 190–191.

Johnson, Burges. Review of *That Men May Understand*. *Nation* 152 (10 May 1941): 563–564.

Josephine, Sister M. Review of *Foundations for American Education*. *America* 79 (8 May 1948): 116–119.

G.R.K. Review of *American Life and the School Curriculum*. *Progressive Education* 14 (February 1937): 138–140.

Kelly, Florence Finch. Review of *The Child-Centered School*. *New York Times,* 10 February 1929, sec. 4, p. 6.

Lasker, Bruno. Review of *Social Reconstruction*. *Survey* 70 (July 1934): 235.

Loomis, A. K. Review of *Changing Governments and Changing Cultures*. *School Review* 40 (June 1932): 472–473.

———. Review of *An Introduction to Problems of American Culture*. *School Review* 40 (June 1932): 473–475.

McAndrew, William. Review of *A Primer of Graphics and Statistics for Teachers*. *Educational Review* 70 (October 1925): 153.

Mearns, Hughes. Review of *Culture and Education in America*. *Progressive Education* 8 (May 1931): 411–414.

Mohr, Louise M. Review of *An Introduction to American Civiliza-tion. School Review* 38 (March 1930): 230.

Niebuhr, Reinhold. Review of *Culture and Education in America. World Tomorrow* 14 (December 1931): 407.

Olson, Edward G. Review of *Foundations for American Education. Social Education* 12 (May 1948): 235–236.

Owen, William Bishop. Review of *Scientific Method in the Recon-struction of Ninth Grade Mathematics. School Review* 26 (June 1918): 451–455.

Parker, Edith. Review of *Changing Civilizations in the Modern World. School Review* 38 (December 1930): 790.

Parker, Franklin. Review of *Imagination. Saturday Review of Litera-ture* 46 (17 August 1963): 49.

Phillips, Burr W. Review of *Changing Countries and Changing Peoples. Elementary School Journal* 39 (June 1939): 796.

———. Review of *Changing Governments and Changing Cultures. Elementary School Journal* 33 (January 1933): 395–397.

———. Review of *Mankind Throughout the Ages. Elementary School Journal* 39 (June 1939): 796.

Pierce, Bessie Louise. Review of *An Introduction to American Civilization. Elementary School Journal* 30 (May 1930): 711–712.

Poore, Charles. Review of *That Men May Understand. New York Times,* 9 April 1941, p. 23.

Redefer, Fredrick L. Review of *The Great Technology. Progressive Education* 10 (April 1933): 236–237.

Review of *The Child-Centered School. Progressive Education* 6 (November 1929): 294–296.

Scates, Douglas E. Review of *A Primer of Graphics and Statistics for Teachers. Elementary School Journal* 26 (October 1925): 151–152.

Shoben, Edward J. Review of *Imagination. Teachers College Record* 65 (October 1963): 95–96.

Shuster, George M. Review of *That Men May Understand. New York Times,* 27 April 1941, sec. 6, p. 5.

Snedden, David. Review of *Citizenship and Civic Affairs. School and Society* 52 (5 October 1940): 305–306.

Spaulding, Willard B. Review of *Foundations for American Educa-tion. Progressive Education* 25 (May 1948): 141–142.

Stetson, Paul C. Review of *Statistical Methods Applied to Education*. *Elementary School Journal* 18 (December 1917): 314–316.

_____. Review of *Statistical Methods Applied to Education*. *School Review* 25 (December 1917): 765.

Storck, John. Review of *Now Is the Moment*. *New York Times*, 16 May 1943, sec. 7, p. 20.

Sturges, W. A. Review of *The Great Technology*. *Yale Review* 23 (Autumn 1933): 162.

Taba, Hilda. Review of *American Life and the School Curriculum*. *Social Frontier* 3 (March 1937): 184–185.

Tead, Ordway. Review of *Foundations for American Education*. *Saturday Review of Literature* 31 (10 January 1948): 13.

Temple, Jean D. Review of *The Child-Centered School*. *New Republic* 57 (2 January 1929): 199.

Waterman, W. C. Review of *A History of American Civilization*. *Historical Outlook* 22 (January 1931): 34–35.

Wesley, Edgar. Review of *The First Book of the Earth, Nature Peoples, Communities of Men*, and *Peoples and Countries*. *Elementary School Journal* 37 (December 1936): 315–316.

Books and Pamphlets

Baier, Kurt. *The Moral Point of View: A Rational Basis of Ethics*. Ithaca, N.Y. Cornell University Press, 1958.

Beale, Howard K. *Are American Teachers Free?* New York: Charles Scribner's Sons, 1936.

Benn, S. I., and Peters, R. S. *Social Principles and the Democratic State*. London: George Allen and Unwin, 1959.

Bergson, Henri. *An Introduction to Metaphysics*. Translated by T. E. Hulme. New York: The Liberal Arts Press, 1950.

Birdwhistell, Ray L. *Introduction to Kinesics*. Louisville, Ky.: University of Louisville Press, 1952.

Bode, Boyd H. *Progressive Education at the Crossroads*. New York: Newson and Co., 1938.

Bowers, Claude A. *The Progressive Educator and the Depression: The Radical Years*. New York: Random House, 1969.

Brameld, Theodore. *Toward a Reconstructed Philosophy of Education*. New York: The Dryden Press, 1956.

Brauner, Charles J. *American Educational Theory*. Englewood Cliffs, N.J.: Prentice-Hall, 1964.

Brooks, Van Wyck. *America's Coming of Age.* New York: B. W. Huebsch, 1915.

_____. *Letters and Leadership.* New York: B. W. Huebsch, 1918.

Broudy, Harry S. *The Scholars and the Public Schools.* Columbus: The College of Education, The Ohio State University, 1964.

Brubacher, John S. *Modern Philosophies of Education.* 2d ed. New York: McGraw-Hill Book Co., 1950.

Bruner, Jerome S. *The Process of Education.* Cambridge: Harvard University Press, 1960.

Buckingham, R. B. *The Rugg Course in the Classroom: The Junior High School Program.* Boston: Ginn & Company, 1935.

Chambers, Clarke A. *Seedtime of Reform: American Social Service and Social Action 1918–1933.* Minneapolis: University of Minnesota Press, 1963.

Chambliss, J. J. *Boyd H. Bode's Philosophy of Education.* Columbus: Ohio State University Press, 1963.

Chase, Stuart. *Technocracy, an Interpretation.* New York: The John Day Co., 1933.

Childs, John L. *American Pragmatism and Education.* New York: Henry Holt & Co., 1956.

Chisholm, R. M. *Perceiving: A Philosophical Study.* Ithaca, N.Y.: Cornell University Press, 1957.

Combs, Arthur W., and Snygg, Donald. *Individual Behavior: A Perceptual Approach to Behavior.* Rev. ed. New York: Harper & Row Publishers, 1959.

Committee of Parents and Tax-Payers, T. H. P. Sailer, chairman. *Statements Regarding the Use of the Rugg Social Science Texts in the Englewood School System.* Englewood, N.J.: The Committee, 1940.

Counts, George S. *Dare the School Build a New Social Order?* New York: John Day Co., 1932.

Cowley, Malcolm. *Exile's Return: A Literary Odyssey of the 1920's.* New York: W. W. Norton & Company, 1934.

Cox, Donald William. *The City as a Schoolhouse: The Story of the Parkway Program.* Valley Forge, Pa.: Judson Press, 1972.

Cremin, Lawrence A. *The Transformation of the School: Progressivism in American Education, 1876–1957.* New York: Alfred A. Knopf, 1961.

_____; Shannon, David A.; and Townsend, Mary Evelyn. *A History* of Teachers College, Columbia University. New York: Columbia University Press, 1954.

Curti, Merle. The Social Ideas of American Educators. New York: Charles Scribner's Sons, 1935.

Dewey, John. The Child and the Curriculum. Chicago: The University of Chicago Press, 1902.

_____. Democracy and Education. New York: The Macmillan Co., 1916.

_____. Individualism, Old and New. New York: Minton, Blach and Co., 1930.

_____. Liberalism and Social Action. New York: G. P. Putnam's Sons, 1935.

_____. The Public and Its Problems. New York: Henry Holt & Co., 1927.

_____. The School and Society. New York: McClure, Phillips and Co., 1900.

Dilling, Elizabeth. The Red Network: A "Who's Who" and Handbook of Radicalism for Patriots. Kenilworth, Ill.: The Author, 545 Essex Road, 1934.

Ewing, A. C. Reason and Intuition. London: Humphrey Amen House, E.C., 1941. (First published in Proceedings of the British Academy, vol. 27 [Oxford: Oxford University Press, 1941].)

Frank, Waldo. Our America. New York: Boni and Liveright, 1919.

Frankena, William K. Ethics. Englewood Cliffs. N.J.: Prentice-Hall, 1963.

Gambrill, J. Montgomery. Experimental Curriculum-Making in the Social Studies. Philadelphia: McKinney Publishing Co., 1924.

Gellermann, William. The American Legion as Educator. New York: Teachers College, Columbia University, 1938.

Ghiselin, Brewster, ed. The Creative Process. New York: The New American Library (Mentor), 1952.

Goldman, Eric. The Crucial Decade: America, 1945–1955. New York: Alfred A. Knopf, 1959.

Gruber, Howard E; Terrell, Glenn; and Wertheimer, Michael, eds. Contemporary Approaches to Creative Thinking. New York: Atherton Press, 1962.

Gutek, Gerald L. The Educational Theory of George S. Counts. Columbus: Ohio State University Press, 1970.

Hofstadter, Richard. *The Age of Reform: From Bryan to F.D.R.* New York: Alfred A. Knopf, 1955.

———. *The Progressive Movement, 1900–1915.* Englewood Cliffs. N.J.: Prentice-Hall, 1963.

Humphrey, George. *Thinking: An Introduction to Its Experimental Psychology.* London: Methuen & Co., 1951.

Iverson, Robert W. *The Communists and the Schools.* New York: Harcourt, Brace & Co., 1959.

Kazin, Alfred. *On Native Grounds: An Interpretation of Modern American Prose Literature.* New York: Harcourt, Brace & Co., 1942.

Kilpatrick, William H. *Education and the Social Crisis.* New York: Liveright Publishing Corp., 1932.

———, ed. *The Educational Frontier.* New York: The Century Co., 1933.

———. *Foundations of Method.* New York: The Macmillan Co., 1925.

Kimball, Solon T., and McClellan, James E., Jr. *Education and the New America.* New York: Random House, 1962.

Leuchtenburg, William E. *The Perils of Prosperity 1914–32.* Chicago: The University of Chicago Press, 1958.

May, Henry F. *The End of American Innocence: A Study of the First Years of Our Own Time 1912–1917.* New York: Alfred A. Knopf, 1959.

McKinnon, Harold Rickert. *Changing Our Children: Harold Rugg's Crusade to Remodel America.* Berkeley, Calif.: Gillick Press, 1943.

National Education Association, Department of Superintendence. *Social Change and Education,* Thirteenth Yearbook. Washington, D.C.: The Association, 1935.

Nelson, Jack, and Roberts, Gene, Jr. *The Censors and the Schools.* Boston: Little, Brown & Company, 1963.

Niebuhr, Reinhold. *Moral Man and Immoral Society.* New York: Charles Scribner's Sons, 1932.

O'Connor, D. J. *An Introduction to the Philosophy of Education.* New York: Philosophical Library, 1957.

Ogburn, William. *Social Change with Respect to Culture and Original Nature.* New York: B. W. Huebsch, 1922.

Poincaré, Henri. *The Foundations of Science.* Translated by George Bruce Halsted. New York: The Science Press, 1929.

Popper, Karl R. *The High Tide of Prophecy: Hegel, Marx and the Aftermath.* The Open Society and Its Enemies, vol. 2. London: Routledge & Kegan Paul, 1945.

_____. *The Poverty of Historicism.* Boston: Beacon Press, 1957.

_____. *The Spell of Plato:* The Open Society and Its Enemies, vol. 1. 4th ed. rev. London: Routledge & Kegan Paul, 1962.

Price, Kingsley. *Education and Philosophical Thought.* Boston: Allyn and Bacon, 1962.

Progressive Education Association, Committee on Social and Economic Problems. *A Call to the Teachers of the Nation.* New York: The John Day Co., 1933.

Report of Special Committee Appointed to Consider the Attacks on the Books of Harold O. Rugg and Others on the Ground of Subversive Teachings. Edwin C. Broome, chairman. Philadelphia: The Committee, 1941.

Rudd, Augustin G. *Bending the Twig.* New York: American Book–Stratford Press, 1957.

Rushdoony, R. J. *The Messianic Character of American Education.* Nutley, N.J.: Craig Press, 1963.

Ryle, Gilbert. *The Concept of Mind.* London: Hutchinson House, 1949.

Sabine, George H.; Holcombe, Arthur; MacMahon, Arthur W.; Wittke, Carl; and Lynd, Robert S. *The Textbooks of Harold Rugg.* New York: The American Committee for Democracy and Intellectual Freedom, 1942.

Scheffler, Israel. *Conditions of Knowledge: An Introduction to Epistemology and Education.* Chicago: Scott, Foresman & Company, 1965.

Schlesinger, Arthur M., Jr. *The Crisis of the Old Order, 1919–1933.* Boston: Houghton Mifflin Company, 1957.

Scott, Howard. *Introduction to Technocracy.* New York: Technocracy, Inc., 1937.

Tenenbaum, Samuel. *William Heard Kilpatrick: Trail Blazer in Education.* New York: Harper & Brothers, 1951.

Thelan, Herbert A. *Education and the Human Quest.* New York: Harper & Brothers, 1960.

Veblen, Thorstein. *The Engineers and the Price System.* New York: The Viking Press, 1921.

Welter, Rush. *Popular Education and Democratic Thought in America.* New York: Columbia University Press, 1962.

White, Morton. *Social Thought in America: The Revolt Against Formalism.* New York: The Viking Press, 1949.

Whitehead, Alfred North. *Process and Reality.* New York: The Macmillan Co., 1929.

Wilson, Howard E. *The Fusion of Social Studies in Junior High Schools: A Critical Analysis.* Cambridge: Harvard University Press, 1933.

Woelfel, Norman. *Molders of the American Mind.* New York: Columbia University Press, 1933.

Articles in Journals, Magazines, and Books

Adams, James T. "Can Teachers Bring About the New Society?" *Progressive Education* 10 (October 1933): 310–314.

"Advertising Groups Pursuing Professor Rugg's Books." *Publishers' Weekly* 138 (28 September 1940): 1322–1323.

Archambault, Reginald D. "The Concept of Need and Its Relation to Certain Aspects of Educational Theory." *Harvard Educational Review* 27 (Winter 1957): 38–62.

Armstrong, Orland K. "Treason in the Textbooks." *American Legion Magazine* 29 (September 1940): 8, 51, 70–72.

Bair, Frederick H. "A Social Philosophy of Education Challenges the Teacher." *New York State Education* 24 (October 1936): 26–27.

Beck, Robert H. "Educational Leadership, 1906–1956." *Phi Delta Kappan* 37 (January 1956): 164.

Berlin, Isaiah. "Equality as an Ideal." In *Justice and Social Policy,* edited by Frederick A. Olafson. Englewood Cliffs, N.J.: Prentice-Hall, 1961. (Originally published as "Equality" in the *Proceedings of the Aristotelian Society,* vol. 56, 1955–56 [London: Harrison & Sons, 1956].)

Bode, Boyd H. "Education and Social Reconstruction." *Social Frontier* 1 (January 1935): 18–22.

_____. "The Problem of Culture in Education." *Educational Research Bulletin* 10 (30 September 1931): 339–346.

"Book Burnings." *Time* 36 (9 September 1940): 64–65.

Bourne, Randolph. "Twilight of Idols." *Seven Arts* (October 1917), 688–702.

Bowers, C. A. "Social Reconstructionism: Views from the Left and the Right—1932–1942." *History of Education Quarterly* 10 (Spring 1970): 22–52.

Brameld, Theodore B. "Is the Conservative Right?" *Frontiers of Democracy* 10 (December 1943): 93–94.

_____. "Memories of a Lost Leader." *Educational Theory* 10 (July 1960): 181.

Brown, N. J. "A Layman Speaks About the Rugg Books." *Frontiers of Democracy* 7 (February 1941): 153–155.

Brunner, Edward deS. "The Faith of a Liberal." *Social Frontier* 4 (June 1938): 278–280.

Burr, Samuel Engle. "Democracy Can Bear Comparisons." *Journal of Education* 118 (17 June 1935): 329–330.

Byrns, Ruth K. "Professor Harold Rugg—How an Educator Becomes an Issue." *Commonweal* 35 (31 October 1941): 42–45.

Carbone, Peter F., Jr. "A Critical Analysis of Harold Rugg's Views on Creativity and Knowledge." *Journal of Creative Behavior* 3 (Spring 1969): 128–143.

_____. "The Other Side of Harold Rugg." *History of Education Quarterly* 11 (Fall 1971): 265–278.

_____. "Rugg, Harold Ordway." *Dictionary of American Biography: Supplement Six*. New York: Charles Scribner's Sons, forthcoming.

_____. "The School as an Agent of Social Change in the United States During the 1930s." *Paedagogica Historica* 9 (1969): 20–40.

Childs, John L. "Experimental Morality and the Post-War World." *Frontiers of Democracy* 9 (April 1943): 197–200.

"Collectivism and Collectivisim." *Social Frontier* 1 (November 1934): 3–4.

"College Professors Defend Rugg's Schoolbooks." *Education Digest* 6 (October 1940): 49–51.

"Controversy Continues Over Rugg Books." *Publishers' Weekly* 138 (23 November 1940): 1954–1955.

"The Crusade Against Rugg." *New Republic* 104 (10 March 1941): 327.

De Guire, Olivia. "The Rugg Social Science Series in Silverton Junior High School." *High School* 9 (October 1931): 18–19.

Dewey, John. "Can Education Share in Reconstruction?" *Social Frontier* 1 (October 1934): 11–12.

_____. "The Crucial Role of Intelligence." *Social Frontier* 1 (February 1935): 9–10.

_____. "Education and Social Change." *Social Frontier* 3 (May 1937): 235–238.

"Educators Join Forces to Fight World-wide Ills." *Teachers College Record* 33 (April 1932): 648–649.

Ennis, Robert H. "The Impossibility of Neutrality." *Harvard Educational Review* 29 (Spring 1959): 128–136.

Fairchild, Henry Pratt. "Private or Social Wealth." *Social Frontier* 3 (December 1936): 80–82.

Farley, Belmont. "The Superintendents at St. Louis." *School and Society* 43 (14 March 1936): 345–356.

Fisher, William. "Harold Rugg, 1886–1960." *School and Society* 89 (23 September 1961): 304–305.

"For Better Citizens." *Time* 34 (6 November 1939): 61.

Forbes, Bertie C. "Does This Smell of Sovietism?" *Forbes* 45 (1 February 1940): 10.

"Further Vindication of the Rugg Books." *School and Society* 53 (31 May 1941): 688–689.

Gambrill, J. Montgomery. "Experimental Curriculum-Making in the Social Studies." *Historical Outlook* 14 (December 1923): 384–406.

_____. "Tendencies and Issues in the Making of Social Studies Curricula." *Historical Outlook* 15 (February 1924): 84–89.

"Goodbye, Messrs. Chips." *Time* 57 (25 June 1951): 42–43.

Gray, Roland F. "Teaching About Communism: A Survey of Objectives." *Social Education* 28 (February 1964): 71–72, 80.

Harlow, Rex Francis. "Should the Tail Wag the Dog?" *School and Society* 44 (28 November 1936): 710–713.

Hart, Mervin K. "Let's Discuss This on the Merits." *Frontiers of Democracy* 7 (December 1940): 82–87.

Hayes, Francis. "Gestures: A Working Bibliography." *Southern Folklore Quarterly* 21 (1957): 218–317.

Hook, Sidney. "The New Failure of Nerve." *Partisan Review* 10 (January-February 1943): 2–23.

Hullihen, Walter. "A Further Obligation to the Social Order." In *Proceedings of the National Association of State Universities.* n.p., 1933. Pp. 43–55.

Hutchins, Robert M. "Education and Social Improvement." *Educational Record* 19 (July 1938): 385–392.

Johnson, F. Ernest. "Working Colleague and Personal Friend." *Educational Theory* 10 (July 1960): 178–179.

Kandel, I. L. "Education and Social Disorder." *Teachers College Record* 34 (February 1933): 359–367.

Laski, Harold J. "A New Education Needs a New World." *Social Frontier* 2 (February 1936): 144–147.

Lilge, Frederic. "The Vain Quest for Unity: John Dewey's Social and Educational Thought in Retrospect." In *Dewey on Education: Appraisals,* edited by Reginald D. Archambault. New York: Random House, 1966. P. 64.

Link, Arthur S. "What Happened to the Progressive Movement?" *American Historical Review* 64 (July 1959): 833–851.

May, Henry F. "Shifting Perspectives on the 1920s." *Mississippi Valley Historical Review* 43 (December 1956): 405–427.

Melcher, Frederic G. "Rugg Serves Freedom of Education." *Publishers' Weekly* 139 (12 April 1941): 1533.

Meyer, Ruth. "On Harold Rugg." *Nation* 152 (10 May 1941): 567.

Meyers, Alonzo F. "The Attack on the Rugg Books." *Frontiers of Democracy* 7 (October 1940): 17–22.

Nash, Paul A. "The Strange Death of Progressive Education." *Educational Theory* 14 (April 1964): 65–75, 82.

Newlon, Jesse. "The Rugg Books." *School Executive* 60 (June 1941): 9–10.

Newman, Fred M., and Oliver, Donald. "Education and Community." *Harvard Educational Review* 37 (Winter 1967): 61–106.

Oertel, Ernest. "Education and Social Reconstruction." *New York State Education* 21 (January 1934): 411–413.

Osborn, Robert C. "Art Gets the Tag End of Friday." *American Education* 1 (February 1965): 5–7.

Parker, Franklin. "The Case of Harold Rugg." *Paedagogica Historica* 2 (1962): 95–122. Also *Midwest Quarterly* 3 (Autumn 1961): 21–34.

"The Present Status of the Textbook Controversy." *School and Society* 53 (12 April 1941): 465–466.

"Prof. H. O. Rugg on Carpet in Row over 'Radical' Texts." *Newsweek* 14 (4 December 1939): 47–48.

"Propaganda Over the Schools." *Propaganda Analysis* 4 (25 February 1941): 1–16.

"Propaganda Purge." *Time* 34 (10 July 1939): 42.

"Publishers Protest Removal of Rugg Textbooks." *Publishers' Weekly* 137 (22 June 1940): 2345.

Reed, Truman G. "Delusions of Grandeur." *Junior-Senior High School Clearing House* 7 (January 1933): 266–271.

Reitman, Sandford W. "The Reconstructionism of Harold Rugg." *Educational Theory* 22 (Winter 1972): 47–57.

"Retirement." *School and Society.* 73 (19 May 1951): 318.

Rudd, Augustin G. "Our 'Reconstructed' Educational System." *Nation's Business* 28 (April 1940): 27–28, 93–94.

"Rugg, Harold (Ordway)." *Current Biography,* 1941, pp. 738–740.

"Rugg, Harold Ordway." *National Cyclopedia of American Biography,* 1943–46, pp. 543–544.

"Rugg, Harold Ordway." *Twentieth Century Authors: First Supplement,* 1955, pp. 851–852.

"Rugg Critics Lose Ground." *Publishers' Weekly* 138 (12 October 1940): 1492.

"Rugg Textbooks Receive Favorable Report in Philadelphia." *Publishers' Weekly* 139 (12 April 1941): 1548.

"Rugg Textbooks Restored in Englewood, New Jersey." *Publishers' Weekly* 139 (25 January 1941): 434.

Shaffer, Laurance F. "A Learning Experiment in the Social Studies." *Journal of Educational Psychology* 18 (December 1927): 577–591.

Smith, B. Othanel. "Harold Ordway Rugg, 1886–1960." *Educational Theory* 10 (July 1960): 176–178.

Smith, Timothy L. "Progressivism in American Education." *Harvard Educational Review* 31 (Spring 1961): 168–193.

Sokolsky, George E. "Hard-Boiled Babes." *Liberty* 17 (16 March 1940): 49–50.

_____. "Is Your Child Being Taught to Loaf?" *Liberty* 17 (4 May 1940): 40–42.

_____. "Our Children's Guardians." *Liberty* 17 (6 April 1940): 33, 36.

Studebaker, J. W. "Safeguarding Democracy Through Adult Civic Education." *Office of Education Bulletin,* No. 6, 1936.

Tildsley, John L. "Why I Object to Some Proposals of the Frontier Thinkers." *Social Frontier* 4 (July 1938): 319–322.

Washburne, Carleton. "Harold Rugg and the New Education." *Educational Theory* 10 (July 1960): 179–180.

Whitman, Howard. "Progressive Education—Which Way Forward?" *Colliers* 133 (14 May 1954): 32–36.

Whitmore, Margaret S. "Two Years' Experience with Rugg." *High School* 9 (October 1931): 16–17.

Wilson, Howard E., and Erbe, Bessie P. "A Survey of Social-Studies Courses in 301 Junior High Schools." *School Review* 39 (September 1931): 497–507.

Winters, Elmer A. "Man and His Changing Society: The Textbooks of Harold Rugg." *History of Education Quarterly* 7 (Winter 1967): 493–511.

Yocum, A. Duncan. "Dr. Dewey's 'Liberalism' in Government and in Public Education." *School and Society* 44 (4 July 1936): 1–5.

Newspaper Articles (New York Times)

"Academic Freedom Abused, Says Lawyer." 24 May 1940, p. 21.

"Anti-Liberal Group Scored by Dr. Rugg." 18 July 1941, p. 6.

"Archaic Texts Seen As School Handicap." 11 March 1933, p. 15.

"Art Appreciation Called Basic Need." 28 June 1938, p. 11.

"Asks Ban on Dr. Rugg's Books." 13 April 1940, p. 19.

"Asks Ban on Rugg Books." 13 October 1940, sec. 1, p. 47.

"Asks Teachers Lead in Social Reform." 27 July 1935, p. 14.

"Bronxville Maps Rugg Book Ban." 15 November 1941, p. 23.

"Candidates Give Education Stand." 11 August 1936, p. 9.

"Capitalists Held Our Rulers Still." 28 November 1934, p. 23.

"Censorship Not Wanted." 14 May 1940, p. 22.

"Clear Rugg Books in Philadelphia." 7 April 1941, p. 15.

"Conant Justifies Backing of Russia." 1 July 1941, p. 4.

"Critics of Rugg Termed Unfair." 26 April 1942, sec. 2, p. 6.

"Dr. Dewey's Stand Disputed." 9 May 1940, p. 22.

"Dr. Harold Rugg, Educator, 74, Dies." 18 May 1960, p. 41.

"Education Is Held Democracy Basis." 22 November 1936, sec. 2, p. 4.

"Education Is Seen Injured by Critics." 27 February 1941, p. 21.

"Education Policy of Legion Scored." 24 November 1935, sec. 2, p. 7.

"Educators Assail Church-School Aid." 28 February 1938, p. 17.

"Educators Differ on Retirement Age." 7 March 1937, p. 6.

"Excerpts from Various Textbooks Criticized in the Survey." 22 February 1941, p. 6.

"Forum Discusses Freedom to Read." 18 November 1951, sec. 1, p. 81.

"Freedom to 'Yell' in Theater Urged." 13 March 1938, sec. 1, p. 39.

"Histories of U.S. Held Provincial." 12 November 1941, p. 25.

"Hold Schools Fail to Teach Realities." 20 November 1932, sec. 1, p. 23.

"Investigating Education." 6 May 1940, p. 16.

"Iowa School Bars Rugg Books." 20 June 1940, p. 25.

"Jersey Town Bans Rugg's Textbooks." 23 August 1940, p. 17.

"Kilpatrick Case Stirs Educators." 21 February 1937, sec. 2, p. 9.

"Legion Attacks Rugg's Books." 3 May 1941, p. 21.

"Lilienthal Urges Wide Atom Study." 29 November 1947, p. 11.

"Mt. Kisco Bans Rugg Books." 15 November 1940, p. 18.

"N.A.M. Stand Is Given on Use of Abstracts." 3 April 1941, p. 26.

"National Party of Thinkers Urged." 21 January 1933, p. 9.

"News and Notes of the Advertising Field." 12 June 1939, p. 26.

"Ohio State Trustees Assail Rugg Speech." 5 September 1951, p. 29.

"Ousting of Bridges Favored by Women." 20 January 1942, p. 16.

"Ousts Prof. Rugg's Books." 18 April 1940, p. 24.

"Paranoia in Germany Is Subject of Forum." 6 June 1943, p. 23.

"'Patrioteers' Are Scored." 31 July 1935, p. 20.

"Ridgefield Backs Rugg Books." 12 February 1941, p. 15.

"Role of the Schools in Defense Studied." 30 November 1940, p. 6.

"Rugg's Books Are Upheld." 23 October 1940, p. 21.

"Rugg's Books Barred from More Schools." 29 August 1940, p. 17.

"Rugg Defends His Textbooks Long Attacked" 5 January 1941, sec. 2, p. 6.

"Rugg Sees Menace in Schoolboy Gang." 4 February 1933, p. 17.

"Rugg Traces Needs in Creative Teaching." 30 November 1929, p. 5.

'Rugg, Whose Texts Drew Wide Criticism, to Retire from Teachers College Faculty." 5 May 1951, p. 15.

"Says Mania for Facts Is Bane of Education." 5 December 1928, p. 20.

"School Bars Textbook." 3 December 1952, p. 42.

"Schoolbook 'Trial' Staged in New Jersey." 21 November 1939, p. 25.

"700 At Columbia Hit By Doak Ban On Jobs." 28 September 1932, p. 21.

"Social Teaching Splits Educators." 27 February 1935, p. 17.

"Subversive Education." 15 June 1952, sec. 4, p. 8.

"Teachers Censure Yale and St. Louis." 28 February 1937, sec. 2, p. 1.

"Teachers Divided on New Deal Aims." 27 February 1934, p. 17.

"Teaching Techniques." 29 June 1952, sec. 4, p. 8.

"Teaching Three R's Held Time Waster." 11 March 1928, sec. 2, p. 4.

"Textbook Critics Assailed by Rugg." 16 March 1941, p. 38.

"Textbook Digests for N.A.M. Finished." 2 January 1941, p. 21.

"Textbook Writers Reply to Attack; 'Censor' Fight On." 23 February 1941, sec. 1 & 3, pp. 1, 47.

"Topics of the Times." 18 March 1941, p. 22.

"Topics of the Times." 4 May 1941, sec. 4, p. 8.

"Topics of the Times." 15 November 1941, p. 16.

"Un-American Tone Seen in Textbooks on Social Sciences." 22 February 1941, pp. 1, 6.

"Urges Fair Deal for Oil Industry." 15 November 1940, p. 11.

"Viewpoint on Education." 30 March 1941, sec. 2, p. 5.

"Warn Nation's Hope Is Adult Education." 19 November 1932, p. 17.

"Would Bar Reds As Teachers." 9 February 1941, p. 29.

"Would Debunk Debunkers." 21 March 1941, p. 20.

"'Yes! We Have No Bananas'—and Why." 12 August 1923, sec. 3, pp. 8, 25.

Unpublished Manuscripts

Graham, Patricia. "A History of the Progressive Education Association, 1919–1955." Ph.D. dissertation, Teachers College, Columbia University, 1964.

Liles, Jesse S., Jr. "Contributions of William Heard Kilpatrick and Theodore Brameld toward a Definition of the Relationship between Education and Social Change." Ph.D. dissertation, Duke University, 1970.

Phillips, Mark. *"The Seven Arts* and Harold Rugg: A Study in Intellectual History." Master's thesis, Columbia Univeristy, 1961.

Seguel, Mary Louise. "The Shaping of a Field of Specialization, Curriculum-Making: A Critical Study of the Selected Writings of Charles and Frank McMurry, Franklin Bobbitt, W. W. Charters, Harold Rugg, Hollis Caswell and John Dewey." Ed.D. project report, Teachers College, Columbia University, 1964.

Wilson, Virginia S. "Harold Rugg's Social and Educational Philosophy as Reflected in His Textbook Series, 'Man and His Changing Society,'" Ph.D. dissertation, Duke University, 1975.

Winters, Elmer Arthur. "Harold Rugg and Education for Social Reconstruction." Ph.D. dissertation, University of Wisconsin, 1968.

INDEX